W9-AYP-418

Praise for *Advancing Differentiation*

"Amazingly comprehensive . . . [this] book is an excellent resource for administrators and classroom teachers alike. Dr. Cash provides countless practical applications [and] makes a case for differentiation for the purposes of raising student achievement and Response to Intervention (RTI), in addition to the increasingly diverse populations our districts encounter in the twenty-first century."

—Anne Roloff, Ph.D., president of Illinois ASCD and assistant superintendent for Curriculum and Instruction, Niles Township High School District, Skokie, Illinois

"How I wish I had this book when I was a principal. I had many new, young teachers, and this outstanding approach to teaching would have made my life as a mentor much easier. The clear writing, commonsense approaches, and suggestions and charts will give any teacher—new or seasoned—confidence and motivation. A fine, practical addition to our field."

—Judith Roseberry, consultant, past president of California Association for the Gifted

"Cash not only provides the big picture of the landscape of differentiation, he clearly demonstrates his expertise in both the art and the science of teaching. He consistently advances his message that all students can learn at high levels and deserve rigor and challenge. This is an essential book for teachers as they encourage new ideas and creative productivity in their students in the current educational landscape."

—Felicia A. Dixon Ph.D., professor emerita of psychology, Department of Educational Psychology, Ball State University

"Cash's approach to differentiation is refreshing, authentic, and practical. He takes a complex philosophy and brings it alive through his writing . . . This publication should be in the hands of all teachers K–16."

—Jaime A. Castellano, Ed.D., principal and coordinator of gifted education at Ganado Intermediate School in Ganado, Arizona, and author of Special Populations in Gifted Education: Understanding Our Most Able Students from Diverse Backgrounds

"Richard writes with a clarity that appeals to both the novice and the seasoned educator. I've yet to read a more comprehensive teacher guide. *Advancing Differentiation* just moved to the top of my recommended list!"

—Jeff Danielian, M.Ed., teacher resource specialist, editor-in-chief of Teaching for High Potential, *National Association for Gifted Children*

Advancing Differentiation

Thinking and Learning for the 21st Century

Richard M. Cash, Ed.D.
Foreword by Diane Heacox, Ed.D.

free spirit
PUBLISHING®

Copyright © 2011 by Richard M. Cash, Ed.D.

All rights reserved under International and Pan-American Copyright Conventions. Unless otherwise noted, no part of this book may be reproduced, stored in a retrieval system, or transmitted in any form or by any means, electronic, mechanical, photocopying, or otherwise, without express written permission of the publisher, except for brief quotations or critical reviews. For more information, go to www.freespirit.com/company/permissions.cfm.

Free Spirit, Free Spirit Publishing, and associated logos are trademarks and/or registered trademarks of Free Spirit Publishing Inc. A complete listing of our logos and trademarks is available at www.freespirit.com.

Library of Congress Cataloging-in-Publication Data
Cash, Richard M.
Advancing differentiation : thinking and learning for the 21st century / Richard M. Cash ; foreword by Diane Heacox.
p. cm.
Includes bibliographical references and index.
ISBN-13: 978-1-57542-357-9 (diskette : alk. paper)
ISBN-10: 1-57542-357-X (diskette : alk. paper)
1. Individualized instruction. 2. Thought and thinking—Study and teaching. 3. Education—Curricula. I. Title.
LB1031.C38 2010
371.39'4—dc22

2010035009

Free Spirit Publishing does not have control over or assume responsibility for author or third-party websites and their content. At the time of this book's publication, all facts and figures cited within are the most current available. All telephone numbers, addresses, and website URLs are accurate and active; all publications, organizations, websites, and other resources exist as described in this book; and all have been verified as of June 2012. If you find an error or believe that a resource listed here is not as described, please contact Free Spirit Publishing. Parents, teachers, and other adults: We strongly urge you to monitor children's use of the Internet.

Edited by Meg Bratsch
Cover design by Michelle Lee
Interior design by Michelle Lee and Tasha Kenyon

10 9 8 7 6 5
Printed in the United States of America

Free Spirit Publishing Inc.
Minneapolis, MN
(612) 338-2068
help4kids@freespirit.com
www.freespirit.com

As a member of the Green Press Initiative, Free Spirit Publishing is committed to the three Rs: Reduce, Reuse, Recycle. Whenever possible, we print our books on recycled paper containing a minimum of 30% post-consumer waste. At Free Spirit it's our goal to nurture not only children, but nature too!

Free Spirit offers competitive pricing.
Contact edsales@freespirit.com for pricing information on multiple quantity purchases.

Dedication

To my parents, Elizabeth and Cecil Cash, who taught me how to think, encouraged my creativity, and told me I could do anything I set my mind to.

This book was born out of ideas I've gathered and generated throughout my years as a teacher. None of this would have been possible if it weren't for the exceptional mentoring and guidance I received from my friend and colleague, Mrs. Barbara Ford. Mrs. Ford, thank you for helping me become who I am today.

Acknowledgments

Thank you to Craig Feltmann for always believing in me, supporting me, and cheering me on in this process, and making it a big deal. I don't think I could have done it without you there.

Special thanks to Dr. Diane Heacox, whose work has been a catalyst for change in classrooms around the world. Diane, you are a great collaborator, someone who makes me think at that next level *and* is fun to be around.

To the best editor I've ever had, Meg Bratsch at Free Spirit Publishing: your finesse with my thoughts made me look good. You were a joy to work with.

I also want to thank my brothers, Robert and John Cash, my sister, Susan Swinick, and my dear friend Jennifer Stevens, for never letting me get too big for my britches.

I greatly appreciate all the support and encouragement I received from my colleagues in the Bloomington Minnesota Public Schools, especially Dr. Tim Anderson and Sue Ostlund. You work hard to keep me humble.

Finally, I extend my sincerest appreciation to my goddesses: Barbara Dullaghan and Julie Donaldson. Your passions for excellence, insights into learning, and love for the students keeps me grounded in why we do what we do!

Contents

Reproducible Pages viii

Figures ix

Foreword x

Introduction 1

The Next Level of Differentiation 1

The Importance of Thinking Skills in Today's World 2

About This Book and Digital Content 2

How to Use This Book 5

Part One
Taking Differentiation to the Next Level 7

Chapter 1: Defining How Differentiation Looks in Today's Classroom 8

GT Stands for Good Teaching 8

Dispelling the Myths of Differentiated Instruction 8

Technology Use in the Differentiated Classroom 12

Chapter 2: Defining the Essentials of a Differentiated Curriculum 13

Skills for a New Century 13

A Hierarchy of Knowledge: Factual, Procedural, Conceptual 14

Four Steps to Defining the Essentials of Curriculum 15

Chapter 3: Advancing Differentiation to New Levels Through a Rigorous Curriculum 28

What Is a Rigorous Curriculum? 28

Hallmarks of a Rigorous Curriculum: Effective, Engaging, Exciting, Enriching (E^4) 29

Infusing Rigor Into Your Curriculum 32

Chapter 4: Motivating and Engaging Learners 36

What Is Motivation? 37

Understanding How the Brain Learns 38

Strategies to Motivate and Engage Students 49

Using Assessment to Motivate and Engage 62

Chapter 5: Developing Student Self-Regulation 71

Self-Regulation Theory 71

Building Self-Regulation Through Goal Setting 72

Building Self-Regulation Through Mindset 73

The Student-Centered Classroom 73

Chapter 6: The Teaching and Learning Continuum: Building Success Through Autonomy 80

What Is the TLC? 81

Why Build Autonomy? 81

Framework Supporting the Teaching and Learning Continuum (TLC) 84

The Four Levels of the TLC Model 85

Assessment That Builds Autonomy 88

Part Two
Putting Thinking Skills to Use in the Classroom 91

Chapter 7: The Thinking Classroom 92

What Is Thinking? 92

Divergent Thinking vs. Convergent Thinking 93

Characteristics of a Thinking Student 94

Characteristics of a Thinking Classroom 94

Characteristics of a Thinking Curriculum 94

Methods for Developing Intellectually Disciplined Thinkers 95

General Strategies to Improve Student Thinking 99

Chapter 8: A Framework for Thinking: Digging Deeper into Bloom's Taxonomy 111

A Brief Introduction to Bloom's Taxonomy 111

Performing Automatically to Performing Consciously 112

Building on Bloom's 112

Putting It All Together: The Digging Deeper Matrix (DDM) 122

Chapter 9: Critical Thinking: Developing Reasoned Thought 125

What Is Critical Thinking? 125

General Critical Thinking Strategies 126

Critical Thinking Strategies in Reading 136

Critical Thinking Strategies in Writing 136

Critical Thinking Strategies in Mathematics 137

Critical Thinking Strategies in Science 137

Seven Critical Questioning Strategies to Use Daily 137

Critical Thinking Tools 139

Chapter 10: Creative Thinking: Stepping Outside the Box 150

What Is Creative Thinking? 151

Characteristics of Creative Individuals 152

Creative Thinking Strategies 152

Creative Thinking Activities 155

Creative "Sponge" Activities 159

Additional Creative Activity Ideas 159

Building a Creative Classroom 160

Chapter 11: Problem Finding, Problem Solving, and Decision Making 162

Characteristics of Effective Problem Finders, Problem Solvers, and Decision Makers 162

Finding Problems 163

Solving Problems 163

Decision Making 168

A Final Note: Pulling It All Together 179

Conclusion 181

References and Resources 183

Index 187

About the Author 193

Reproducible Pages

(You may download these forms at **freespirit.com/advancing-differentiation-forms**. Use password **2thrive**.)

Chapter 1

10 Elements of a Differentiated Classroom 11

Chapter 2

Concept Development Worksheet 20

Breaking Down the Essentials 27

Chapter 3

Principles of Curriculum and Instruction for Advancing Learning 33

Classroom Practices for Advancing Learning 34

Walkthrough Checklist of Differentiation for Advancing Learning 35

Chapter 4

25 Strategies for Developing a Boy-Friendly Classroom 44–45

Strategies for Creating a Brain-Compatible Learning Environment 46

Brain Breaks 47

I Chart 48

What Interests Me: Topic Preview 50

KIQ Chart 51

Rank Your Interests 52

Guidelines for Creating a Passion Project 54–55

Motivation Strategies Based on Student Interests 56

Sternberg Model of Abilities: Learning Styles Activity 59–60

Motivation Strategies Based on Student Learning Preferences 61

Four Square Concept Map 63

3–2–1 Exit Slip/Entrance Ticket 67

Roundtable Review 68–69

Motivation Strategies Based on Assessment 70

Chapter 5

Student Checklist for a Student-Centered Classroom 78

Teacher Checklist for a Student-Centered Classroom 79

Chapter 6

The Teaching and Learning Continuum (TLC) 82–83

Chapter 7

Checklist of Characteristics of a Thinking Student 100

Checklist of Characteristics of a Thinking Classroom 101

Checklist of Characteristics of a Thinking Curriculum 102

Teaching Thinking Skills: Lesson Format Template 103–104

Guided Thinking Template 105

Student Perception Questionnaire 108

Work Plan 109

Student Reflection Log 110

Chapter 8

Digging Deeper Matrix (DDM) 124

Chapter 9

Spider Diagram 129

Compare and Contrast Graphic Organizer 130

Cross-Impact Matrix (CIM) 132

Positive, Negative, Interesting (PNI) 142

Consider All the Issues (CAI) 145

Priority Ladder Template 147

Synthesis 3 + 1 148

Structured Thinking Organizer 149

Chapter 10

Norms of the Creative Classroom 161

Chapter 11

5 Whys to Therefore 165

If-Then Mind Map for Decision Making 172

What Would Happen If . . . ? 175

What? So What? Now What? 177

12 Steps to Group Decision Making 178

Figures

Figure 1.1 The Pros and Cons of Technology Use 12
Figure 2.1 21st Century Workforce Skills 13
Figure 2.2 21st Century Curriculum Model 15
Figure 2.3 200 Abstract Concepts 16
Figure 2.4 Concept Development Lesson Sample 18
Figure 2.5 Relationships–Rigor–Relevance: The 3 Rs 17
Figure 2.6 Concept Development Worksheet: Example 21
Figure 2.7 The Pyramid of Knowledge 22
Figure 2.8 Breaking Down the Essentials: Example Science Standard 24
Figure 2.9 Breaking Down the Essentials: Science Example (Upper Grades) 25
Figure 2.10 Breaking Down the Essentials: Math Example (Lower Grades) 26
Figure 4.1 The Cycle of Motivation 37
Figure 4.2 The Brain's Domains 38
Figure 4.3 The Hindbrain 38
Figure 4.4 The Midbrain 39
Figure 4.5 The Reptilian Brain 39
Figure 4.6 The Cerebral Cortex 40
Figure 4.7 The Four Lobes of the Cortex 40
Figure 4.8 Pathway to a Motivating and Engaging Classroom 42
Figure 4.9 Rank Your Interests: Example—The Nervous System 53
Figure. 4.10 Using Assessment as Feedback to Students 62
Figure 4.11 Four Square Concept Map: Example 64
Figure 4.12 Read-Write-Pair-Share and Think-Pair-Share 65
Figure 4.13 1–3 Minute Coaching/Consultation 66
Figure 4.14 Tiered Review/Practice 66
Figure 5.1 Four Phases of Self-Regulation 71
Figure 5.2 Cycle of Progression of Achievement 72
Figure 5.3 10:2/20:2 Rule 76
Figure 6.1 Gradual Release of Responsibility Model 84
Figure 6.2 TLC Level 1: Didactic Instruction 86
Figure 6.3 TLC Level 2: Facilitated Instruction 87
Figure 6.4 TLC Level 3: Coached Instruction 87
Figure 6.5 TLC Level 4: Consultative Instruction 88
Figure 6.6 Assessment That Builds Autonomy 89
Figure 7.1 Divergent Thinking 93
Figure 7.2 Convergent Thinking 93
Figure 7.3 Teaching Thinking Skills Lesson Format: Example 96
Figure 7.4 Guided Thinking: Math Example 106
Figure 7.5 Guided Thinking: History Example 107
Figure 8.1 Bloom's Taxonomy 1956 112
Figure 8.2 Implementing Bloom's Revised Taxonomy 116
Figure 8.3 Bloom's Revised Taxonomy with Additional Assessment Layer 114–115
Figure 8.4 Digging Deeper into Bloom's: Science Example (Lower Grades) 117
Figure 8.5 Digging Deeper into Bloom's: History Example (Upper Grades) 118
Figure 8.6 The Three Stages of the *Understand* Level 119
Figure 9.1 Spider Diagram: Example—Biological Systems 128
Figure 9.2 Advanced Compare and Contrast Graphic Organizer: Examples 131
Figure 9.3 CIM: Examples 133
Figure 9.4 Sequencing and Prioritizing Graphics 134–135
Figure 9.5 PNI: Examples (Lower Grades) 143
Figure 9.6 PNI: Example (Upper Grades) 144
Figure 9.7 Priority Ladder: Example 146
Figure 11.1 A Linear-Cyclical Problem-Solving Process 164
Figure 11.2 5 Whys to Therefore: Example 166
Figure 11.3 If-Then Mind Map for Decision Making: Example 171
Figure 11.4 What Would Happen If . . . ? Example 173–174
Figure 11.5 What? So What? Now What? Example 176
Figure 12.1 Connecting Differentiation and 21st Century Thinking and Learning 180

Foreword by Diane Heacox, Ed.D.

As teachers, we are frequently presented with new educational paradigms, school and government initiatives, and an ever-expanding list of "do's." This is what keeps us engaged and learning, but it can also feel a bit overwhelming.

Twenty-first century skills, dispositions, and attitudes are the topics of current discussions, debates, and a good deal of research and writing. These discussions center on the increased diversity of our classrooms as well as our preparation of students for success in an increasingly complex and connected global society.

Today's students differ greatly from each other and their learning needs vary even more dramatically than ever. Such classroom disparities require educators to think differently about teaching and learning. Richard Cash's *Advancing Differentiation: Thinking and Learning for the 21st Century* is a comprehensive resource that enables teachers to deepen their understandings of differentiation as well as prepare our students for their tomorrow.

The Framework for 21st Century Learning[1] presents four critical components to educate students for success in the future:

- deep content knowledge and the ability to apply this knowledge across disciplines
- information, media, and technology skills that respond to new needs and interests of tech-savvy students
- life and career skills, including dispositions and attitudes such as personal initiative and self-direction
- learning and innovation skills, including creative and critical thinking, problem solving, and decision making

Richard Cash provides not only the theoretical foundations that ground these critical components, but also the instructional strategies and classroom applications that enable us to see how these components look in practice.

Teaching for the twenty-first century infuses more complexity and rigor in learning, focuses on conceptual knowledge beyond subject-specific knowledge, employs strategies to engage and motivate learners, builds student self-regulation skills and learning autonomy, and develops students' thinking proficiencies. This is no small charge. However, this book's checklists enable you to critically examine your current classroom practices, while planning templates easily guide you in developing new teaching habits and routines.

> Teaching for the twenty-first century . . . is no small charge.

The first six chapters provide ideas for optimizing curriculum and instructional practices to increase student achievement. Richard defines the essential elements of curriculum for the twenty-first century, as well as ways to motivate and actively engage students in the learning process. Focusing on best practices, he also includes an overview of how the brain learns, as well as the impact of culture and gender on learning.

Advances in technology have altered the very nature of pedagogy. The tools of technology and the tremendous access to information have changed the act of teaching. Richard considers both the positives and negatives of classroom technology and challenges us to consider that the efficiency of technology in supporting learning is enhanced through the thinking and learning habits of our students.

1 The Partnership for 21st Century Skills (www.p21.org).

The Teaching Learning Continuum (TLC) in Chapter 6 may be of particular interest to teachers. We want our students to take more responsibility for and control of their learning. However, students do not necessarily develop skills of autonomy independently as they mature. The TLC model suggests that in order to move all students toward greater autonomy, we must change the role of the teacher and the learner. Specific strategies for guiding students to greater levels of autonomy are clearly outlined in this chapter and throughout the book.

The final four chapters focus on twenty-first century thinking skills. Richard introduces us to the foundations of thinking proficiency: critical reasoning, creative idea generation, problem finding and solving, and decision making. He coaches us in our efforts to formally introduce thinking skills to students, bring the skills to the students' consciousness, and embed them in our curriculum and lessons. He provides generous examples of lessons bridging many grade levels and curriculum topics. Graphic organizers provided for thinking skills will save you preparation time. Richard's concept of "digging deeper into Bloom's" will change the way you use the Bloom's Taxonomy model in your classroom.

Advancing Differentiation is your go-to resource as you extend your practices in differentiation and increase your focus on twenty-first century skills, dispositions, and attitudes. All educators—from novices to master teachers—will find next steps in their professional development within the pages of this comprehensive book. Strategies, templates, tools, and examples will make your work in preparing your students for their future both doable and practical. Enjoy this engaging and enlightening book as Richard Cash guides and coaches you in developing new habits in teaching and learning.

Diane Heacox, Ed.D.
Author of *Differentiating Instruction in the Regular Classroom* and *Making Differentiation a Habit* and Associate Professor of Education at St. Catherine University in St. Paul, Minnesota

Introduction

> We are now at a point where we must educate our children in what no one knew yesterday, and prepare our schools for what no one knows yet.
>
> —*Margaret Mead, cultural anthropologist*

Mrs. Donaldson is a sixth-grade teacher in a suburban school district. Her 30 students come from four continents, speak seven different languages, represent every major ethnic group, range in economic status from disadvantaged to wealthy, differ intellectually from developmentally delayed to gifted, and are a genuine cross-section of social and emotional needs. One thing that her students have in common is: *they are all learning*. She has made an effort to know each student as an individual, understands their preferred learning styles, is familiar with their interests and cultural backgrounds, and continually assesses them to find out what they know and don't know. While she has constant demands on her time as a teacher, she's made it a priority to differentiate her instructional strategies as well as her learning environment. It's paying off in her students' success and in her classroom's efficiency. Mrs. Donaldson's not an expert on differentiation—and she doesn't need to be—but she's on the journey toward proficiency.

I have observed and worked with numerous teachers like Mrs. Donaldson; they inspired me to write this book. In our challenging time of standards-based learning, high-stakes testing, efforts to close the achievement gap, and initiatives such as No Child Left Behind and Race to the Top, I am continually amazed by these teachers' passions for ensuring every child is not only prepared to meet standards and pass tests, but is truly prepared for future success.

The Next Level of Differentiation

Today's classroom is far different from the one many teachers, parents, and business professionals encountered during their own 13-plus school years. Advances in technology including interactive white boards and other computerized classroom tools, developments in learning theory, and expansion of knowledge are just a few of the forces requiring educators to change the way they teach children. In addition, student needs today vary more dramatically than ever. Students come to our classrooms with preparation ranging from early exposure to vast amounts of information to limited access to reading materials. Student learning differences are developing and being identified earlier and are more wide-ranging. These differences include sensory processing disorders; emotional and behavioral issues; differences in memory, abstraction, or sequencing ability; dyslexia; ADHD; autism; Asperger's syndrome; degrees of English language proficiency; and various levels and types of giftedness, among many others. Such disparities require us to think differently about how we design our curriculum and deliver instruction.

When we truly know our students, we are better able to meet their needs and direct our curriculum and instruction toward ensuring their success. However, the curriculum many of us use in our classrooms, in the form of textbooks and other classroom learning materials, is often not enough to meet the myriad needs of learners and prepare them for their futures.

While retaining fidelity to a standards-based curriculum is essential, it also is our job as teachers to adapt and enhance this curriculum when needed to ensure our students' success. This often means infusing more rigor and conceptual knowledge into the curriculum, employing specific strategies to engage and motivate students, building students' self-regulation skills and learning autonomy, and, perhaps most importantly, making certain our students are not just learning, but also are *thinking*.

The Importance of Thinking Skills in Today's World

Beyond the need for a rigorous curriculum and differentiated instruction is the core need for thinking skills. In today's differentiated classroom, students and teachers must work together toward a common goal of thinking proficiency. Beyond subject-specific knowledge, thinking skills are crucial to students' future success in their work, personal, and community lives. Thinking skills, most generally, include the ability to take in and make sense of new information, and connect, apply, and transform that information into unique and novel ideas. Proficiency in thinking involves the capacity to analyze information and find problems, evaluate evidence through critical reasoning, and then creatively synthesize ideas to generate new knowledge.

Our students must be equipped to think differently, cogently, and flexibly to thrive in today's world. A 1991 school improvement research report cited, "In the twentieth century, the ability to engage in careful, reflective thought has been viewed in various ways: as a fundamental characteristic of an educated person, as a requirement for responsible citizenship in a democratic society, and, more recently, as an employability skill for an increasingly wide range of jobs."[1] Now—more than a decade into the twenty-first century, with the fast and furious advances in technology, vast increases in the amount of information at our fingertips, diversification of the workforce, and the "flattening" of the world through global trade and communication—it is more crucial than ever that our students be taught these skills of effective thinking. Being able to think, both critically and creatively, is the characteristic that will determine whether our students succeed as members of today's workforce and society, and tomorrow's.

The Partnership for 21st Century Skills, a U.S. national advocacy organization, has defined five essential competencies that help employees and citizens be successful in this century. They include *adaptability*, *self-direction*, *cross-cultural skills*, *productivity*, and *leadership*. In addition, the organization has identified the five major interdisciplinary themes these thinking skills will likely be centered on: *global awareness* and *financial*, *civic*, *health*, and *environmental* literacy.[2] Thus, effective thinking skills are imperative for our students to develop into individuals who are able to locate and prioritize information, employ new technologies, retain and continually build on essential knowledge and skill-sets, and contribute innovative solutions to increasingly complex societal and environmental problems. Proficient thinking will also enable them to relate to people of diverse backgrounds, maintain functional relationships, manage their individual goals and identity, make wise financial and personal health choices, and participate as informed citizens in a democracy.

Being able to think, both critically and creatively, is the characteristic that will determine whether our students succeed as members of today's workforce and society, and tomorrow's.

An engaging, rigorous curriculum that infuses high-level thinking skills, delivered through authentic differentiated instructional practices within a student-centered classroom environment—this is what will ultimately guarantee our students' current and future success.

About This Book and Digital Content

Advancing Differentiation provides numerous strategies, templates, tools, and ideas to help you progress to the next level in differentiating curriculum and instruction. The work within this book comes from my years spent teaching gifted children and working with teachers across the United States and internationally.

As suggested in the title, *Advancing Differentiation: Thinking and Learning for the 21st Century* is intended to move you from where you are now in the procedures of differentiation to the next level of infusing the thinking

1 Kathleen Cotton, North West Regional Educational Laboratory (NWREL), School Improvement Research Series report, 1991.

2 The Partnership for 21st Century Skills (www.p21.org).

and learning skills essential for student success in the twenty-first century. The book is divided into two parts, both focused on evolving your practice of differentiation. Part One helps you better articulate the content (what you are teaching) and how you organize the environment (brain-compatible learning) so that your students are more successful in acquiring and achieving standards and goals. You will be introduced to methods for defining the essential components of your curriculum and ways to motivate, engage, and build your students' responsibility in the learning process. Part Two is focused on the process (how students think through the learning) and products (how students can eloquently show what they have learned). The book's second half guides you through infusing and implementing 21st Century Skills. It defines the various levels of thinking and provides a wealth of practical strategies that can be applied in any classroom.

Together, the two parts of this book combine the concept of differentiation with the skills our students need for success in the twenty-first century. When considering the actions of differentiating content, teachers must be aware of the concepts, facts, and procedures they want their students to know, be able to do, and understand. Conceptual levels of learning are supported through the execution of procedures and implementation of facts. It is these understandings of concepts that move our students to greater degrees of success in today's world. Being able to aptly apply skills and procedures in multiple contexts and in automatic ways gives students the mental time and energy to problem solve, reason critically, and think creatively. This all is supported with a strong knowledge base in and among disciplines.

The essential goal of this book is to help teachers create a classroom environment that identifies and embeds twenty-first century skills within the curriculum, reinforces these skills through instructional practices, and requires the generation of creative and original products. Additional goals are included in the following list.

The Goals of *Advancing Differentiation*

- To clarify how differentiation can be taken to the next level in today's classroom
- To provide methods for defining the key components of your curriculum: what students should know, be able to do, and understand
- To offer ideas for creating effective unit-based and essential questions
- To examine what constitutes a quality, rigorous, concept-based curriculum
- To lay out a framework to help you create effective, engaging, exciting, and enriching learning opportunities that guide all students to deeper levels of thinking
- To present research-based information on student motivation and engagement
- To offer an overview of how the brain learns, including the impacts of gender, ethnicity, and cultural background on learning
- To supply useful strategies and helpful assessment formats that can increase student achievement
- To provide valuable tools for developing student self-regulation and responsibility in learning
- To offer a unique design for increasing student autonomy in the learning process
- To outline numerous strategies for infusing the skills of critical and creative thinking, problem finding, problem solving, and decision making
- To define essential tools for building a classroom centered on student learning and thinking proficiency

▶ **Part One** (Chapters 1–6) leads you through the process of taking your current differentiation practices to the next level. In order to masterfully differentiate instruction, you must have articulate knowledge about how your curriculum is designed. Knowing what goes into the construction of curriculum will help you define what is essential, learn how to increase rigor, motivate and engage your students, and thus develop lifelong learners.

The essential goal of this book is to help teachers create a classroom environment that embeds twenty-first century skills within the curriculum, reinforces them through instructional practices, and requires the generation of original products.

Chapter 1 explains how, with the ever-changing demographics and needs of students, differentiation takes on a new immediacy in today's classrooms. *Differentiated instruction* is a crucial strategy within leading instructional paradigms such as Response to Intervention (RTI). Many myths surround differentiation: what it is and is not, what it can and cannot do. This chapter dispels these myths in both the classroom and school culture of student success. It also presents Figure 1.1 The Pros and Cons of Technology, and discusses the impact of technology use on classroom instruction.

Chapter 2 outlines the *essentials of the curriculum* you deliver in the process of differentiating. The focus of this chapter is to relate the three levels of knowledge construction: what your students should know, be able to do, and understand. These levels also relate to the three types of knowing: factual knowledge, procedural knowledge, and conceptual knowledge. Factual knowledge includes the terminology, specific details, and basic elements that students must be acquainted with to work within the discipline. Skills, procedures, techniques, and thinking strategies are all examples of procedural knowledge. The highest level of learning is conceptual knowledge, which provides students with a framework for understanding the relationships between disciplines—from classifications, to principles and generalization, to theories and models.

Chapter 3 defines and asserts the need for a *rigorous curriculum* that is effective, engaging, exciting, and enriching (an "E^4" curriculum). The chapter highlights the need for all students to engage in conceptually based complex learning tasks that allow them to explore content through various learning modes. Students are stretched in their learning when they complete authentic tasks. Additionally, students gain ownership of the learning when they engage in substantive conversations about content that is relevant to their lives.

Chapter 4 guides you in creating a learning environment in which students develop the intrinsic desire to learn. *Intrinsic motivation* is achieved when learning tasks are stimulating to students, develop their interests, and foster appropriate skill development. Engaging students in interesting, fun, and personally meaningful tasks makes them want to learn. This chapter offers suggestions for developing a classroom that is based on student choice and is intrinsically motivating. It explores learning preferences and how you can use them to improve achievement. It provides instructional ideas related to gender and cultural differences, as well as various brain-compatible learning strategies and examples. Robert Sternberg's model of "Successful Intelligence" also is explained and related curricular formats are offered. Finally, this chapter outlines a *three-phase assessment process* that both motivates students and helps you determine their readiness levels. Assessment *before* learning identifies which skills and processes students possess at the beginning of each lesson. Assessment *for* learning is the systemic, ongoing, dynamic process of collecting and analyzing data to improve student learning. Assessment *of* learning identifies how close the student came to achieving the learning goal. This section offers tips and suggestions for assessment application and grading practices.

Chapter 5 provides strategies for encouraging *self-regulation* and building a student-centered classroom. When students have an awareness of their own learning process, it helps them monitor their progress, make changes and adaptations when necessary, understand the usefulness of various learning strategies, and recognize the direct relationship between effort and learning. Five key elements are defined for mobilizing resources to improve student self-regulation. The chapter also shows you how to use the theory of mindset to assist learners in developing metacognitive awareness to achieve their goals. Finally, reflection on the learning process is critical to understanding successes and gaps in learning. Several ideas are offered for developing efficient reflective practices.

Chapter 6 discusses the benefits and goals of student *learning autonomy* and introduces the Teaching and Learning Continuum (TLC) model. Teaching students to be self-directed learners is fostered through a gradual transformation in student and teacher roles. Without a progressive instructional design, students may struggle in conducting quality independent learning. Building on a synthesis of research on teaching and learning, the TLC offers a framework for the changing roles and responsibilities of both teacher and student. As the learner gains skills toward self-guidance, the teacher becomes more consultative. Also suggested are classroom strategies and practices for developing each level of student independence.

▶ **Part Two** (Chapters 7–11) guides you in implementing effective high-level thinking skills in your differentiated classroom. This section articulates and defines the concept of thinking and offers ways to integrate thinking skills into any curricular area, topic, or grade level. It also provides a template to use as an overlay to enhance and extend material offered in textbooks.

Chapter 7 asserts that the foundations of *thinking proficiency* are critical reasoning, creative idea generation, problem finding and solving, and decision making. This chapter explains the need for both divergent and convergent thinking, and defines the characteristics of a thinking student, a thinking classroom, and a thinking curriculum. It also provides methods for developing intellectually disciplined thinkers.

Chapter 8 constructs a *framework for thinking* by using Benjamin Bloom's Taxonomy of Learning and Robert Marzano's Advanced Taxonomy of Learning to explore various questioning techniques and lesson designs. This chapter provides you with strategies to move learners from basic to complex levels of thinking, and from automatic reproduction to conscious self-awareness in the learning process.

Chapter 9 discusses *critical thinking*, which entails making decisions based on the evidence at hand. Without sufficient training in critical thinking and reasoning, students often use emotion, opinion, or instinct to make decisions. This chapter presents strategies and curricular ideas for how students can form questions to build relevant claims and inform the decision-making process. Helpful graphic organizers are also included.

Chapter 10 emphasizes the importance of *creative idea generation* in the classroom. As our world changes more rapidly each year, our students must be provided with the skills to develop their own creativity and creative thinking abilities. The ability to think "outside the box" is framed through fluency, flexibility, originality, and elaboration (FFOE). This chapter defines these four elements and articulates curricular connections. Strategies for supporting a creative learning environment are also introduced.

Chapter 11 illustrates the process of approaching learning through the lens of *problem finding and solving* in order to engage learners more completely. For students to solve problems, they need a tool kit filled with many diverse tools. This chapter provides problem-finding techniques, problem-solving strategies, as well as decision-making skills.

Finally, the **Final Note** and **Conclusion** review the key points in the text and also revisit the issue, presented in Chapter 1, of technology in the classroom and discuss how it can be successfully incorporated as an important component in thinking and learning for the twenty-first century. Included is a graphic depicting the connection, made throughout the book, between differentiation and twenty-first century thinking and learning.

The digital content (see page viii for how to download) includes all of the reproducible forms from the book as PDFs. Many of the forms are able to be customized on-screen before printing out. In addition, there is a PowerPoint presentation for use in professional development.

If you wish to use the book in a professional learning community or book study group, a PLC Guide with chapter-by-chapter discussion questions and teaching suggestions is available. You may download the free guide at freespirit.com.

How to Use This Book

Advancing Differentiation brings together essential elements of curriculum design and the latest research on thinking and learning. This book is a culmination of my journey as a student of learning. I've connected the theoretical ideas into practical, proven strategies that can increase students' achievement and ultimately lead to their future success.

My intent with this guide is to support classroom teachers, teacher coaches, school administrators, and curriculum developers in enriching and enhancing the learning experiences of all students. I also believe this book serves as an excellent resource for teacher education college courses. The ideas, strategies, and techniques fit within any content area, grade level, or ability level. While sample figures and templates may illustrate higher grade levels, they can easily be adjusted for lower grade levels, and vice versa.

The ideas, strategies, and techniques fit within any content area, grade level, or ability level.

You may choose to go through the book chapter by chapter, building a rigorous curriculum and a thinking classroom from the sequential flow of the text. Or, you may choose to review the text in its entirety, examine your current practices, and then select individual chapters that can help you refine what you are already doing to ensure all of your students are thinking and learning. For example, you may find that your existing textbook curriculum does not offer enough information about concept development or provide for rigorously engaging activities. You will then want to focus your attention on Chapter 3: Advancing Differentiation to New Levels Through a Rigorous Curriculum.

If you are a specialist outside the role of a classroom teacher—such as a teacher coach, curriculum coordinator, gifted and talented specialist, or school administrator—this book can be a valuable resource. How do you help teachers understand how curriculum is designed? In what ways can you help teachers and students create their own essential questions? How do you get students to think effectively in this age of standardized testing and No Child Left Behind? How do you infuse thinking skills without having to remove something else from the curriculum? You will find the answers to these questions and more within these pages.

You may be asking yourself, "Where do I begin? How do I get started? What do I need to know?" I suggest starting small. Get a taste for success. Take one idea or topic from this book and make it work for you and your students. I've arranged each chapter to provide a general overview of the theory that grounds the practices, and then give plenty of examples of how to apply the ideas to your classroom. Not every idea presented here will work for you, but many can be adjusted and modified to fit your students and curricular needs. I hope that you will find this text to be an essential resource in your classroom, school, and district to engage your students in the art of thinking, increase their achievement, and ensure lifelong success.

Enjoy!

Richard M. Cash, Ed.D.

Part One
Taking Differentiation to the Next Level

The following six chapters serve as a valuable resource in building your portfolio of differentiated curriculum and instruction practices. The art of differentiation is about being proactive in meeting *all* of your students' learning needs. Having a greater storehouse of ideas, strategies, and techniques can better prepare you for the diversity of these needs in the twenty-first century.

Chapter 1

Defining How Differentiation Looks in Today's Classroom

> Differentiated instruction is a way of taking into account the needs and wants of others without relinquishing our own needs and wants, or dominating and controlling the other person. In that way, differentiated instruction is more than just a method of teaching; it is a way of being human.
>
> —*Carol Ann Tomlinson, author and educator*

GT Stands for Good Teaching

As a teacher these days, you have likely been introduced to a plethora of "new" initiatives that can improve how your students learn. New math, whole language, outcome-based education, the content standards movement—the list goes on. For years, teachers of gifted and talented students (such as myself) have been required to use the strategies of differentiated instruction, because not all gifted students are gifted in the same way. Outstanding pioneers of gifted education such as Lewis Terman, Paul Torrence, Letta Hollingworth, John Feldhusen, and Joe Renzulli instructed teachers of gifted kids how to identify their students' strengths and weaknesses, build units based on higher order thinking skills (or HOTS), and create lessons that were loaded with critical reasoning and creative thinking. This education of gifted and talented students was known by the acronym "GT." I see now, however, after many years working with a broader group of students, that what we have learned in gifted and talented education can be applied to *all* students at varying degrees of sophistication. I now call GT: good teaching! This book is full of GT ideas, strategies, and techniques for every learner.

> What we have learned in gifted and talented education can be applied to *all* students at varying degrees of sophistication.

Dispelling the Myths of Differentiated Instruction

Many teachers fear differentiated instruction. The numerous myths that surround the idea can sometimes stifle a teacher's willingness to begin the process of differentiating. Following is a collection of some of those myths and how they might be addressed to encourage teachers to move forward.

Myth #1: Differentiation is another word for individualization.

▶ **Reality:** Differentiation is *not* synonymous with individualization. All teachers individualize to some extent. When a teacher meets one-on-one with a student, individually answers questions, or modifies instruction based on an individual need, this is both individualization as well as differentiation.

Individualization gained a bad reputation during the 1970s when teachers were expected to write individual lessons for students. This is not differentiation. Differentiation aims to meet individual needs through a quality curriculum and effective and efficient instructional practices that target groups of students based on learning readiness, individual interests, and preferred ways of learning—not to create thirty separate lesson plans for every unit.

Myth #2: In a differentiated classroom you will see all the kids doing something different.
▶ **Reality:** All students should be provided relevant, meaningful, and challenging learning opportunities. Every lesson and activity should consider the individual students within the class, but not every child will be doing something different. There will be times when small groups of students or individuals will be engaged in different projects or independent studies, and other times when all or most students are engaged in the same activity. Teachers in a differentiated classroom take on the role of managing the learning process. Just like in any work setting, not every worker is doing the same thing, but the good manager is clear as to what each worker is doing and where he or she is in the process. So too in a differentiated classroom, the teacher, like the good manager, oversees and coordinates the learning process of each student, some in groups and some individually.

Myth #3: Differentiation will change everything and solve all of our teaching problems.
▶ **Reality:** Differentiation will not solve all your problems; it is not the magic potion that will raise student achievement. Being a teacher who is mindful of his or her students' academic, social, and emotional needs is what will help address learning gaps, increase motivation to learn, and ultimately raise student achievement. Differentiating curriculum and instruction means providing intervention strategies and techniques so that every student is successful. Differentiation doesn't happen in isolation or without a team effort. Just like in the Response to Intervention (RTI) model, differentiated instruction requires teachers to use effective practices and to reflect on the outcomes of its implementation. This is what differentiation can do to ensure all students meet or exceed expectations.

Myth #4: In a differentiated classroom the teacher does not teach.
▶ **Reality:** In a differentiated classroom the teacher is the key to student achievement. However, the role of teacher changes from the "sage on the stage" to the "guide on the side." There will be times when teachers may need to directly instruct, as well as times for students to direct their own learning. Chapter 6 presents a teaching and learning continuum that supports students toward more autonomy in their learning. Though differentiation is nothing new, teachers must now be proactive about planning instruction so as to optimize student learning. They research effective practices; implement quality strategies before, during, and after instruction; continually monitor student learning; and reflect on how well students have mastered material before moving on to the next topic.

Myth #5: You can't differentiate when you are trying to prepare for high-stakes testing.
▶ **Reality:** "Evidence clearly suggests that for most students, mastery and understanding come through, not after, meaningful interaction with ideas."[1] The first important objective of differentiation is for students to understand the content deeply. When students understand the content, they are *more* prepared for standardized tests rather than less. Students learn more deeply when allowed to connect information to previous experiences and knowledge, apply learned material in authentic situations, and exercise skills in problem solving, creative thinking, and critical reasoning. The second important objective of a differentiated classroom is to prepare students for all kinds of content delivery, including those that are undifferentiated (such as standardized tests). All assessments, including standardized tests, are tools that direct the plans for instruction as well as offer feedback to the learner. Teachers who differentiate use quality assessment strategies throughout the learning process including those that model standardized tests.

Myth #6: Differentiation is mainly for gifted students.
▶ **Reality:** Differentiation is for all students. A differentiated classroom is centered on students' readiness, interests, and learning profiles—not on ability alone. Some students will require more complex and in-depth material, while other students will require more scaffolding and foundation construction to support their learning experiences. When differentiating

1 Tomlinson, Carol Ann, and Jay McTighe. *Integrating Differentiated Instruction & Understanding by Design: Connecting Content and Kids.* Alexandria, VA: Association for Supervision and Curriculum Development, 2006, p. 8.

based on your students' abilities or achievement, it is critical to keep in mind that your gifted and advanced students do not get "more" work, but get "more challenging" work. Tasks must be respectful not only of students' abilities but also of their time. In differentiated classrooms, teachers apply principles of gifted education to all students.

Myth #7: Differentiation is just a way to group or track students.
▶ **Reality:** Tracking is the practice of permanently assigning students to a particular level of instruction with very little differentiation included. In a differentiated classroom, teachers employ the strategy of flexible grouping practices, which include grouping students by interest, ability, learning style, academic strength/weakness, or gender. Teachers plan instruction so that students will move in and out of groups so as to interact with a variety of peers throughout the learning process. Sometimes students will work with like-ability students and sometimes with students who have different skills and/or ability. In other cases you may find that some students learn best while working with others and some learn best by working alone. This strategy takes into account the students' interpersonal and intrapersonal strengths. It all depends on what outcome you expect from the activity.

Myth #8: There is no fair way to grade in a differentiated classroom.
▶ **Reality:** Not all kids learn at the same rate. Therefore, grading in a differentiated classroom takes on an entirely different meaning. When teachers know *what* they want students to know, be able to do and understand; *how* they want students to represent that knowledge; and have developed quality grading criteria, then grading becomes about identifying students' acquisition of knowledge and mastery.

Grading in a differentiated classroom must be equitable and represented through a "photo album" of student growth. Three types of assessment are used in a differentiated classroom to ensure students are learning the material. Preassessments are used to find out what students know and don't know before instruction begins. Formative assessments are used as checkpoints for how well the students are accumulating the information taught and provide the teacher with feedback about teaching strategies and pace. Summative assessments are used to mark students' achievement of goals set forth in a unit of study. You will employ all three of these assessment strategies to create a "grade" of how well the student gathered information and mastered content. Remember, it is *not* about the grade, but rather about what the student learned.

Myth #9: With everything teachers have to do, they can't be expected to differentiate, too.
▶ **Reality:** Differentiation of curriculum and instruction should not be separate from all other school initiatives. Differentiation is Response to Intervention (RTI); Structured Instruction, Observation Protocol (SIOP); Positive Behavioral Intervention and Support (PBIS); Achievement Via Individual Determination (AVID); Guided Reading; new math; preparation for post-high school; and the list goes on. All initiatives schools employ to provide safe and quality learning environments and to improve student achievement are methods of differentiation. Simply put, whatever it takes to ensure that every child is ready for the next step is differentiation. Differentiation is embedded within the educational systems, not a separate initiative.

Myth #10: Differentiation takes too much time that I don't have.
▶ **Reality:** Differentiation *will* require a considerable time investment initially, but in the long run it will actually save you time as a teacher and increase the overall efficiency of your classroom. Begin by creating your own mindset of doing whatever it takes to get students to be proficient in what you know to be essential about your content. Start small, work on one strategy at a time, develop expertise, and build a knowledge base. Every hour you invest now in planning and implementing differentiation will save you an hour in the future and will enable your students to succeed and progress more quickly.

Differentiating curriculum and instruction is *not* easy. It takes many hours for teachers to define what is essential for students to know, be able to do, and understand; figure out how best to provide engaging experiences for students to acquire this information; present information through multiple activities that assist students in applying the learning; create effective assessment strategies that can appraise where students are at in the learning process; and finally, offer authentic modes of production where students can demonstrate their knowledge. Differentiation is a teaching process that takes time and patience . . . but it is entirely doable.

The 10 Elements of a Differentiated Classroom on page 11 is for you to refer to as you read this book. Each of these elements will be explored in more detail throughout.

10 Elements of a Differentiated Classroom

1. **Content goals** are defined.
   - Know: Factual Knowledge
   - Able to do: Procedural Knowledge
   - Understand: Conceptual Knowledge

2. **Learning differences** are acknowledged.
   - Interests
   - Learning Styles
   - Readiness

3. The three types of **assessment** are employed.
   - Preassessment
   - Formative Assessment
   - Summative Assessment

4. Curriculum and instruction foster **brain-compatible learning**.

5. The classroom environment respects **active learning**.

6. Learners develop **21st Century Skills**.
   - Higher Order Thinking Skills (HOTS)
   - Creative Thinking
   - Critical Reasoning
   - Self-Regulation

7. **Flexible grouping** is used to achieve optimal learning.

8. **Tiered assignments and activities** respond to learning needs and differences.

9. The learning environment is **interesting, enjoyable, challenging,** and **choice-filled** for all students.

10. Students develop **learning autonomy.**

From *Advancing Differentiation: Thinking and Learning for the 21st Century* by Richard M. Cash, Ed.D., copyright © 2011. Free Spirit Publishing Inc., Minneapolis, MN; 800-735-7323; www.freespirit.com. This page may be reproduced for use within an individual school or district. For all other uses, contact www.freespirit.com/company/permissions.cfm.

Technology Use in the Differentiated Classroom

As a teacher today, you likely employ many different forms of technology in your classroom to assist you in differentiating curriculum and instruction, ranging from interactive white boards to wireless slates to electronic student response systems. These devices can be of great assistance in customizing lesson plans, tasks, activities, and assessments for students of diverse abilities and preferences. This book does not directly address technology use or computer literacy in today's classrooms; that topic is for another volume altogether (or, rather, multiple volumes). And yet the use of technology pervades nearly all of the book's contents. The tools and skills being used by you and your students to achieve the goals presented here are becoming more and more computer-based and technology-specific each year.

Depending on your viewpoint, technology has made our lives more efficient or more difficult. Technology has definitely improved our society and our schools, but in some cases it may have caused our students to rely too much on the technology to where they have become intellectually lazy or unimaginative. Other possible pros and cons of technology are highlighted in **Figure 1.1.**

Chances are, you've heard a student say, "If the calculator can figure it out for me, why should I learn how to do the equation?" or "Why do I have to study this information if all I have to do is an Internet search to find the answers?" This line of thought, while at times showing a student's resourcefulness, can also lead to chronic intellectual laziness. As teachers, we have a duty to cure and prevent this laziness through persistently and routinely infusing differentiation practices, rigorous tasks, and thinking skills into our daily classroom routines, into every lesson and unit, as well as into our own practices.

Above all, we must keep in mind that technology is only as effective as the person who has created it and the person who is using it. This book's focus is on the learning habits and the thoughts of the minds behind, and the students seated in front of, the computers. Our responsibility as teachers is to facilitate and coach our students to use thinking as a tool to enhance the efficiency of technology.

Figure 1.1 The Pros and Cons of Technology Use

PROS	CONS
Expands the possibilities of thought	May limit imagination
Allows ready access to multiple views and limitless information	Encourages instant gratification and information overload
Enables users to customize content to meet their individual needs	Reduces shared language and experience
Requires the use of thoughtful examination and filtering of information	Increases impulsivity and reduces perseverance
Enables virtual connections with people around the world from diverse backgrounds	Fosters working in isolation without physical human contact
Provides access to a greater degree of global information media	Media can be formulaic, passive, and present an inaccurate view of the world
Encourages the use of ethics and open-mindedness in dealing with diversity	Encourages an egocentric view of the world
Increases productivity	Wastes time
Produces highly trained workers with new and malleable skills	Reduces workforce by automating jobs
Increases profits through reduced waste and higher productivity	Is often costly to build and maintain technology
Provides ease of communication	Increases cyberbullying and security threats

Chapter 2

Defining the Essentials of a Differentiated Curriculum

> The principal goal of education is to create [people] who are capable of doing new things, not simply of repeating what other generations have done.
>
> —*Jean Piaget, cognitive psychologist*

Skills for a New Century

The world has changed dramatically over the last 50 years. Advances in technology have altered both the educational and workforce landscapes. During the past two centuries, students could graduate from high school and expect to obtain a job that would sustain their own lives, and perhaps their families' lives, for decades. The workforce needs of the nineteenth and early twentieth centuries were based primarily on the lower-level skill of application, the ability to work with one's hands. Schooling, therefore, taught the skills of remembering and application.

Figure 2.1 21st Century Workforce Skills[1]

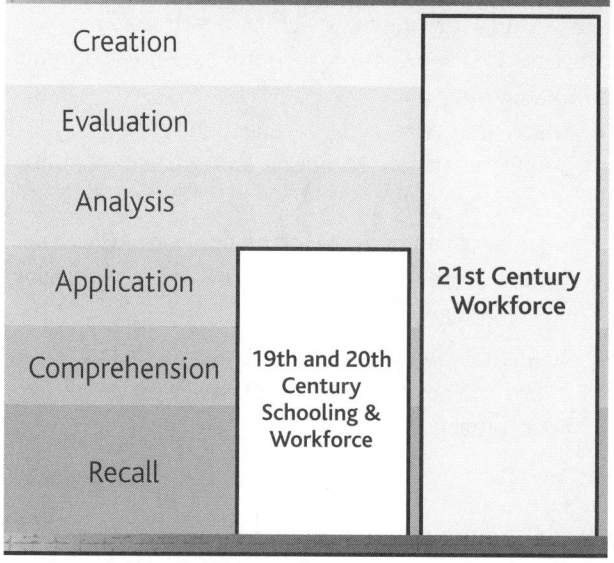

Today's careers, however, demand more sophisticated skills beyond application. "Of all the big developed countries, America now has the smallest proportion of factory workers in its labor force."[2] In the twenty-first century, the growing need in the workforce—of the United States and of most developed countries—will be for knowledge workers: those who analyze, evaluate, and create new knowledge within and across fields of discipline **(Figure 2.1).** The knowledge workers of tomorrow are the classroom students of today. We must have a curriculum that will prepare our students for their futures.

Essential to this curriculum development process is having a clear understanding of the content (what you are teaching) to ensure that you are addressing the wholeness of the goals and standards. Additionally, to effectively differentiate you must know what you are differentiating. This chapter will help you identify those essential components of your curriculum.

1 Based on Anderson, Lorin W., and David R. Krathwhol, eds. *A Taxonomy for Learning, Teaching, and Assessing: A Revision of Bloom's Taxonomy of Educational Objectives.* New York: Longman, 2001.

2 Drucker, Peter F. "The Next Workforce: Knowledge Workers Are the New Capitalists." *The Economist* (November 2001).

In the twenty-first century, the growing need in the workforce will be for knowledge workers.

According to the Partnership for 21st Century Skills[3], the five essential competencies of the new century are:

1. Flexibility and adaptability
2. Initiative and self-direction
3. Social and cross-cultural skills
4. Productivity and accountability
5. Leadership and responsibility

Today's curriculum and instruction must ensure that students are proficient in these competencies.

The Partnership for 21st Century Skills also defines a framework for curriculum and instruction as one that accomplishes the following:

- Teaches students thinking skills embedded within core subjects and twenty-first century interdisciplinary themes; these themes include:
  - global awareness
  - financial, economic, business and entrepreneurial literacy
  - civic literacy
  - health literacy
  - environmental literacy
- Requires students to apply thinking skills across content domains through performance-based activities
- Allows students to utilize technology and resources beyond the classroom walls

A Hierarchy of Knowledge: Factual, Procedural, Conceptual

This new idea of curriculum is a design that concentrates on the essentials of what students should know, be able to do, and understand in the twenty-first century. With advances in neuroscience, it is clear that the brain learns most efficiently through the following three dimensions of knowledge: factual (knowing the facts), procedural (doing the tasks), and conceptual (understanding the concepts) knowledge. Based on this finding, we should develop curricular activities that emphasize these dimensions. The design laid out for you in this chapter will help you define what is essential for your students to know, be able to do, and understand. This design is grounded in brain research, reflecting the knowledge built from both cognitive science and motivational theory.

"If a student engages in a curriculum that is well beyond that student's level of readiness, stress results, and the brain overproduces key neurotransmitters that impede learning."[4] Conversely, if the curriculum is redundant for the child—beneath that student's level of readiness—the brain is not inclined to engage or respond and, consequently, does not release the levels of dopamine, noradrenalin, serotonin, and other neurochemicals needed for optimal learning. The result is apathy.[5] Understanding this hierarchy of knowledge construction provides teachers a more refined way of approaching the development of unit and lesson design.

In today's classroom, however, most curriculum and instruction is anchored in factual and procedural knowledge. Most assessments that are critical to student and school reporting are regenerations of factual and procedural knowledge. The essential twenty-first century tool missing from many curriculum, instruction, and assessment equations is *conceptual* knowledge; specifically, the creative idea generation and critical reasoning that is grounded in conceptual levels of thinking. Experts think conceptually; they use creativity and critical analysis, and make efficient use of facts and procedures when solving problems. For our students to be effective thinkers we must ensure that our curriculum and instruction scaffolds them toward conceptual levels of thinking.

As we review our curriculum and instructional practices for the twenty-first century, we must commit to the following goals:

- Ensure that our standards reflect and specifically articulate factual, procedural, and conceptual levels of learning
- Focus equal amounts of instructional attention on factual, procedural, and conceptual levels of thinking and learning
- Guarantee that *all* our students are proficient in factual knowledge, procedural abilities, and conceptual understandings

3 The Partnership for 21st Century Skills (www.p21.org).

4 Koob, G. F., B. J. Cole, N. R. Swerdlow, and M. le Moal. "Stress, Performance, and Arousal: Focus on CRF." *National Institute on Drug Abuse Research Monograph*, No. 97-163176. LaJolla, CA: Research Institute of Scripps Clinic, Department of Neuropharmacology, 1990.

5 Schultz, Wolfram, P. Dayan, and P. R. Montague. "A Neural Substrate of Prediction and Reward." *Science*, 275 (1997): 1593–1599.

Four Steps to Defining the Essentials of Curriculum

Step 1: Define the Key Components of Curriculum

The model in **Figure 2.2** ilustrates how twenty-first century curriculum is constructed. Curricular materials are developed with a broad foundation of factual knowledge, moving toward procedural knowledge, and finally up to conceptual levels of thinking. This model is framed not only in the foundations of brain-compatible learning, but also in the taxonomy of educational objectives defined by Benjamin Bloom in 1956, with updates in 2001. (See Chapter 8 for an in-depth discussion of Bloom's Taxonomy.)

Factual Knowledge

At the foundation of all curricula is the factual level of knowledge. This level contains all of the basic elements of vocabulary or the language of the discipline, symbols, resources, and other components of indisputable evidence that students must know to be acquainted with a subject. Factual knowledge can most easily be represented and assessed using tests or quizzes centered on information recall and remembering.

Figure 2.2 21st Century Curriculum Model

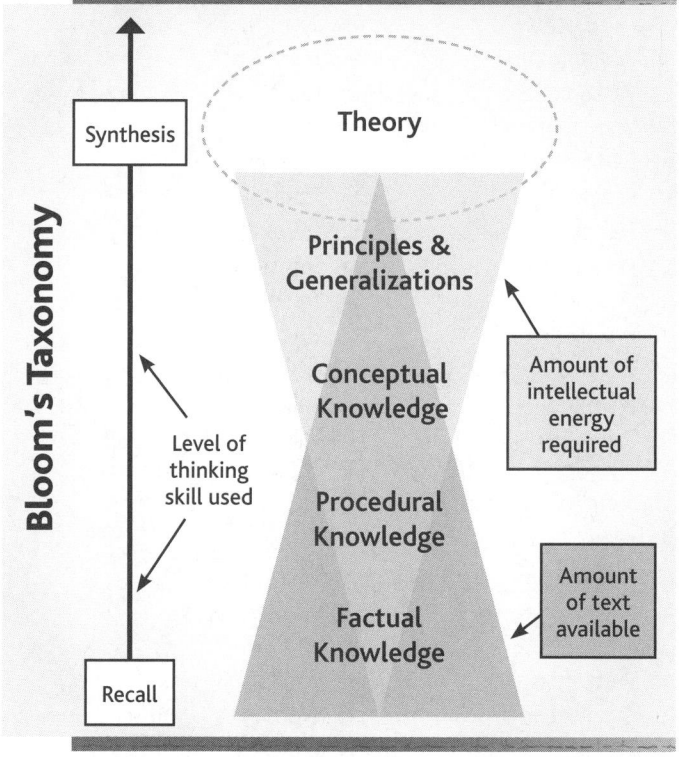

Procedural Knowledge

Progressing from factual knowledge, students then begin to interact with procedural knowledge, or the "know-how" of a discipline. Procedural knowledge includes actions or tasks to be learned and carried out, such as thinking skills, writing processes, experiments, and rules of doing. Also, at this level students are introduced to the tools of the discipline, such as editing, calculating, research, measurement, or any of the other tools a disciplinarian would use to solve problems, create, or produce within a domain of study.

Conceptual Knowledge

As students become more proficient in the areas of factual and procedural knowledge, they solidify their conceptual knowledge. Conceptual knowledge refers to the broad, overarching ideas, generalizations, principles, and theories that are found within and across disciplines. Concepts help students understand the deeper meanings within a discipline, as well as across a curriculum. Concepts offer avenues toward interdisciplinary study by helping students see the similarities and differences a single concept can possess in many different domains. Ultimately, concepts help students go more deeply into the subject matter by building connections and relationships between and across content areas. Concepts naturally inspire a sense of curiosity and provide students entries into the curriculum and ways to attach learning to their interests.

Concepts naturally inspire a sense of curiosity and provide students entries into the curriculum and ways to attach learning to their interests.

Conceptual knowledge can be divided into two general types:

- **Concrete** (it can be seen, touched, heard, smelled, or tasted). Examples of concrete concepts are home, dog, music, sour, and sweet.
- **Abstract** (it cannot be seen, touched, heard, smelled, or tasted, and it is a public idea rather than a personal belief). Examples of abstract concepts include such ideas as freedom, history, change, and beauty. (See **Figure 2.3** on page 16 for more examples.)

Figure 2.3 200 Abstract Concepts

1. Adaptation	51. Engagement	101. Justification	151. Rationality
2. Alienation	52. Engineering	102. Knowledge	152. Reality
3. Attitude	53. Environment	103. Language	153. Reason
4. Authenticity	54. Equality	104. Learning	154. Reductionism
5. Authority	55. Essence	105. Life and death	155. Reflection
6. Autonomy	56. Eternity	106. Literature	156. Rejection
7. Awareness	57. Ethics	107. Love	157. Relationships
8. Beauty	58. Evolution	108. Loyalty	158. Religion
9. Behavior	59. Existence	109. Man	159. Resolution
10. Being and becoming	60. Experience	110. Management	160. Responsibility
11. Beliefs	61. Experimentation	111. Materialism	161. Revolution
12. Caring	62. Exploration	112. Meaning	162. Rituals
13. Cause & effect	63. Extinction	113. Meditation	163. Scale
14. Certainty	64. Faith	114. Memory	164. Science
15. Change	65. Falsity	115. Metaphor	165. Self
16. Childhood	66. Family	116. Method	166. Self-esteem
17. Classification	67. Fantasy	117. Migration	167. Self-image
18. Commitment	68. Feelings	118. Mind	168. Self-knowledge
19. Communication	69. Free will	119. Models	169. Sensitivity
20. Community	70. Freedom	120. Moral	170. Service
21. Compassion	71. Global	121. Morality	171. Socialization
22. Conflict	72. Good and evil	122. Mystery	172. Society
23. Conflict resolution	73. Goodness	123. Myth	173. Soul
24. Conformity	74. Group	124. Nature	174. Spirituality
25. Connectedness	75. Growth	125. Negotiation	175. State
26. Conscience	76. Habit	126. Objectivity	176. Story
27. Consciousness	77. Harmony	127. Openness	177. Subjectivity
28. Conservation	78. Having	128. Origins	178. Survival
29. Constancy	79. Holism	129. Ownership	179. Systems
30. Consultation	80. Humankind	130. Paradigm	180. Teacher
31. Contemplation	81. Human rights	131. Paradox	181. Teamwork
32. Control	82. Idea	132. Participation	182. Time
33. Cooperation	83. Ideals	133. Patterns	183. Tolerance
34. Courage	84. Identity	134. Peace	184. Tradition
35. Creativity	85. Imagination	135. Perception	185. Training
36. Crisis	86. Independence	136. Personhood	186. Transformation
37. Culture	87. Individuality	137. Perspective	187. Truth
38. Cycles	88. Indoctrination	138. Philosophy	188. Understanding
39. Decision	89. Infinity	139. Physical	189. Utilitarian
40. Democracy	90. Information	140. Planning	190. Validity
41. Destruction	91. Initiation	141. Play	191. Value
42. Detachment	92. Insight	142. Poetry	192. Violence
43. Development	93. Instinct	143. Politics	193. Vision
44. Discipline	94. Integrity	144. Positivism	194. Voice
45. Discovery	95. Intelligence	145. Potential	195. Volition
46. Dualism	96. Interdependence	146. Power	196. Wholeness
47. Education	97. Intuition	147. Principles	197. Will
48. Emotion	98. Invention	148. Problem-solving	198. Wisdom
49. Empathy	99. Judgment	149. Qualitative	199. Woman
50. Energy	100. Justice	150. Qualities	200. Work

Have you ever put together a jigsaw puzzle? If so, you probably looked at the box cover to see what the puzzle should look like when you are finished. You used the box cover as a model to see the "big picture" of where you are going and how all of the pieces fit together. This is how learning should happen in the classroom. Starting a unit of study from the concept view can offer students the "big picture"; give them direction as to where they are headed; show them how the facts, skills, and processes all link together; and provide them with a connection to their prior knowledge of the content area.

Generalizations

From conceptual knowledge, we can draw generalizations and principles. Both generalizations and principles are the "big ideas," or universal and enduring beliefs, of a content area. Generalizations are formed from the relationship between concepts and are not factual in nature. Generalized statements can be said to be either always true or almost always true. Factual examples of the generalization are used in the content lessons to provide a common understanding. Teaching through generalizations gives students context to remember facts and procedures. Examples of generalizations include the following (notice the qualifiers: *often*, *may*, *can*):

- People are often willing to move to improve their lives.
- Animals and plants can be affected by their environment.
- Algebra can be used to solve problems.
- Literature often reflects culture.

Figure 2.4 on pages 18–19 presents a sample lesson plan for helping you and your students first make connections between concepts and then develop generalizations. When students make connections to the concepts, they find *relevance* in a concept, which makes the curriculum pertinent and meaningful to their lives. In creating generalizations from these concepts, students form a *relationship* to the unit of study—a sense of personal ownership of the content. This now supports your development of a *rigorous* curriculum, because students have formed relevance to the concept and a relationship with the content. (See **Figure 2.5**.)

This model in Figure 2.4 involves both inductive and deductive reasoning processes. Used as a beginning lesson in the unit, the model focuses on the creation of generalizations from a student-derived list of created concepts and essential questions. This lesson is comprised of six steps and involves student participation at every step. Students begin with a broad concept, determine specific examples and non-examples, create appropriate categorization systems, establish a generalization from those categories, and then create either an individual or group essential question that will be the focus of the unit of study. (See page 23 for rules that help create quality essential questions.) This activity works best by dividing the class into small groups for initial work, followed by whole class discussion after each stage of the process. Figure 2.4 illustrates the use of the model around the concept of change.

A Concept Development Worksheet follows on page 20, with an example worksheet presented in **Figure 2.6** on page 21. Students should keep the resulting question in a notebook throughout the unit of study and continue to try to answer the question until the end of the unit. Alternately, you can take one essential question and display it on a bulletin board for the entire class to try to answer throughout the unit. Encourage students to post answer ideas and bring in news articles or website links that help answer the question. This also acts as a reminder to you to focus all activities and lessons on providing students with information to answer their own essential question or the class essential question. If you develop a class essential question, inform students at the beginning of the unit that it will be included on the final exam and that they should be continuously looking for information to answer the question and prepare for the exam.

Figure 2.5 Relationships–Rigor–Relevance: The 3 Rs

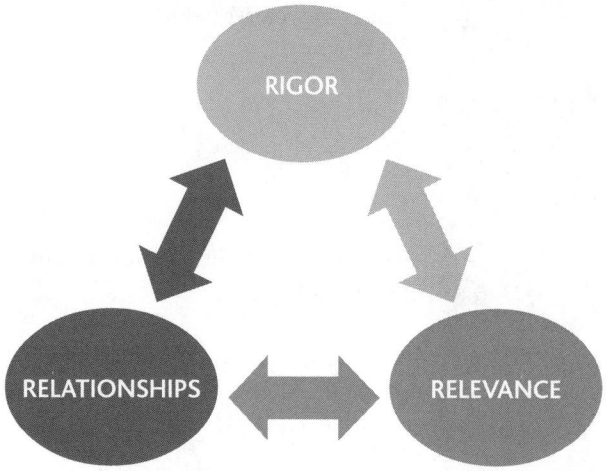

Figure 2.4 Concept Development Lesson Sample[6]

Concept: **Change**

Materials:

- Concept Development Worksheet
- Different color highlighters for each group of students
- Bulletin board or individual notebooks for the unit

	BEHAVIORAL OBJECTIVES	FOCUSING QUESTIONS
Step 1	**Students generate examples and non-examples of change derived from their own understanding and experiences with changes in the world.**	What examples of change have you read about or experienced? Why do these things change? Now list examples of things that do not change. Why do these things *not* change?
Step 2	**Students group words that are alike.**	Think about what the words in your lists have in common. Group words that are alike. *Note:* You might not use all of the words, and you may use some words twice if they fit into more than one category.
Step 3	**Students label the categories.**	Create a label for each category you created.
Step 4	**Students write generalizations.**	Review all of the categories you have created. Write at least three statements or generalizations about change. Plan to share with your group.
Step 5	**Students create essential questions.**	Using at least one of the generalizations you have created, turn that statement into a good question. Remember, good questions are open-ended and have more than just one right answer.
Step 6	**Students post their generalizations and essential questions.**	As a group, decide which of your generalizations and essential questions your team would like to investigate and attempt to answer throughout this unit.

6 Based on the curriculum model in *Curriculum Development: Theory and Practice* by Hilda Taba. New York: Harcourt Brace and World, 1962.

NOTE: The final step can be done as a class. Instead of each student having their own essential question, the class decides upon one question they would like to answer as a team. This generalization and corresponding question are then posted on a bulletin board. Throughout the unit, students can post notes, ideas, suggestions, websites, and news or magazine articles on the bulletin board to help answer the question. This question is then used as the final question on the unit summative assessment.

SUPPORT PROCEDURES

Have students form groups and generate at least 15 examples. These words are placed in the **+** side of the Concept Development Worksheet.

Encourage students to think carefully about non-examples of the concept of change. Each group should list five to six non-examples. These words are placed in the **–** side of the Concept Development Worksheet.

Have students explain their reasoning for assigning categories and seek clarification from each other as a class. Ensure that students have accounted for all (or most) of their items through the categories established.

Students categorize the words on their Concept Development Worksheet by circling or highlighting with different colors. Have students look for categories that can be combined with other categories to make bigger or more general categories.

Have students work in groups to create generalizations. To advance this activity, have students write their own generalizations. If students struggle, assist them by offering some examples of generalizations about change:
- *Change is everywhere.*
- *Change may happen naturally or be caused by people.*
- *Change may be perceived as orderly or random.*
- *Change can be positive or negative.*
- *Change is linked to identity.*
- *Change influences identity.*

In their groups, students decide on at least one of the generalization statements to turn into an essential question. Examples include:
- *In what ways is change linked to time?*
- *Why is it important that we understand change is everywhere?*
- *In what ways is change orderly and/or random?*
- *In what ways does change happen naturally or with the help of humans?*

Student groups decide on one generalization and the corresponding essential question to answer during the unit. Students either post the generalization and question on a bulletin board or write it in their unit notebooks. Throughout the unit, students take notes to supply an answer to their essential question.

Remind students that their essential question will be the final question on the summative assessment for the unit. They will be allowed to use their notes to answer the question, so they should be encouraged to take succinct notes during every class period and after every major activity.

Concept Development Worksheet

Instructions:

1. Write the concept in the concept square.
2. In the **+** (plus) box, list words or simple statements that represent or define the concept.
3. In the **–** (minus) box, list words or simple statements that do *not* represent or define the concept.
4. Review the list and categorize the words or statements in both boxes.
5. In the ∴ (therefore) box, create statements that explain your categorizations. (These are called *generalizations*: statements that are always or almost always true.)
6. In the **?** (question) box turn each of your generalizations into an open-ended question. These questions are your *essential questions*.

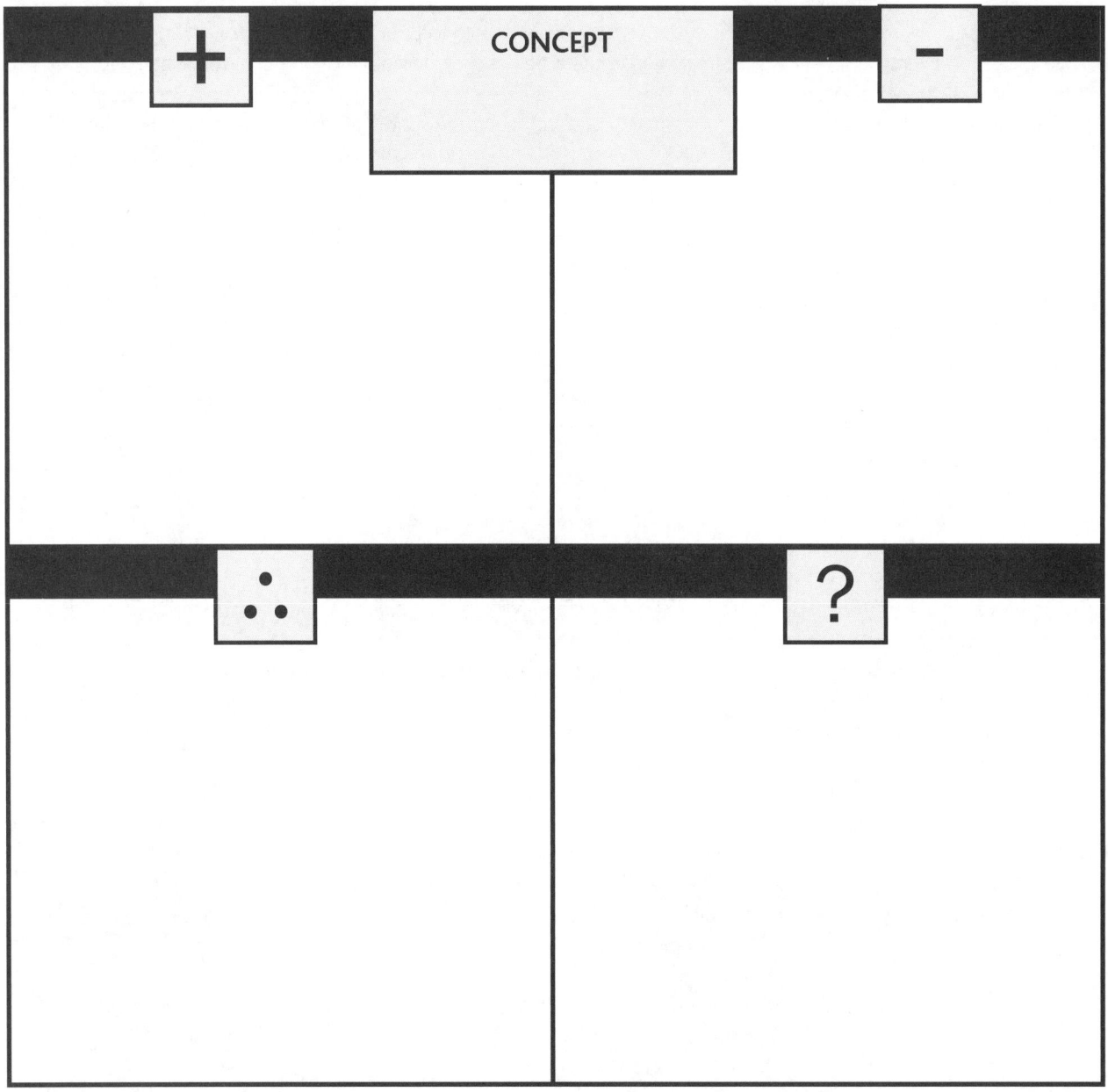

Based on the curriculum model in *Curriculum Development: Theory and Practice* by Hilda Taba. New York: Harcourt Brace and World, 1962.

From *Advancing Differentiation: Thinking and Learning for the 21st Century* by Richard M. Cash, Ed.D., copyright © 2011. Free Spirit Publishing Inc., Minneapolis, MN; 800-735-7323; www.freespirit.com. This page may be reproduced for use within an individual school or district. For all other uses, contact www.freespirit.com/company/permissions.cfm.

Figure 2.6 Concept Development Worksheet: Example

+	CONCEPT Change	-
People Time Earth Styles Beliefs Money		Your parents Teachers during the school year
∴		?
More things change than don't change. Change can be man-made or natural. Change can be good or bad.		Why do more things change than don't change? In what ways do humans change nature? In what ways does nature change humans? In what ways can change be good or bad?

Principles

Principles, like generalizations, are derived from the content area's concepts. Whereas generalizations are broad, principles are mostly specific in nature and usually refer to the rules, laws, codes, truths, or assumptions within a content domain. Examples of principles include the following (notice the lack of qualifiers such as *sometimes, generally, almost always, usually, mostly,* etc.):

- Science seeks to understand the natural world through experimentation and observation.
- The law of supply states that supply increases as prices increase and decreases as prices decrease.
- The rules of the English language require a sentence to include a verb.

Theories

Out of generalizations and principles comes theory. Theories explain, in relatively simple terms, ideals or abstract thoughts structured from the content area. Theories are not often developed or created in the K–12 setting, but are used as guides to the larger intent of the curriculum. Here are some examples of theories:

- The theory of relativity
- Number theory
- Direct reference theory
- Social distance theory
- Music composition theory
- The theory of aesthetics

At each level of the 21st Century Curriculum Model (Figure 2.2)—from factual knowledge to theory—learners go through a thought process that requires intellectual energy. At the lowest level of this design, very little intellectual energy is expended to recall information. As learners progress upward toward conceptual knowledge into generalizations and principles, they are required to use more areas of their brain and engage in deeper levels of thought.

Most curriculum materials do not provide for this advanced level of thinking. Therefore, it is up to you as the teacher to develop activities and performances that engage your students in more sophisticated levels of thinking. This can be accomplished through an awareness of how content standards are structured. When you are able to define what students should know, be able to do, and understand, you can more easily guide them toward high levels of thinking.

Most curriculum materials do not encourage an advanced level of thinking. It is up to you to develop activities that engage your students in more sophisticated levels of thinking.

Step 2: Form Objectives for What Students Will *Know, Be Able to Do, and Understand*

To Know

To know something is to be able to directly recognize it, recite it, or tell it to others in concrete language. In the classroom, what we want students to know are the facts, terms (language of the discipline), symbols, and specific factual details of the domain of study. These are "Students will know . . . " objectives within content standards. Here are some examples:

- Students will know the multiplication tables 0 through 9.
- Students will know the capital cities of each state in the United States.
- Students will know all of the elements in the periodic table.
- Students will know the elements of art (form, shape, line, color).

To Be Able to Do

This objective involves using the procedures and processes, tools, or techniques of the subject. Procedures are those step-by-step actions a student takes to solve a problem. Processes are the thinking skills a student uses to solve or think through a problem such as specific problem-solving strategies of the content area. Procedural knowledge is built by the actions that students participate in and can demonstrate. These are the "Students will be able to do . . . " objectives within standards. Here are some examples:

- Students will be able to write a five-paragraph essay.
- Students will be able to do an experiment.
- Students will be able to multiply fractions.
- Students will be able to use graphs and charts to solve problems and identify trends.
- Students will be able to design a map using a compass, key, and symbols.
- Students will be able to analyze information to identify trends.

To Understand

Concepts, as stated previously, are those big ideas that students will understand through the content delivery. When students understand a concept, they have grasped the meaning and significance of the content area, as well as the interrelationship between disciplines. Understanding is an abstract intellectual process built on the foundation of factual knowledge and procedural abilities. These are the "Students will understand . . . " objectives. Here are some examples:

- Students will understand the concept of change.
- Students will understand the theory of relativity.
- Students will understand the concept of multiplication.
- Students will understand the impact of language on culture.

Figure 2.7 illustrates the three levels of the Pyramid of Knowledge. **Figure 2.8** (page 24) shows how a science standard has been broken down into the concepts, procedures, and facts. **Figure 2.9** (page 25) shows the same standard diagrammed on a Breaking Down the Essentials template, while **Figure 2.10** (page 26) shows an example of a lower grades math standard. Page 27 is a blank template for Breaking Down the Essentials.

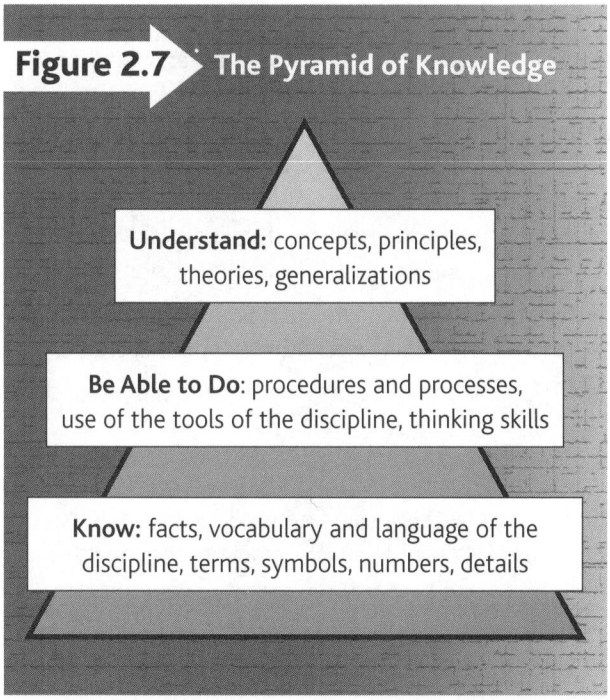

Step 3: Create Essential Questions

From here you can now construct the essential questions related to the learning. Essential questions are created by using the concepts embedded within the content. These questions are the most relevant aspects of the unit or subject. The answering of an essential question is a journey through the curriculum. Students may never come to a conclusion on an essential question, but they will have constructed content knowledge through the exploration of various answers. Remember, answering an essential question is a process, *not* an end product. As mentioned earlier, students can construct their own essential questions or you may construct them as a teacher.

Essential questions help students transcend the discipline and connect it with other disciplines. These provide students with a framework of reference within the content. Ultimately, essential questions should cause students to generate more questions than answers. The technique of constructing quality essential questions is predicated on the design of a well-formed question. Writing an effective question can engage students in higher levels of thinking, as well as problem solving and decision making. Also, well-formed questions can illicit deeper levels of conversation about the content, thus making it relevant to the learner.

We all know the categories of questions: Who? What? When? Where? Why? Which? and How? (6 Ws and H). Unfortunately, in many cases, the 6 Ws and H questions can produce a single response from students when ill formed. Here are some examples:

- Who is the leader of the United States?
- What is photosynthesis?
- When did the industrial revolution occur?
- Where is the continent of Africa?
- Why are there 60 minutes in an hour?
- Which flavor of ice cream is the most popular?
- How do animals adapt to various climates?

Well-crafted essential questions should be written open-ended and in ways that challenge and intrigue the students in discourse. They should also be uncluttered: straightforward and containing only one question. To form quality essential questions, keep the following rules in mind:

- *Who* questions should engage the students in making choices.
- *What* questions should involve students in hypothesizing.
- *When* questions should require students to predict.
- *Where* questions should have students developing plans.
- *Why* questions should use the students' skill of analysis.
- *Which* questions should provoke students to use criteria and evidence to make decisions and reason arguments.
- *How* questions should compel students to synthesize meaning by gathering information on the manner or method of solving problems.

Using the science standard example provided in Figure 2.8, well-formed essential questions for this unit of study would be:

- In what ways do causes have multiple effects?
- How do causes predict effects?
- Why does changing a cause change the effects?

Here are the previous ill-formed questions rewritten as well-formed ones:

Ill-Formed Question	Well-Formed Question
Who is the leader of the United States?	Who do we depend upon to lead the United States and for what reasons?
What is photosynthesis?	What could occur if one step in the photosynthesis process were changed?
When did the industrial revolution occur?	When might we encounter another industrial revolution?
Where is the continent of Africa?	Where is the heart of Africa?
Why are there 60 minutes in an hour?	Why do we use the units of minutes and hours to define a day?
Which flavor of ice cream is the most popular?	Which flavor of ice cream is predicted to remain popular into the next decade?
How do animals adapt to various climates?	How might animals adapt to natural or man-made disasters?

Finally, essential questions should spark curiosity, provoke wonder, require multidisciplinary approaches to answering, and use the skills of inference and interpretation. Here are some more examples:

- In what ways can causes have multiple effects?
- When might conflict be positive?
- Where is the most ideal location on Earth?
- Why do patterns occur?
- Which is more important: love or money?
- How do systems break down?

Step 4: Develop Unit Questions

Unit questions are formed as subordinate questions to the essential questions, nested within the essential question. Unit questions build an understanding of the content and support the approaches to the essential question. They are used as the framework for the activities that lead to the demonstration of understanding of the content and concepts.

Unit questions are specific to the lesson or unit of study and use the vocabulary of the discipline. They often provide the guiding questions for a particular activity or expected outcome of the lesson or unit. Using the science standard example in Figure 2.8 and the example essential questions on page 25, the unit or lesson questions might be:

- How does the transfer of energy and motion of Earth contribute to global climatic processes?
- What impact does the movement of carbon and water through the lithosphere, hydrosphere, atmosphere, and biosphere have on living and nonliving things on Earth?
- What effects do Earth's tilt, rotation, and revolution have on you each day, month, and year?
- Why is there a need for quality water reuse, recycling, and conservation?
- How have human activities impacted Earth's climate?

In completing these four steps in defining the essentials of the curriculum, you are constructing lessons and activities that are meaningful to your students. Your curriculum design provides a roadmap for the teaching of skills, processes, and concepts through an interdisciplinary approach; it is infused with authentic experiences and assessments; and it enables students to think innovatively, critically, and thoughtfully. In essence, a twenty-first century curriculum design blends thinking skills with content knowledge so that your students are well prepared for future success.

Designing this roadmap means that you are able to identify and define what is essential for our students to know, be able to do, and understand. In the process of differentiating, you must have solid knowledge of these essentials of the curriculum. In my experience, teachers have been trained to deliver curriculum, but were not necessarily taught how to develop curriculum. Understanding these basic components of the curriculum will make differentiation a more doable task.

Figure 2.8 **Breaking Down the Essentials: Example Science Standard**

CONTENT STANDARD:

Explain the **causes and effects** of Earth's atmospheric and hydrologic process.[7]

KEY:
Concept
Procedure
Facts

BENCHMARKS:

1. The student will *explain how* the transfer of energy and motions of Earth contribute to global climatic processes including wind, waves, and ocean currents.
2. The student will *trace* the cyclical movement of carbon and water through the lithosphere, hydrosphere, atmosphere, and biosphere. **(Cycles)**
3. The student will *demonstrate* the effect of Earth's tilt, rotation, and revolution on the seasons, day length, and tides.
4. The student will *identify, predict, and investigate* the factors that influence the quality of water and how it can be reused, recycled, and conserved.
5. The student will *discuss* the impact of the use of natural resources and other human activities on Earth's climate.

7 Adapted from Minnesota Academic Standards, Grades 9–12, Earth and Space Science.

Figure 2.9 Breaking Down the Essentials: Science Example (Upper Grades)

CONTENT STANDARD

Explain the causes and effects of Earth's atmospheric and hydrologic process.

ESSENTIAL QUESTIONS

- In what ways do causes have multiple effects?
- How do causes predict effect?
- Why does changing a cause change the effect?

PROCEDURAL KNOWLEDGE

Students will be able to:

- Explain
- Trace
- Demonstrate
- Identify
- Predict
- Investigate
- Discuss

CONCEPTUAL KNOWLEDGE

Students will understand:

- Cause & effect
- Cycles

FACTUAL KNOWLEDGE

Students will know:

- Earth's atmospheric and hydrologic process
- The transfer of energy and motions of Earth contribute to global climatic processes including wind, waves, and ocean currents
- The cyclical movement of carbon and water through the lithosphere, hydrosphere, atmosphere, and biosphere
- The effect of Earth's tilt, rotation, and revolution on the seasons, day length, and tides
- The factors that influence the quality of water and how it can be reused, recycled, and conserved
- The impact of the use of natural resources and other human activities on Earth's climate

UNIT QUESTIONS

- How does the transfer of energy and motion of Earth contribute to global climatic processes?
- What impact does the movement of carbon and water through the lithosphere, hydrosphere, atmosphere, and biosphere have on living and nonliving things on Earth?
- What effects do Earth's tilt, rotation and revolution have on you each day, month, and year?
- Why is there a need for quality water reuse, recycling, and conservation?
- How have human activities impacted Earth's climate?

Figure 2.10 Breaking Down the Essentials: Math Example (Lower Grades)

CONTENT STANDARD

Represent data and use various measures associated with data to draw conclusions and identify trends.

ESSENTIAL QUESTIONS

How do you use data to draw conclusions?
How do you use data to define trends?
How do trends assist you in drawing conclusions?

PROCEDURAL KNOWLEDGE

Students will be able to:

- Create and label graphs, surveys, experiments, and tables
- Use data sets
- Use fractions
- Use percentages
- Compare
- Contrast
- Measure

CONCEPTUAL KNOWLEDGE

Students will be able to:

- Draw conclusions
- Identify trends

FACTUAL KNOWLEDGE

Students will know:

- How graphs match to data sets
- The process for comparing data sets using fractions and percentages
- The process for collecting and representing data
- Mean, mode, and median

UNIT QUESTIONS

- What information can you gather from graphs, surveys, and tables?
- In what situations would you use mean, median, and mode?
- Why is it important to know how to change fractions into percentages?
- Why is it important to know how to read graphs and interpret data sets?

Breaking Down the Essentials

CONTENT STANDARD

ESSENTIAL QUESTIONS	FACTUAL KNOWLEDGE

PROCEDURAL KNOWLEDGE

CONCEPTUAL KNOWLEDGE

UNIT QUESTIONS

From *Advancing Differentiation: Thinking and Learning for the 21st Century* by Richard M. Cash, Ed.D., copyright © 2011. Free Spirit Publishing Inc., Minneapolis, MN; 800-735-7323; www.freespirit.com. This page may be reproduced for use within an individual school or district. For all other uses, contact www.freespirit.com/company/permissions.cfm.

Chapter 3

Advancing Differentiation to New Levels Through a Rigorous Curriculum

> What we want is to see the child in pursuit of knowledge, and not knowledge in pursuit of the child.
>
> —*George Bernard Shaw, playwright*

With the advent of 21st Century Skills and the continued nationalization of the learning standards movement, it is more urgent than ever for teachers to examine what is taught and why. The first step is for you to know the essentials of the curriculum and how they are connected to what your students are expected to know, be able to do, and understand. Then, to better equip yourself for meaningful differentiation, you must also ensure that all students are challenged, engaged, and motivated to reach high expectations. This is achieved by articulating a rigorous curriculum that prepares your students for success in today's world.

Differentiation expert Carol Ann Tomlinson has often said that you can't differentiate garbage. If a curriculum is not solid with clearly defined goals, standards, expectations, and outcomes, it won't matter how many different ways you offer the information; it will not be effectively learned. Quality differentiation can only be achieved when we can clearly articulate what we want students to know, be able to do, and understand, and build a curriculum that is coherent with a focus on our students' future success. This is why teachers should understand the essence of a rigorous curriculum, know how to define it, and be able to construct activities that guide students toward deep levels of learning.

What Is a Rigorous Curriculum?

What exactly is a "rigorous" curriculum? Answer: One that stretches each learner to grow intellectually, through engaging and challenging activities, to a point where the learner is self-directed, autonomous, and able to contribute successfully to society. See Figure 2.2 on page 15.

A rigorous curriculum:

- is inquiry based
- relies less on facts, more on concepts
- involves critical reasoning
- infuses creative idea generation
- requires problem finding and solving
- employs authentic tasks and products
- necessitates the application of knowledge
- encourages reflection
- integrates assessment *for* and *of* learning

Building a rigorous curriculum requires teachers to have:

- a thorough knowledge of the content
- a complete understanding of the concepts that underlie the content
- a solid grasp of instructional skills
- autonomy to make judgments of what is taught and how
- quality assessment practices
- a deep comprehension of how students learn

Hallmarks of a Rigorous Curriculum: Effective, Engaging, Exciting, Enriching (E^4)

Russian psychologist Lev Vygotsky defined intellectual growth as a process that moves the learner from observation, to mimicking, and ultimately to independence of thought. Vygotsky's theory of the "zone of proximal development" (ZPD) suggests that learning happens when a person is challenged to stretch beyond what is comfortable to that which is difficult. For students to be challenged, they must be provided instruction that levels support from *guidance* to *autonomy*, and curriculum that scaffolds information from *basic* to *complex*. This scaffolding of information can be accomplished through four main traits: complex, ambiguous, provocative, and personally or emotionally challenging[1]. Curriculum can be varied in degree of rigor by increasing any or all of the four traits just listed, which could also be described as: **effective** (complex), **engaging** (personally or emotionally challenging), and **exciting** (provocative and ambiguous), as well as **enriching** (authentic and substantive).

Effective—Create Complexity Through Concept-Based Learning

For curriculum to be effective, it must offer students a variety of complex activities. Complex activities are those that go deeply into the content, allow students to explore content through different learning styles, or expose students to new ways of thinking and doing. This is best achieved when curriculum is organized around complex and interrelated *concepts*. Concepts are those universal thoughts or ideas that transcend and unite disciplines. They might be discipline specific (such as multiplication and sums in math, transportation and government in social studies, temperature and gravity in science, or vowels and folktales in language arts) or interdisciplinary general (such as change, systems, models, or loyalty). Concepts help students organize ideas and categorize information in a coherent fashion. You can increase curriculum rigor by using multifaceted concepts that require a greater understanding of content principles.

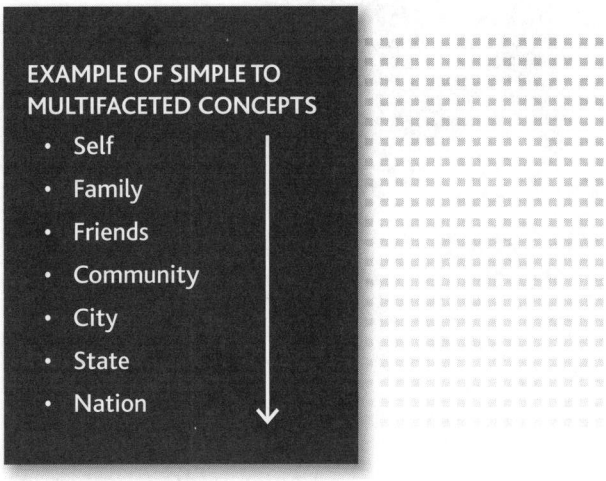

Conceptual development and design is explored in greater detail in Chapter 2.

Engaging—Challenge Students Personally and Emotionally

Emotional engagement drives attention; attention drives learning. Students will not engage in a learning situation unless they have some personal or emotional relevance to the content being delivered. Getting students emotionally engaged in learning begins with focusing on student interests and passions. Using these interests, you can motivate learners to find new connections to old information, and to make information personally relevant and worthwhile. This emotional engagement piques students' desires to go deeper into topics or areas of study. The more emotionally charged a topic is, or the more the student feels personally connected to it, the more rigorous and engaging that topic becomes for the student.

The more emotionally charged a topic is, or the more the student feels personally connected to it, the more rigorous and engaging that topic becomes for the student.

1 Strong, Richard W., Harvey F. Silver, and Matthew J. Perini. *Teaching What Matters Most: Standards and Strategies for Raising Student Achievement.* Alexandria, VA: Association for Supervision and Curriculum Development, 2001.

STRATEGIES TO ENGAGE STUDENTS

- Conduct an interest survey at the beginning of a major unit.
- Preview the topic with students. Have them look through the text and flag pages or pictures that pique their interest.
- Share your own interest in the topic.
- Have students bring in items from their personal lives that connect to the topic.

Exciting—Choose Ambiguous and Provocative Topics

Ambiguity is an exceptional learning tool. When material, issues, or solutions are less obvious, the learner must invest greater amounts of mental energy to develop knowledge. Curriculum that allows for ambiguity forces students to look for multiple meanings within the context of the information. When students deal with ambiguity they learn how to deal with uncertainty, develop perseverance, make personal sense of the information, rationalize debates, and form solid independent opinions. Curriculum that infuses greater ambiguity, such as focusing on symbols and images full of multiple meanings, raises the level of rigor. Dealing with ambiguity helps students understand the richness and intricacy of the world around us.

Ambiguous topics are often also provocative. A provocative curriculum is one that centers on problems within and across disciplines, and that challenges students' beliefs, understandings, and prior knowledge. These issues elicit responses from students, evoke feelings, and excite students to find solutions or resolutions. See examples of topics in the right column.

Enriching—Create Authentic Tasks and Substantive Conversations

Another way to ensure curriculum rigor is to have students practice operations and skills in authentic ways and engage in meaningful discussions.

Create Authentic Tasks

Tasks are authentic when students are using content skills and knowledge in real-world applications found outside of the classroom walls, such as at home or in the workplace. An authentic task is most often constructed so that there is not one right way to complete the task, nor one right answer. These tasks require students to use the content skills and knowledge holistically and in interdisciplinary context. Students are motivated to persevere and put forth greater effort.

Examples of Provocative Discussion Topics

- Abortion rights
- Advertising in schools
- Affirmative action
- Allowance
- Alternative medicine
- Animal rights
- Bioethics
- Biological weapons
- Bullying/Cyberbullying
- Capital punishment
- Cell phones in school
- Censorship
- Chores
- Citizenship
- Cloning
- Conflict vs. cooperation
- Consumerism
- Curfews
- Drug legalization
- Drug testing
- Eating disorders
- Environment
- Euthanasia
- Evolution
- Family
- Fast food in schools
- Foreign policy
- Friendship
- Gambling
- Genetic engineering
- Genocide
- Global warming
- Grief and loss
- Gun control
- Hairstyles/clothing
- Hate crimes
- Healthcare
- Helmet laws
- HIV/AIDS
- Homelessness
- Homeschooling
- Immigration
- Internet use in school
- Nuclear weapons
- Obesity
- Parental consent/supervision
- Piercings/tattoos
- Prayer in school
- Punishment at home/school
- Racism
- Ratings for movies, TV, games
- Rules for classroom/school
- Same-sex marriage
- School uniforms
- School violence
- Sex education
- Sexual harassment
- Smoking bans
- Stem-cell research
- Steroid use
- Suicide
- Teamwork vs. independence
- Teenage pregnancy
- Terrorism
- Video games
- Welfare
- Women's rights

While engaged in authentic tasks, students are motivated to persevere and put forth greater effort.

A hallmark of quality authentic tasks is *student collaboration*. When students collaborate they build community by working together toward a common goal. Interactions between diverse learners (whether the diversity be academic, social, or cultural) provide new opportunities for ideas to blossom and grow. Collaborative efforts in authentic tasks require students to use higher order thinking skills, critical reasoning, and problem-solving strategies.

The real problems presented in authentic tasks require more careful attention to finding real solutions, thus forcing students to employ *valid research strategies*. Students are challenged to plan initiatives, organize materials, develop new ideas, assess while learning, and evaluate outcomes. Students build ownership, foster a sense of community, and develop an entrepreneurial spirit in learning. There is a greater chance that learning developed through authentic tasks will transfer outside of the content area, as well as beyond the classroom walls.

Authentic tasks also employ the use of *expert sources*, from materials to individuals. For students to solve real problems they must use materials that reflect the causes and effects of the problem. For instance, for students to understand how to represent data they must work with actual charts and graphs that hold meaning for them, such as those found in the newspaper or on the Internet.

EXAMPLES OF AUTHENTIC TASKS

- project-based learning
- student-designed experiments, questions, or problems
- service learning projects
- science experiments
- WebQuests
- simulations
- debates

Ignite Substantive Conversations

Students crave the chance to discuss, debate, and challenge each other's ideas. In a rigorous curriculum, students put new information to work and engage in exchanges of ideas that build on prior knowledge. Taking part in substantive conversations with peers as well as experts in the field helps students clarify ideas, form opinions based on fact or experience, and grasp a deeper understanding of and connection to issues in the real world. At the center of a rigorous curriculum are those issues that provoke students to wrestle with real problems that challenge their ideas, beliefs, and prior knowledge.

For students to engage in substantive conversations, the content must be emotionally enlivened enough for students to interact with the information. Enlivening content requires the use of relevant and current issues that relate to what is being taught. Students will converse when they feel ownership of the issue, and so making a topic relevant to students will engage them in discussion. By taking stories from the news, students' daily lives, or general social issues and weaving the content through these stories, you are helping students emotionally engage in discussions.

Strategies to Incorporate Substantive Conversations

- **Debate** controversial issues in your discipline; *for lower elementary students:* Debate the actions of a character in a story.
- **Discuss** alternative/risky solutions that characters/individuals might have considered; *for lower elementary students:* Discuss alternative observations made during a science experiment by asking, "What else can account for the outcome of this experiment?"
- **Question** methods/ulterior motives of famous figures; *for lower elementary students:* Question a famous person from history about why they did what they did, using role play or writing a letter to the person.
- **Mediate** the pros and cons of political decisions; *for lower elementary students:* Mediate an argument between two characters from a story using role play.

KEY WORDS TO IGNITE CONVERSATION

- Debate
- Ponder
- Argue
- Dispute
- Contend
- Deliberate
- Confer
- Discuss
- Question
- Inquire
- Interrogate
- Arbitrate
- Mediate
- Reconcile
- Deduce
- Reason
- Interpret
- Infer
- Construct

Infusing Rigor Into Your Curriculum

Many teachers believe their curriculum to be the textbook. While the textbook is one source within a curriculum it is *not* the only source. Textbooks rely on providing a broad general sweep of a content area. A curriculum is more than just the textbook. It includes the standards of the discipline, knowledge within and around the content, and skills and practices used within the subject matter. Curriculum is also the teacher's content expertise and knowledge that is infused to excite students to pursue deeper understanding of the subject. All of the strategies and ideas listed in this section are ways teachers can excite students. Rigor is achieved when students have identified relevance to the topic and then can form a relationship to the learning.

To help in creating a school culture of rigor I've created the principles of curriculum and instruction that advance learning (page 33), and classroom practices that advance learning (page 34). These lists can be used by a site team to define how content is delivered beyond the textbook or by individual teachers as a reminder of ways to ensure rigor. I suggest these lists be publicly posted throughout the school or classroom so students and families are also aware of the implementation of principles and practices of a rigorous school culture.

Also included is a Walkthrough Checklist of Differentiation for Advancing Learning on page 35. This can be used by school administrators, peer coaches, or content specialists when doing brief classroom walkthroughs. Walkthroughs are a powerful tool educational leaders use to assist and guide teachers toward fidelity of implementation of a rigorous curriculum and instructional practices.

Strategies to Develop a Rigorous (E^4) Curriculum

- Engage students in the learning by piquing their interests in the topic of study. This can uncover hidden talents or undiscovered areas of interests.
- Anchor enrichment activities to the regular curriculum through either concept or process.
- Unite content through the use of interdisciplinary topics or a single theme.
- Allow students to wrestle with ambiguous case studies or authentic issues that require them to use higher level thinking skills and creativity.
- Encourage students to better know themselves as scholars by assessing their learning modes and styles.
- Establish an open environment within your classroom where students are encouraged to take risks, voice opinions, debate ideas, and tackle controversial issues.
- Orchestrate flexible instructional groups in the classroom allowing students to work both with peers who are alike and peers who are different.
- Teach using multiple learning modes to encourage students to reach beyond their comfort zones and seek sources of information.
- Use humor in your classroom to create a more enjoyable learning setting and to relieve stress.

Principles of Curriculum and Instruction for Advancing Learning

- Present content that is related to broad-based issues, themes, or problems.
- Integrate multiple disciplines into the area of study.
- Present comprehensive, related, mutually reinforcing experiences within an area of study.
- Allow for the in-depth learning of a self-selected topic within an area of study.
- Develop independent or self-directed study skills.
- Develop productive, complex, abstract, or higher order thinking skills.
- Focus on open-ended tasks.
- Develop research skills and methods.
- Integrate basic skills and higher level thinking skills into the curriculum.
- Encourage the development of products that challenge existing ideas and produce "new" ideas.
- Encourage the development of products that use new techniques, materials, and forms.
- Encourage the development of self-understanding (i.e., recognizing and using one's abilities, becoming self-directed, appreciating likenesses and differences between oneself and others).
- Evaluate student outcomes by using appropriate and specific criteria through self-appraisal, criterion referenced, or standardized instruments.

From *Advancing Differentiation: Thinking and Learning for the 21st Century* by Richard M. Cash, Ed.D., copyright © 2011. Free Spirit Publishing Inc., Minneapolis, MN; 800-735-7323; www.freespirit.com. This page may be reproduced for use within an individual school or district. For all other uses, contact www.freespirit.com/company/permissions.cfm.

Classroom Practices for Advancing Learning

- Create an open environment
- Use flexible instructional groups
- Include multiple approaches to information
- Use multiple learning modes
- Be aware of student strengths
- Use humor (not sarcasm)
- Draw on multiple and varied resources
- Build an inquisitive atmosphere
- Encourage acceptance of diversity (in people and ideas)
- Provide independent and small group instruction
- Teach and use research skills

From *Advancing Differentiation: Thinking and Learning for the 21st Century* by Richard M. Cash, Ed.D., copyright © 2011. Free Spirit Publishing Inc., Minneapolis, MN; 800-735-7323; www.freespirit.com. This page may be reproduced for use within an individual school or district. For all other uses, contact www.freespirit.com/company/permissions.cfm.

Walkthrough Checklist of Differentiation for Advancing Learning

CONTENT	PROCESS	PRODUCT
☐ Content is linked to broad issues, themes, or problems ☐ Content reinforces interdisciplinary study ☐ Content is linked to fields of study or discipline ☐ Students are provided choices in topics within an area of study ☐ Students have the opportunity to pursue independent or self-directed studies ☐ The content has direct relevant links to students' experiences and lives ☐ The curriculum is grounded in conceptual, procedural, and factual knowledge ☐ The teacher knows and focuses student attention on conceptual, procedural, and factual knowledge ☐ The curriculum is directly linked to state or national standards ☐ Formative assessment is utilized to guide students toward success ☐ Summative assessment is used to inform achievement	☐ Teacher knows and utilizes advanced levels of Bloom's Taxonomy ☐ Students are offered in-depth learning opportunities ☐ Students are guided toward higher levels of thought through open-ended questions ☐ Students problem find and solve issues that are relevant and worth solving ☐ Students know and utilize research skills ☐ Students know and utilize creative thinking skills ☐ Students know and utilize critical reasoning tools ☐ Students make connections between self and the curriculum ☐ The classroom environment is welcoming and accepting of all students ☐ Flexible instructional grouping practices are used ☐ Multiple instructional strategies are used to engage students in understanding ☐ A variety of resources are available to and used by students ☐ Teacher acts as guide in learning and discovery	☐ Students are encouraged to create new products and ideas ☐ Students create products that incorporate techniques, materials, and forms taught throughout the unit of study ☐ Students are allowed choices to work on projects collaboratively or independently, depending on the requirements of the project ☐ Assignments are tiered by the readiness, interest, or learning style of the students ☐ Students are given choices in how to represent knowledge acquisition ☐ Students use technology in the creation and presentation of projects ☐ Student products represent an accumulation of knowledge rather than a regeneration of facts ☐ Students are encouraged to act as scholars ☐ Student products are authentic and are presented to an authentic audience

From *Advancing Differentiation: Thinking and Learning for the 21st Century* by Richard M. Cash, Ed.D., copyright © 2011. Free Spirit Publishing Inc., Minneapolis, MN; 800-735-7323; www.freespirit.com. This page may be reproduced for use within an individual school or district. For all other uses, contact www.freespirit.com/company/permissions.cfm.

Chapter 4

Motivating and Engaging Learners

> There is a brilliant child locked inside every student.
>
> —*Marva Collins, educator*

In today's classroom, students come with differing complexities, experiences, interests, and learning abilities. As a teacher, you must be prepared to meet the needs of every learner with a variety of strategies and techniques to differentiate the curriculum and activities so that all your students are successful. This chapter defines some of the variances students possess and offers valuable differentiation strategies that motivate and engage learners.

Think back to a time when you were required to attend a workshop or staff meeting. List all the reasons why you did not want to be in that workshop or meeting. Now list all the reasons why you wanted to be there. It's likely that many of the reasons why you did *not* want to be there included these:

- You were forced to be there.
- You knew you had someplace more important to be.
- You'd rather be doing something else.
- You felt that you already knew the information being presented.
- You were tired, hungry, angry, or upset.

And perhaps the reasons why you *did* want to attend the workshop or meeting included these:

- You thought you would gain new knowledge or skills.
- You wanted to meet new friends or connect with colleagues.
- You hoped the presenter would be engaging and interesting.
- You were hoping for some inspiration and encouragement.

These are the same reasons our students do or don't want to be in our classrooms. How often do you ask your students, "Who *doesn't* want to be here today and why?" or "Who *does* want to be here and why?" If you asked this more often of your students, you may be surprised how similar their responses are to your own. Also, if you ask your students to honestly tell you *why* they don't want to be in your classroom, you may then be able to address their needs so they can spend more of their mental energy on learning, rather than on resisting learning.

Emotion ➡ Attention ➡ Learning

A fundamental of brain-compatible learning is that emotion drives attention, and attention drives learning. Students underachieve or underperform for a variety of reasons. They may:

- perceive a lack of challenge in the content
- be uninterested in the content
- lack self-efficacy
- lack key skills
- not have practice in perseverance or the ability to control it
- be unable or unwilling to see the purpose of learning the content
- have too much or too little self-confidence
- be overinvolved with other activities
- have difficulty getting product-oriented
- lack task follow-through
- have a fear of failure

- tend to procrastinate
- be overly focused on personal difficulties
- depend too much on others to do it for them
- be highly distractible
- be experiencing distress in their personal or family lives

What this all comes down to is that students lack *motivation*. In my work with teachers throughout the United States, I hear this over and over again: "I just can't get my students motivated to learn!" Many teachers, administrators, and parents are frustrated by the lack of commitment that some students have toward learning and producing. So how do we get our kids motivated to learn what we need them to learn? How do we motivate them to do well on the products, performances, and those ever-present tests? Students' motivation to learn and perform to the highest levels of their potential has puzzled researchers for years. Understanding what motivates and engages individuals and why is a very complex issue.

What Is Motivation?

If you break down the word *motivation*, you get *motive + action*. A *motive* is "something that causes a person to act in a certain way or do a certain thing." In other words, it is an incentive to perform. *Action* is "doing." So *motivation* is "a desire to do or a drive to complete." In the classroom we want our students to be motivated to achieve, to be "achievement motivated." Achievement motivation is about striving for competence. To attain achievement motivation, students must feel and recognize their own competence.

Two highly regarded experts in the study of motivation, Andrew Elliott and Carol Dweck, state that competence is "a condition or quality of effectiveness, ability, sufficiency, or success."[1] All people want to be competent at meaningful tasks—it's part of being human. We naturally aspire to competence at meaningful tasks, because it defines who we are, promotes self-esteem, and makes us valuable to others. Achievement motivation occurs when the learner feels a sense of ownership of the learning, has a level of skill development to expand upon, desires the incentive offered, and feels good about the accomplishment. Knowing this reality, you might think differently about why your students may or may not be motivated to learn what you want them to learn.

Two Types of Motivation: Extrinsic and Intrinsic

Generally, we can divide motivation into two types: *extrinsic* and *intrinsic*.

Extrinsic motivation comes from outside the learner in the form of such things as stickers, money, rewards/awards, grades, trophies, and diplomas. These types of external incentives can help learners acquire self-regulating strategies, and they can support the development of intrinsic motivation. Research suggests that there is little long-term retention of learning through the extensive use of extrinsic motivation.[2]

Intrinsic motivation is the internal drive to perform regardless of the external reward. All people are naturally intrinsically motivated (or "self-motivated") to do things they find interesting, fun, personally meaningful, or relevant. Intrinsic motivation can assist people in overcoming difficult situations or tasks, or provide the extra effort required to complete a task. Research also suggests that when the learner has the intrinsic desire to learn, there is greater longer-term retention of the learning.[3] Although motivation can be categorized as either extrinsic or intrinsic, both types are dependent upon each other. A person usually cannot be intrinsically motivated without some form of extrinsic motivation. For example, even though you may love the art of teaching, would you be willing to come to work every day if you were not paid? Realizing the cyclical effect of both types of motivation can help you understand how to move your students from purely extrinsic motivation ("I'm only doing it for the grade") to more intrinsic motivation ("I'm learning this because I want to be better at this skill"). See **Figure 4.1.**

Figure 4.1 The Cycle of Motivation

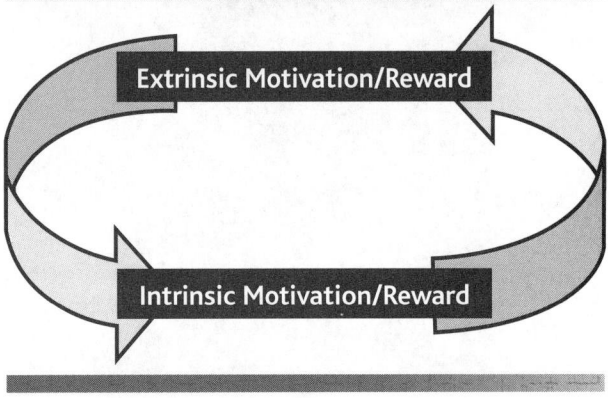

1 Elliot, Andrew J. and Carol S. Dweck. *Competence as the Core of Achievement Motivation: Handbook of Competence and Motivation.* New York: Guilford Press, 2005.

2 *How People Learn: Brain, Mind, Experience, and School* (Expanded Edition). National Research Council. Washington, DC: National Academies Press, 2000.

3 Ibid.

Understanding How the Brain Learns

You can assist students in building intrinsic achievement motivation by providing a classroom environment that addresses the students' basic human needs and offers engaging, relevant, and meaningful tasks. To fully understand basic human needs, you must have a rudimentary understanding of how the brain works. In general, all brains are *organized* in the same way, but not all brains *learn* in the same way. Research findings support that a person's environment can actually change his or her brain[4]. Therefore, your job as a teacher is to create learning experiences and opportunities for your students to develop talent and achieve success; in short, you must provide your students with *brain-compatible learning*.

Note: The following section is a general overview of the human brain and is not intended to be comprehensive, nor is it complete. The intent is to point out a few highlights of how the brain is organized and the significance of how the parts work together.

The Three Brain Domains

In the most general of terms, the brain can be divided into three domains: the cerebral cortex, the midbrain, and the hindbrain (see **Figure 4.2**). Each area has significance to the learning process working in tandem with the other areas. What follows is a broad representation of how the brain is organized. Having this knowledge will help you attune your learning environment and instructional practices to address the workings of the brain, so your students will be more motivated and engaged to find greater success in the classroom.

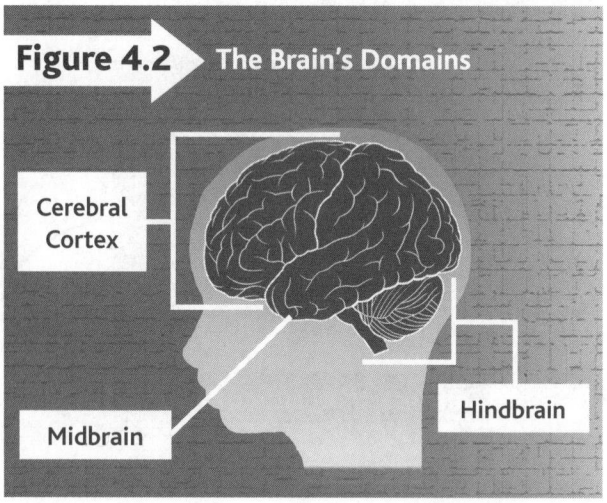

All brains are *organized* in the same way, but not all brains *learn* in the same way.

The Hindbrain

Starting in the back of the brain coming up out of the spinal column is the brain stem. The oldest and most primitive part of the organ, the brain stem controls and organizes the autonomic systems of our body (circulatory, digestive, respiratory, and nervous). While the brain stem is the smallest part of your brain, it performs an extremely important function: keeping your body alive so the rest of your brain can keep working. Motor and sensory information coming into and out of the brain pass through this area. The information corresponding to attention, arousal, and consciousness is evaluated at this point for the purposes of survival. If the information is deemed to be threatening to the body, the brain stem will pull energy away from the other parts of the brain to protect itself and the body as a whole. When students enter your classrooms lacking the basic survival needs of food, shelter, and water, their brains are likely to be paying attention to those needs rather than to lessons on nouns, fractions, or chemical compounds.

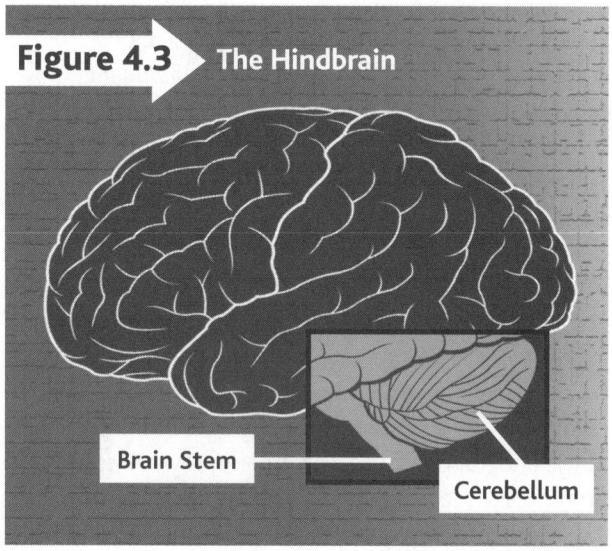

The cerebellum, two fist-shaped bundles of brain matter at the back of your brain, controls your body's movements, balance, and coordination. It is also important to the procedural memories you develop by practicing movements or actions. For instance,

4 Nussbaum, P. D. and W. R. Daggett, *What Brain Research Teaches About Rigor, Relevance, and Relationships and What It Teaches About Keeping Your Own Brain Healthy.* Rexford, NY: International Center for Leadership in Education, 2008.

take the act of driving a car. Have you ever said, "My car just *knows* the way to work"? Actually, it's your cerebellum that knows the way to work. It processes the information of how much pressure to put on the gas or brake pedal, when to turn your signal on, how to move your arms to turn the steering wheel, and so forth. This type of automatic brain processing allows the other more conscious parts of your brain to perform more advanced levels of thinking and doing, such as listening to songs on the radio, thinking about your plans for the day, or processing a fight you had with your friend.

Therefore, the cerebellum is a significant component to the thinking and learning process, in that it regulates the rote parts of process and actions, while allocating energy to the upper areas of the brain to process high-level thoughts and actions. For students in your classroom, this means that they require sufficient practice to develop *automaticity* of the skills and strategies learned, so they can reserve brain energy for more advanced levels of thinking. If students have deficits in what is considered basic knowledge, they will spend precious brain energy processing low-level skills, such as multiplication facts.

The Midbrain

Also called the limbic system, the midbrain is a set of structures that play a critical role in learning, memory, and emotion. This very complicated interrelated system spans across to your sensory system and motor system. The limbic system also has an influence on the executive functioning of the prefrontal cortex. The two areas of the limbic system that are most involved in the learning, memory, and emotion are the hippocampus and the amygdala.

- The *hippocampus* plays an important role in the process of long-term memory and spatial orientation. In fact, it is one of the first areas of the brain that is affected by Alzheimer's disease. It has densely packed layers of neurons, the underlying cellular structure of learning and memory. The female brain is believed to have a larger hippocampus, which means that girls have a greater advantage in school-based learning, especially in the language arts[5].
- The *amygdala* provides the emotional coloring of your experiences. As information passes through the midbrain, the amygdala stimulates a chemical reaction within the brain to affect an emotional state. The amygdala also plays a role in regulating attention, forming perceptions, and recalling specific memories, possibly through the interplay of emotional memories. When you feel good about an experience, you are more likely to repeat the experience or attempt a variation of the experience. During adolescence, emotional responses may be considered irrational or impulsive. That may be due to the fact that the prefrontal cortex (which forms reasoned responses to emotion) is not well developed in the adolescent brain, so the amygdala is in action instead.

Safety and Survival: The Reptilian Brain

In a very general sense, the lower parts of the brain (brain stem, cerebellum, and limbic system) can be considered the reptilian brain. These older and smaller regions of the brain are the least evolved, and they resemble and function similar to the brains of present-day reptiles. The processes mediated in these regions lack language and are impulsive, instinctual, and ritualistic. The reptilian

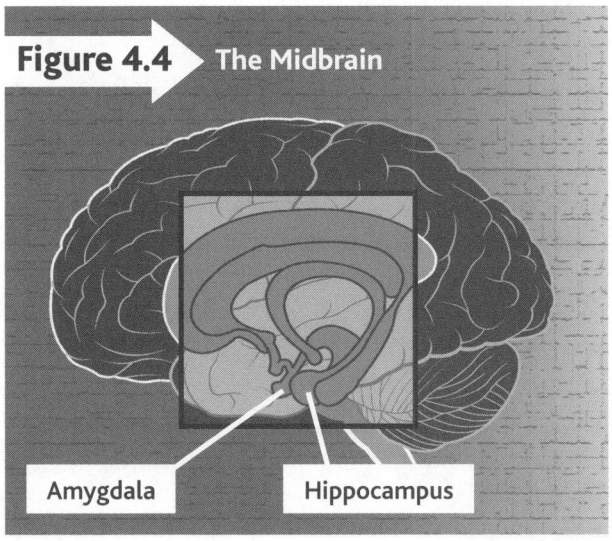

Figure 4.4 The Midbrain

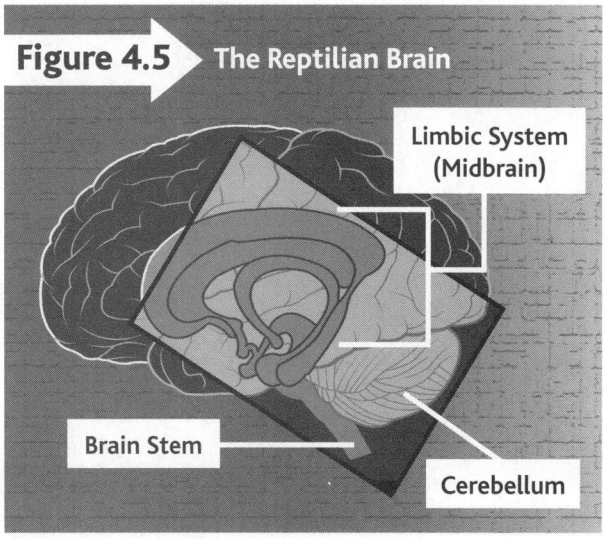

Figure 4.5 The Reptilian Brain

5 Gurian, M. and K. Stevens. *The Minds of Boys: Saving Our Sons from Falling Behind in School and Life.* San Francisco: Jossey–Bass, 2005.

brain is concerned with the fundamental needs of survival, protection, and mating. When needs within the reptilian brain are not being met or are challenged, a person naturally goes into what is called a "downshift." Energy is pulled away from the more conscious or thinking parts of your brain and directed toward the lower parts of the brain in a "fight or flight" action. Think about the last time someone confronted you. You more than likely said something that you should not have said, and it wasn't until later that you thought of a more articulate response. This is the process of downshifting; you responded from a relatively unevolved part of your brain, and after your brain had time to reorganize the energy back to the thinking part of the brain, you were able to think more clearly and "smarter."

To avoid the downshifted response in an argument or difficult situation:

- Take a deep breath (this floods your brain with oxygen-rich blood for better processing).
- Count to 10 (this gives your brain time to upshift and send energy to the cerebral cortex, and gives the limbic system time to process the chemical reaction of emotion).
- Then, respond.

The Cerebral Cortex

The cerebral cortex (*cerebral=brain; cortex=bark*) is the outer mantel of cells encasing the two hemispheres of the brain. The cortex ranges in thickness from between one and four millimeters. The elaboration of the cortex is the most distinguishing characteristic of the human brain. The specific functions of the various areas of the cerebral cortex allow us to use language, have conscious thoughts and movements, think through difficult situations, understand emotions, remember past experiences, learn new ideas, and perform other higher-order cognitive operations. These abilities are what make our brain unique from any other animal.

Figure 4.6 The Cerebral Cortex

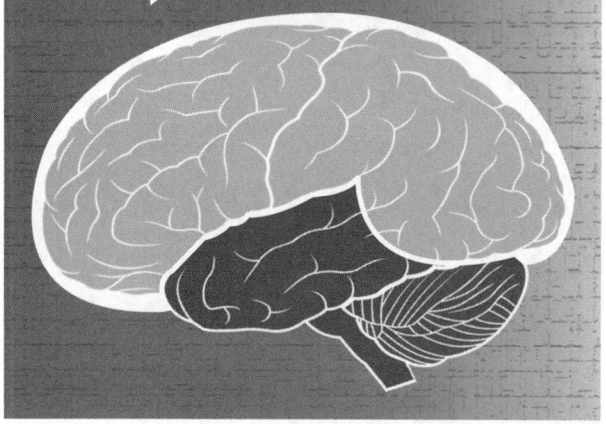

The cerebral cortex is divided into four major interrelated lobes (see **Figure 4.7**). Understanding the functions of each of these lobes can help you better meet the needs of your students.

Figure 4.7 The Four Lobes of the Cortex

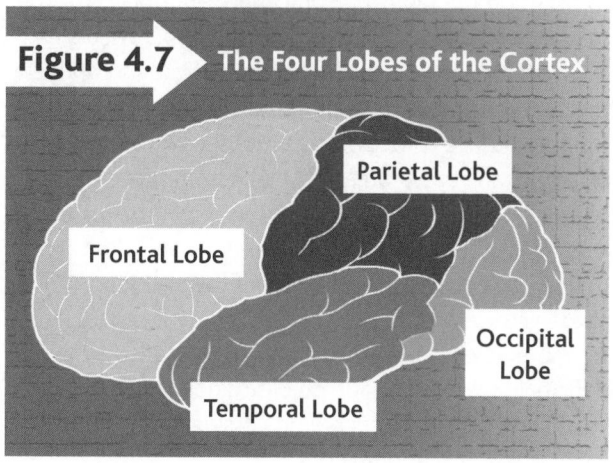

The **frontal lobe** is our primary motor cortex. This area is responsible for our planning, initiating, and follow-through of our movements, as well as higher-level cognitive functioning. This high-level cognitive functioning, or "executive functioning," is carried out in a part of the frontal lobe called the *prefrontal cortex*. The prefrontal cortex acts as your brain's CFO (Chief Functioning Operator) in that it:

- controls your planning and organization
- is the seat of your working memory
- modulates your moods
- inhibits your behavior (impulse control)
- controls empathy, insight, reason, and introspection

This area of the brain is under a great deal of development during the adolescent years. Therefore, it is essential that you provide opportunities in your classroom for students to develop these skills.

The **parietal lobe** runs across the top of your brain. This area is responsible for the processing of:

- sensory information that comes in from the body (touch, pain, the feel of your body in space)
- written language (this is critical to the acts of reading and writing)

The **occipital lobe**'s primary function is visual. You process visual stimuli in this area of the brain.

The **temporal lobe** is primarily responsible for processing auditory information. The understanding of language and facial recognition are also functions of the temporal lobe. Learning and memory are greatly enhanced because of the temporal lobe's direct connection to the hippocampus.

The brain is a fascinating and complex organ that forms the seat of all learning, and yet it is first and foremost concerned with safety and survival. When you want to ensure that students feel they can survive in your classroom, you must first pay attention to their basic needs for food, water, shelter, and safety. Students who are well nourished and hydrated, have a home or feel at home in your classroom, and feel safe in and around school are ready to learn. In addition, students need to feel safe within the content of what they are learning. Consider, for example, a girl who is math phobic, or a boy who has repeatedly been told he can't read. These children are less ready to learn new information because they have downshifted, fearing for their academic survival. When students feel safe and have a sense of belonging, they are ready to take on learning tasks.

Gender Differences in Learning

Human beings are very social animals. When students can make social connections in the school environment, they have a greater chance for learning and understanding. Making personal connections with both the content and the community of learners helps students build responsibility for their own learning, as well as engage the midbrain process of memory and emotional connection. However, making connections to the learning community and the content can mean different things for male students and female students.

Recent brain research has found that generally girls' brains develop differently from boys' brains[6]. This developmental difference may have significant implications for how we teach girls and boys. What follows are some significant discoveries from recent studies on brain development. Keep in mind that the connections between the research and educational practices have not been fully validated. Also, the generalizations about girls versus boys are just that: generalizations. There will always be exceptions to the rules.

In general, girls have a greater advantage in school because of the way their brains are organized. Girls are believed to have stronger neural connectors in the temporal lobe, which may be why they typically have better listening skills, provide greater detail in their writing, and often are able to remember information more holistically, especially sensually. Girls also have a more active prefrontal cortex that can assist in making fewer impulsive decisions. And they use more of the cortical areas of the brain for verbal and emotional functioning, which may explain why girls often use words and emotions to connect with or hurt others. On the other hand, girls' learning is inhibited by the stress of competition, while boys' learning is enhanced by it. This may help explain why girls' achievement often falls off and boys' achievement rises at the high school level, where the stress of competition becomes greater.

Boys are thought to have a more sophisticated occipital lobe. The occipital lobe is primarily responsible for visual processing. This makes sense, as prehistorically, the male's job was to hunt and gather food. Hence, males relied on their vision not only for protection, but also survival. Males are therefore more visually stimulated, which may explain why explicit magazines, websites, and video games are more attractive to boys than to girls. Because of this need for greater visual stimulation, it is recommended that teachers provide boys with visual images of directions and graphic organizers to visualize their thoughts.

Boys lateralize brain activity with less blood flow extending across the entire brain, meaning that they are often poor multitaskers, have a shorter attention span, and find it difficult to quickly transition from one activity to another. Boys also use more of their cortical areas for spatial understanding, meaning that they move objects three-dimensionally in their head. In addition, boys have lower levels of serotonin and oxytocin (the human bonding chemicals) in their brains, which may explain why they are more physically impulsive and less likely to bond with others through language and emotions.

Due to the way boys' brains are organized, we may be disadvantaging them in school because of the way we teach. Using high levels of auditory information with limited amounts of visual stimuli may inadvertently disengage the boy brain. (See pages 44–45: 25 Strategies for Developing a Boy-Friendly Classroom.)

6 Eliot, Lise. "The Truth About Boys and Girls." *Scientific American Mind,* May/June 2010.

The Impact of Race, Ethnicity, and Culture on Learning

The biological systems of the brain develop and change based on the influences of the social, cultural, and familial world. All kids have varying degrees and types of opportunities prior to starting school. This may be due to economic status or cultural backgrounds. These experiences or lack of experiences may affect the way students' brains are processing information, how they prefer to learn, their interests, and ultimately how they personally connect or interact with the curriculum and with other learners.

Students who perceive themselves to be chronic targets of others' discrimination or mistreatment often lose confidence in themselves and in their self-efficacy. Students who are part of a cultural or linguistic minority often experience such adverse effects from the stereotyping and social isolation that can happen in school. Their loss of confidence can contribute to academic disengagement and other problem behaviors at school. In effect, these students' brains may be in perpetual downshift during the majority of their school day, which prevents them from thinking or acting at higher levels.

Those students who have formed a positive racial identity are more likely to have higher academic achievement than their counterparts with negative racial identity. They may have developed strategies to upshift their thinking[7]. The key to success in school for culturally or linguistically diverse students appears to be the development of a strong bicultural or bilingual competence, or the ability to function effectively in the dominant culture while retaining a primary ethnic identity. Always keep in mind that the number one factor in increasing achievement motivation is a caring adult who can guide, coach, and encourage the learner—no matter the learner's gender, race, ethnicity, or cultural background.

Pathway to a Motivating and Engaging Classroom

Taking into account all that has been stated about how the brain learns, how boys and girls learn differently, and how race and ethnicity impacts learning, I have developed a pathway to building a motivating and engaging classroom (see **Figure 4.8**).

First, students must feel **competent** in the content and know that you, their teacher, are competent in instructing and guiding them through the content. While you may not have all the answers, you must be able to help the learner find the answers.

Closely aligned with competence is the need for the learner to feel **connected** to the content and find relevance in it. If learners can't attach themselves to the information, or if you're unable to assist them in making those connections, it is highly likely that your students will not engage in future learning.

As students begin the process of learning, they must feel **supported** and allowed to make mistakes. Taking intellectual risks should be expected and nurtured as part of the learning process. Students must have the support through all phases of learning, from you and from others in the learning community.

When they feel competent, connected, and supported, your students can start to feel **responsible** for their learning. This includes initiating their own learning as well as being accountable for what they have learned. Responsible learners hone the skills of being prepared every day for learning, sharing in the operations of the classroom procedures, and developing independence and organizational techniques for success.

Next, learners become able to take **control** of their learning. Control in learning is about setting goals, managing the process to reach the goal, and monitoring and evaluating goal attainment. As the "guide on the side," you must allow for **choices** in what the students learn, where they learn it, and how they learn it. Students build self-efficacy, self-esteem, and confidence in their capabilities when they engage in **challenging** activities. Your role becomes one of improving learners' capacity for self-guided learning. (See Chapter 6 for more on developing learner autonomy.)

Finally, learning should be **fun**! As students build their competence and confidence in learning, they experience greater feelings of intrinsic motivation. Learning becomes fun because the students have committed themselves to studies they are interested in.

7 Graham, S. and C. Hudley. "Race and Ethnicity in the Study of Motivation and Competence." *Handbook of Competence and Motivation.* New York: The Guildford Press, 2007.

Figure 4.8 Pathway to a Motivating and Engaging Classroom

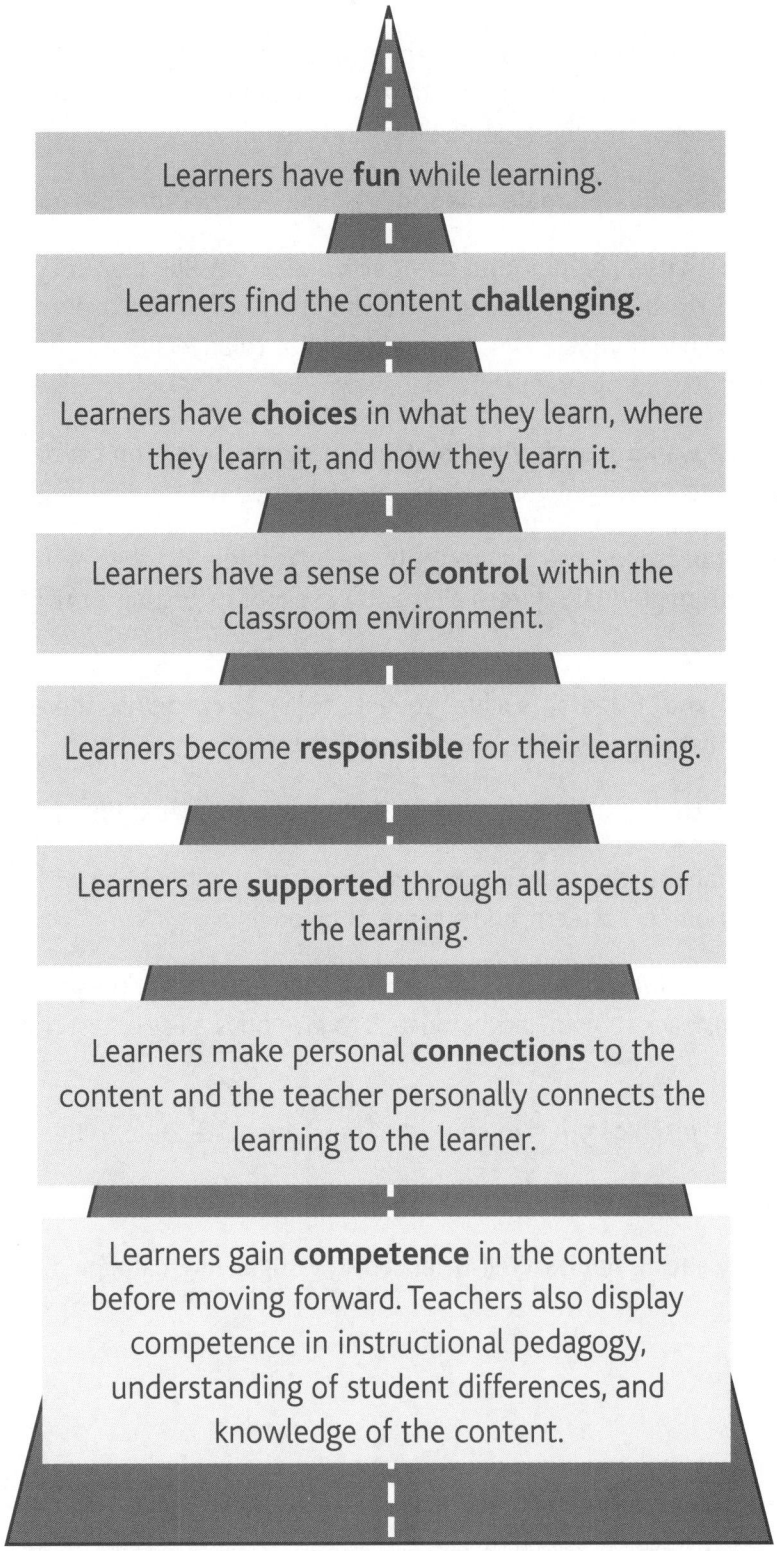

25 Strategies for Developing a Boy-Friendly Classroom[8]

1. **Create a "Success Team"** for each boy to act as a support system that can intervene when issues arise. Boys work best in a team mentality. The team can be made up of family, friends, relatives, religious leaders, teachers, counselors, and peers.

2. **Find successful, well-adjusted male role models** who can mentor boys in school and in life.

3. **Provide physical activities, games, and competitions** to develop resiliency and give boys chances to bond with others. Boys who are involved in organized sports or other team activities are more likely to be healthy, well adjusted, and resistant to adversity and delinquent activities (such as gangs, graffiti, and other unlawful behavior).

4. **Use the "talk while walking or driving" method of counseling**. Don't expect boys to maintain eye contact when dealing with stressful issues or concerns.

5. **Celebrate "rites of passage"** as a way to motivate boys and build their self-esteem. These rites could be anything from graduating from elementary school to getting a driver's license and beyond.

6. **Use "brain breaks" and "fidgets"** (such as squeeze balls). Boys can use these while at school or while doing a task that requires long periods of attention.

7. **Provide intricate activities** such as beadwork that can help develop fine motor skills.

8. **Provide experiential and kinesthetic outings**. These outings should be with specific groups to build social interaction, self-esteem, and a sense of belonging.

9. **Reduce verbal instructions**, or repeat the verbal directions several times and then have boys repeat the directions back to you. Another idea is to give boys a list of directions along with the verbal instructions.

10. **Lower the tone and pitch of your voice** so that boys are better able to hear you.

11. **Increase a sense of attachment** by allowing boys to personalize their own spaces.

12. **Encourage healthy eating habits**. Well-balanced, low-sugar, low-caffeine diets are crucial for many boys.

continued ➡

8 Gurian and Stevens, *The Minds of Boys: Saving Our Sons from Falling Behind in School and Life*. San Francisco, CA: Jossey-Bass, 2005.
Lise Eliot, "The Truth About Boys and Girls." *Scientific American Mind*, May/June 2010.
Neu, Terry W. and Rich Weinfeld. *Helping Boys Succeed in School: A Practical Guide for Parents and Teachers*. Waco, TX: Prufrock Press, 2006.

From *Advancing Differentiation: Thinking and Learning for the 21st Century* by Richard M. Cash, Ed.D., copyright © 2011. Free Spirit Publishing Inc., Minneapolis, MN; 800-735-7323; www.freespirit.com. This page may be reproduced for use within an individual school or district. For all other uses, contact www.freespirit.com/company/permissions.cfm.

25 Strategies for Developing a Boy-Friendly Classroom[8] (continued)

13. **Ask parents to become "homework coaches."** Homework for boys can be tedious and laborious. Show boys' parents how they can spend this time with their sons, keeping them focused and supported throughout the work.

14. **Consider brain injury** when faced with a learning disability. During rough play at an early age, some boys may have experienced a brain injury, which may not have been diagnosed and could lead to later learning problems.

15. **Place books around the classroom** to encourage boys to read.

16. **Set up "Boys Only" book clubs** to bridge the gap in academic language acquisition and break down the stigma of reading being a feminine activity. Use literature as a way of shaping identity and forming social groups.

17. **Offer boy-friendly reading choices,** which may include action, gore, fun, and purposeful adventures. These types of choices can often be found in comic books, graphic novels, magazines, cartoon anthologies, or "How Things Work" books.

18. **Provide plenty of technological outlets** to stimulate creativity. Computer graphics and screen animations are excellent ways to engage boys in research and investigations.

19. **Limit screen time**. While computer time is highly beneficial for boys, it must be monitored and used in moderation. Also encourage parents to limit the amount of television their boys watch.

20. **Focus curriculum and instruction on the self.** Adolescence, particularly for boys, is a period of egocentric development. Focusing the content on how boys fit within the topics will engage and encourage them to participate more completely.

21. **Make learning experiences meaningful, rigorous, and active**. Boys are often more physically active than girls. Therefore, by making the learning more authentic and active, boys will have a better chance of engaging in the tasks.

22. **Provide opportunities for safe risk taking**. The competitive nature of boys may stunt their intellectual risk taking. Ensure that your classroom is free of intimidation and is supportive when mistakes happen.

23. **Allow for choices.** When boys (particularly adolescent boys) don't have power within a situation, they will often rebel and are less likely to participate in the learning activities.

24. **Use bright natural light** for reading. Boys are generally more visually stimulated than girls.

25. **Use stories** to encourage social cohesion, build empathy, transmit knowledge, persuade, challenge, and develop boys' social acumen.

---

8 Gurian and Stevens, *The Minds of Boys: Saving Our Sons from Falling Behind in School and Life.* San Francisco, CA: Jossey-Bass, 2005.
Lise Eliot, "The Truth About Boys and Girls." *Scientific American Mind,* May/June 2010.
Neu, Terry W. and Rich Weinfeld. *Helping Boys Succeed in School: A Practical Guide for Parents and Teachers*. Waco, TX: Prufrock Press, 2006.

From *Advancing Differentiation: Thinking and Learning for the 21st Century* by Richard M. Cash, Ed.D., copyright © 2011. Free Spirit Publishing Inc., Minneapolis, MN; 800-735-7323; www.freespirit.com. This page may be reproduced for use within an individual school or district. For all other uses, contact www.freespirit.com/company/permissions.cfm.

Strategies for Creating a Brain-Compatible Learning Environment

1. **Create a safe and nonthreatening atmosphere.**
   - Get to know each student as an individual.
   - Ensure the learning environment is free of intimidation, threats, bullying, sarcasm, stereotyping, and fear.
   - Let students know it is okay to be many different things, such as smart, athletic, attractive, quirky, popular, introverted, *and* funny.
   - Avoid the "pop quiz." Let students know what they will be assessed on and when.
   - Use a "fist to five" ranking method to assess understanding (for example, "If you don't understand show me a fist. If you totally get it show me five.")
2. **Provide stimulation of all five senses and allow for various learning styles.**
   - Teach using varied learning styles and techniques.
   - Use authentic learning experiences, mentors, role models, and field trips.
   - Make sure to offer students three ways of acquiring the information by seeing it, then saying it, and ultimately doing it.
   - Introduce content that encourages discussions and debates and challenges beliefs.
   - Allow students to do projects creatively and think outside the box.
   - Emphasize student independence rather than dependence on the teacher to always lead the learning.
3. **Offer opportunities for physical action and connections to the learners' prior experiences.**
   - Get students up and moving. Use activities such as "four corners."
   - Use "essential questions" to connect learning to students' interests.
   - Relate material to the learner.
   - Use graphic organizers to help learners attach new information to prior knowledge.
   - Use service learning approaches, role plays, and case studies.
4. **Provide accurate, efficient, relevant, and timely feedback.**
   - Use authentic assessments.
   - Teach students self-regulating strategies such as setting goals, monitoring those goals, and evaluating personal growth.
   - Provide specific feedback focused on positive growth.
   - Provide frequent "coaching conferences" as a way to give regular feedback.
   - Show students how effort is the major contributor to achievement.

From *Advancing Differentiation: Thinking and Learning for the 21st Century* by Richard M. Cash, Ed.D., copyright © 2011. Free Spirit Publishing Inc., Minneapolis, MN; 800-735-7323; www.freespirit.com. This page may be reproduced for use within an individual school or district. For all other uses, contact www.freespirit.com/company/permissions.cfm.

Brain Breaks

The brain works and learns best when it has time to process information and shift gears when you move from activity to activity. The following strategies can be helpful in giving the brain time to think and shift between activities.

- Use an "I Chart" to help students process information during instructional time.
- Use word puzzles, cartoons, jokes, and riddles to help relieve stress, transition between topics, or create an enjoyable learning climate.
- Use the 10:2/20:2 Rule to ensure that students have time to think.
- Use creative thinking activities to help students think more broadly.
- Use physical activity to stimulate blood flow such as doing a quick set of jumping jacks, stretching, bending over to touch toes, taking three deep breaths, walking around the room, or singing the song: "Head, Shoulders, Knees, and Toes."
- Have students do facial stretching and relaxing to relieve tension in the head and neck.
- Use cross-lateral brain activity to stimulate the entire brain. Have students do the following activities:
  - Cross your right arm over your left arm and intertwine your fingers. Now, roll your clasped hands toward your body and wiggle your right index finger.
  - Hold up your right index finger and left thumb. Then, switch them back and forth quickly (right thumb/left index, right index/left thumb).
  - Touch your right hand to your left knee, and then your left hand to your right knee. Repeat several times while singing a song.
  - Raise your right hand and cross it behind your head to touch your left shoulder. Do the same thing with your left hand and right shoulder. Repeat while counting backward by 3s from 52.

BENEFITS OF BRAIN BREAKS

- Relieve stress
- Provide physical activity
- Stimulate blood flow
- Energize the students
- "Wake up" students' brains and get them in gear for learning
- Make students more comfortable in the classroom
- Prepare students for presentations
- Help students stay focused
- Help students retain information
- Give students time to think

From *Advancing Differentiation: Thinking and Learning for the 21st Century* by Richard M. Cash, Ed.D., copyright © 2011. Free Spirit Publishing Inc., Minneapolis, MN; 800-735-7323; www.freespirit.com. This page may be reproduced for use within an individual school or district. For all other uses, contact www.freespirit.com/company/permissions.cfm.

I Chart

I wonder	I discovered
I think	I question
I believe	I plan
I connected	I learned

From *Advancing Differentiation: Thinking and Learning for the 21st Century* by Richard M. Cash, Ed.D., copyright © 2011. Free Spirit Publishing Inc., Minneapolis, MN; 800-735-7323; www.freespirit.com. This page may be reproduced for use within an individual school or district. For all other uses, contact www.freespirit.com/company/permissions.cfm.

Strategies to Motivate and Engage Students

As stated earlier, when students are emotionally engaged they are more likely to pay attention to the learning tasks. Also, all students want to be competent at meaningful tasks. Therefore, taking into account how the brain learns best, we should:

- use the students' interests to engage them in the learning process
- use the students' learning preferences to teach new information and confirm preexisting knowledge
- routinely use assessment to motivate students to achieve at the highest level possible

Use Student Interests to Motivate and Engage

Critical to the learning process is getting students interested in what you have to offer. Find out what will hook learners about the topic or the concepts being presented. Integrating student interest in the classroom is a way to add personal meaning and relevance to the content. Additionally, you can help students make connections between what they already know to the new information being generated.

Surveys

Find out what students are interested in and how it can connect to the curriculum. One way to do this is to administer an interest survey or inventory. Many surveys and inventories exist to assist you in fine-tuning curriculum and instruction to address student interests. If you choose to use surveys or inventories, make sure you are willing to change instruction to either address or incorporate the students' responses. Keep the survey results handy, use them often in your planning process, and allow students to adjust their responses at any time. Try to give students the survey or inventory at least two times throughout the year.

Topic Previews

Another way to motivate and engage learners is to get them interested in the topic. This can be done through a preview of a textbook or other source material (see page 50).

KIQ Charts

Another strategy is using a KIQ chart: what I *Know*, find *Interesting*, and have *Questions* about (see page 51). A KIQ chart is similar to a KWI chart (What I *Know*, What I *Want* to Know, What I Find *Interesting*) or a KWL chart (What I *Know*, What I *Want* to Know, What I *Learned*), but the final box is changed to solicit students' questions about a topic. This strategy is very helpful for students to recognize they don't know everything about a topic, and that nobody *can* know everything there is to know about any topic. Even medical students take courses in "what I don't know about medicine." This form can also generate topics for independent research or group projects.

Rank Your Interests Forms

In some cases, you may want students to become "experts" in a certain part of a unit. Using the Rank Your Interests form (page 52) can help guide this practice. Steps to using this form are as follows:

1. Organize the unit around specific concepts, themes, or categories.
2. Offer a mini-lesson (a brief two-minute explanation) of the unit components.
3. Have students rank their preferred topics from high to low.
4. Group students using the ranking. (Tell students you will try hard to give them their first choice, but if there are too many students in one group or you feel some students won't/can't work well together, you may need to go to their second choice. Tell them you will try very hard not to give them their third choice and will almost never give them their fourth choice.)
5. Students work in collaborative groups to build a project that represents their knowledge and research of the topic. The project/presentation must include connections to other content/curricular areas and use students' creative talents.
6. Students present the projects either throughout the unit of study or at the end as a wrap-up to the unit.

An example is provided in **Figure 4.9** on page 53.

What Interests Me: Topic Preview

1. Write the title of the textbook or other source material here:_____

2. What do you think this title means OR what are your thoughts on the title?

_____

_____

_____

_____

3. Look over the contents. List at least three headings that jump out at you.

- _____
- _____
- _____

4. Preview the entire textbook or other source material. Pick out three chapters or sections that seem interesting to you.

- Interesting chapter/section title:_____
- Why I think it's interesting: _____
- Questions I have about this chapter/section: _____

  _____

  _____

- Interesting chapter/section title:_____
- Why I think it's interesting: _____
- Questions I have about this chapter/section: _____

  _____

  _____

- Interesting chapter/section title:_____
- Why I think it's interesting: _____
- Questions I have about this chapter/section: _____

  _____

  _____

5. Find a textbook, website, or other resource that is similar or may deal with the same topic. If possible, bring it in to share with the class. Write the source below:

_____

_____

From *Advancing Differentiation: Thinking and Learning for the 21st Century* by Richard M. Cash, Ed.D., copyright © 2011. Free Spirit Publishing Inc., Minneapolis, MN; 800-735-7323; www.freespirit.com. This page may be reproduced for use within an individual school or district. For all other uses, contact www.freespirit.com/company/permissions.cfm.

KIQ Chart

What I KNOW about this topic	What I find INTERESTING about this topic	What I QUESTION or don't know about this topic

From *Advancing Differentiation: Thinking and Learning for the 21st Century* by Richard M. Cash, Ed.D., copyright © 2011. Free Spirit Publishing Inc., Minneapolis, MN; 800-735-7323; www.freespirit.com. This page may be reproduced for use within an individual school or district. For all other uses, contact www.freespirit.com/company/permissions.cfm.

Rank Your Interests

UNIT TOPICS

Rank the topics below: 1 (your least favorite) through 5 (your favorite).

____ Topic: _____

____ Topic: _____

____ Topic: _____

____ Topic: _____

____ Topic: _____

ASSIGNMENT

You will team with others who have similar interests. Your team will decide on a topic and create a project to present the topic. Your team must connect the project to music, art, literature, math, sports, family life, or the life of a person like you. You must also incorporate the following learning objectives:

- **Know:** _____

  _____

  _____

  _____

  _____

- **Be able to:** _____

  _____

  _____

  _____

  _____

- **Understand:** _____

  _____

  _____

  _____

  _____

Be creative, think outside the box!

From *Advancing Differentiation: Thinking and Learning for the 21st Century* by Richard M. Cash, Ed.D., copyright © 2011. Free Spirit Publishing Inc., Minneapolis, MN; 800-735-7323; www.freespirit.com. This page may be reproduced for use within an individual school or district. For all other uses, contact www.freespirit.com/company/permissions.cfm.

Figure 4.9 Rank Your Interests: Example—The Nervous System

UNIT TOPICS

Rank the topics below: 1 (your least favorite) through 5 (your favorite).

___ Topic: Cerebrum

___ Topic: Autonomic nervous system

___ Topic: Peripheral nervous system

___ Topic: Pons, medulla oblongata, and spinal cord

___ Topic: Midbrain and diencephalons

ASSIGNMENT

You will team with others who have similar interests. Your team will decide on a topic and create a project to present the topic. Your team must connect the project to music, art, literature, math, sports, family life, or the life of a person like you. You must also incorporate the following learning objectives:

- **Know:** how the parts of a system work together to maintain homeostasis.
- **Be able to:** explain how the anatomy of a structure is related to its physiology.
- **Understand:** the human body systems.

Be creative, think outside the box!

You may find that you already have "experts" in your classroom. One strategy to acknowledge these experts is by doing a "passion project" (see passion project guidelines and rubric on pages 54–55). Passion projects can be used as tools to encourage students to share their passions with others, or to enhance a unit of study where students have already gained some valuable working knowledge. Offering students a chance to do a passion project can:

- allow gifted students to share an interest they have spent time studying on their own
- give other students ideas of talent areas and extensions from subjects being learned in school
- give students who may not get the opportunity to share much about themselves a chance to shine

A passion project can be used with every student in your class as a year-long anchoring assignment, or on an individual basis. The project can replace another unit project, be a stand-alone assignment, or be used for extra credit purposes. You will note that when the student makes a presentation about their passion, they are encouraged not to relay everything they know about the topic so as to encourage others to do their own research. Students should give just enough information to pique their audience's interest, and offer lists of resources, websites, books, or other materials that another student could use to start their own investigation.

On page 56 is a list of additional strategies to motivate and engage students based on their interests.

Guidelines for Creating a Passion Project

1. Passions are those things you love, greatly enjoy doing, and have a good storehouse of knowledge about. Clearly explain your passion and why others would want to know about this topic:

_____

_____

_____

_____

_____

_____

_____

_____

_____

_____

2. Meet with the teacher to find an appropriate unit project that can be replaced by your passion project.

Teacher meeting date: _____

Unit project to be replaced by the passion project: _____

Due date for the passion project: _____

Signature of teacher: _____

Signature of student: _____

3. Construct your passion project for presentation to the class.

- Think of an interesting way to present your passion project (PowerPoint, speech, role play, charts/posters, etc.).
- In your presentation, tell the class:
  - How you became involved with the topic
  - How you came to know your topic
  - Why you enjoy your topic
  - What makes your topic interesting
- Provide the class with information that could stimulate them to investigate this topic.
- Offer the class a list of resources, websites, books, or other materials that could get other students started on your topic.

4. Your passion project will be graded based on the rubric attached. Your grade on the passion project will replace the grade on the unit project.

continued ➡

From *Advancing Differentiation: Thinking and Learning for the 21st Century* by Richard M. Cash, Ed.D., copyright © 2011. Free Spirit Publishing Inc., Minneapolis, MN; 800-735-7323; www.freespirit.com. This page may be reproduced for use within an individual school or district. For all other uses, contact www.freespirit.com/company/permissions.cfm.

Rubric for Passion Project

CATEGORY	4	3	2	1
Preparedness	Student is completely prepared and has obviously rehearsed.	Student seems fairly prepared but might have needed a couple more rehearsals.	Student is somewhat prepared, but it is clear that rehearsal was lacking.	Student does not seem prepared to present.
Enthusiasm	Student's facial expressions and body language generate a strong interest and enthusiasm about the topic in the audience.	Student's facial expressions and body language sometimes generate a strong interest and enthusiasm about the topic in the audience.	Student's facial expressions and body language are used to try to generate enthusiasm, but seem somewhat faked.	Student makes very little use of facial expressions or body language and did not generate much interest in the topic in the audience.
Content	Student shows a full understanding of the topic.	Student shows a good understanding of the topic.	Student shows a good understanding of parts of the topic.	Student does not seem to understand the topic very well.
Resources	Student provides a wide range of resources (at least 10) including websites, text, and artifacts.	Student provides a range of resources (at least 8) including websites, text, and artifacts.	Student provides some resources (at least 5) including websites and text.	Student provides few resources (less than 5), which include websites and text.
Connection to Content	Student makes exceptional connections to content including math, science, social studies, language arts, the arts, physical education, and/or other areas of study.	Student makes some connections to content including math, science, social studies, language arts, the arts, physical education and/or other areas of study.	Student makes few connections to content including math, science, social studies, language arts, the arts, physical education, and/or other areas of study.	Student makes no connections to content.

From *Advancing Differentiation: Thinking and Learning for the 21st Century* by Richard M. Cash, Ed.D., copyright © 2011. Free Spirit Publishing Inc., Minneapolis, MN; 800-735-7323; www.freespirit.com. This page may be reproduced for use within an individual school or district. For all other uses, contact www.freespirit.com/company/permissions.cfm.

Motivation Strategies Based on Student Interests

The following activities stimulate students' curiosity and motivation and promote collaboration.

- **Group students by interest**, then jigsaw the material from alike to mixed groups. Students who have deep interest in content areas can be grouped with other like-minded learners, allowing them the opportunity to go into advanced levels of knowledge. The students should then share their interest-based learning with other students.
- **Allow students to opt out of assigned work** by doing a "passion project" that focuses on a complex issue related to the course of study. Students develop passion projects based on personal interests or hobbies. Through this project students discover the skills required and developed by career possibilities within their interest or hobby.
- **Use interest surveys** to develop lessons and projects that require multiple interests to be included, as well as interdisciplinary subjects that encompass the arts, sports, family life, and social and civic issues. Interest surveys can help students define their level of engagement in a topic, specify what they like in learning, and identify assets they bring to their learning environment.
- **Allow students to design units, lessons, or projects** based on a meaningful question. This requires investigation that is semi-structured with articulated benchmarks, produces tangible end products that are presented to an authentic audience, and includes reflection on learning. Students complete the work based on an interest contract developed in concert with you and their parents.
- **Allow independent projects** that require students to use inquiry and discovery that expands and extends the classroom curriculum.
- **Incorporate authentic mentors and coaches** from the wider community within the content areas. Connect students to these adults to explore their areas of interest.
- **Develop community or service projects based** on student interests. Expose the students to the social and civic issues that involve their interests. Engage them in solving an authentic problem through community service or volunteerism.
- **Have students construct an online "wiki" to share information** on a particular topic of study or to assist other learners in gaining the necessary knowledge of a course of instruction.
- **Develop "Special Interest Groups" (SIGs)** that meet throughout the school year to discuss topics, work on tasks, network, create products, and find solutions to authentic student issues. Students learn to collaborate, define problems that are common to a greater number of individuals, share resources, plan and work toward solutions, and develop leadership skills within a community.

From *Advancing Differentiation: Thinking and Learning for the 21st Century* by Richard M. Cash, Ed.D., copyright © 2011. Free Spirit Publishing Inc., Minneapolis, MN; 800-735-7323; www.freespirit.com. This page may be reproduced for use within an individual school or district. For all other uses, contact www.freespirit.com/company/permissions.cfm.

Use Student Learning Preferences to Motivate and Engage

Dr. Robert Sternberg, one of the world's leading cognitive psychologists, has theorized a balance of intellectual abilities that he calls "successful intelligence." According to Sternberg, when people are aware of their strengths and abilities they are more likely to use those strengths to compensate or correct their weaknesses[9]. Also, when people are able to best use those strengths in effective ways, they are more likely to be successful in life. Successful individuals have figured out how to adapt to, shape, or select environments where their abilities and strengths are best used.

Sternberg's design of successful intelligence has three ability dimensions: **creative**, **analytical**, and **practical**. While we all have each of these abilities, we have varying degrees of them. And since we tend to prefer learning styles that match our abilities, we also vary in our learning preferences across the three dimensions. Based on their abilities, most people will prefer one or two of the dimensions when learning, but those individuals who understand all three dimensions collectively can more effectively use them in combination to be more successful.

Creative Dimension

Individuals with creative ability often:

- think outside the box
- generate new and interesting ideas
- make connections between seemingly disjointed information
- may not perform well in school on standardized tests or follow directions well
- come up with novel ways to represent information

Learning activities preferred by creative individuals:

- creating
- inventing
- discovering
- exploring
- imagining
- pretending
- hypothesizing
- postulating
- theorizing
- designing

Assessment or questioning techniques suitable for creative individuals:

- open-ended
- active
- conceptual
- unusual or novel
- techniques that elaborate on information beyond the facts

Analytical Dimension

Individuals with analytical ability often:

- do well in school, especially on standardized tests, and follow directions well
- are book smart
- may recognize flaws in lines of thought or reasoning
- prefer to follow directions rather than come up with their own way of doing things

Learning activities preferred by analytical individuals:

- analyzing
- evaluating
- judging
- critiquing
- comparing/contrasting
- testing
- examining
- studying
- investigating
- questioning

Assessment or questioning techniques suitable for analytical individuals:

- structured
- individually focused
- factual or information rich
- logical
- organized

9 Sternberg, Robert J. and Elena L. Grigorenko. *Teaching for Successful Intelligence: To Increase Student Learning and Achievement (2nd Edition)*. Thousand Oaks, CA: Corwin Press, 2007.

Practical Dimension

Individuals with practical ability often:

- do moderately well in school
- have an abundance of common sense
- are resilient and easily adapt to social situations
- are considered social leaders

Learning activities preferred by practical individuals:

- applying
- using
- implementing
- collaborating
- working with their hands or tools
- operating
- manipulating
- managing
- practicing
- authenticating

Assessment or questioning techniques suitable for practical individuals:

- group process
- authentic application
- process-oriented
- demonstrating feasibility of product
- displaying information in an "everyday" useful manner

Again, to some degree, everyone has all three of these abilities. How we recognize the need for each ability and then use the abilities within a given setting is what determines our success. We must give students a chance to safely explore each of the ability dimensions—not only the ones they are strong in and prefer—through learning activities so they build awareness of how to best employ the skills involved.

One way to help students understand the three dimensions of successful intelligence is through the activity on pages 59–60. Share with students a list of people both famous and not-so-famous who possess strengths in each of the three dimensions. Then have students develop a list of individuals whom they believe to have strengths in the three dimensions. Also, have students recognize when to rely on each of the different dimensions and when using a combination of the dimensions would be most beneficial. Students who are flexible in shifting their thinking depending on the situation will find greater success.

Following on page 61 is a list of additional strategies for motivating based on student learning preferences.

Students who are flexible in shifting their thinking depending on the situation will find greater success.

Sternberg Model of Abilities: Learning Styles Activity

Activity

- Learning Styles

Objectives

- Students will know the characteristics of analytical, practical, and creative abilities.
- Students will be able to define their preferred learning style and strengths.
- Students will understand the differences people bring to every situation and how those differences benefit the learning setting.

Concepts

- Learning differences, strengths, weaknesses

Procedure

1. Ask students what they believe "success" to be. List ideas.
2. Ask students what it takes to be successful. List ideas.
3. Discuss with students how each person comes to a learning setting with a different set of attributes that can be used for success. How we use those abilities to our benefit is what makes us successful. Refer to the list students made of "What it takes to be successful."
4. Explain Robert Sternberg's model of Successful Intelligence, which involves:
   - A set of three abilities needed to attain success
   - A person's ability to recognize and make the most of his or her strengths (nearly everyone is good at something)
   - A person's ability to recognize and compensate for or correct his or her weaknesses (no one is good at everything)
   - Utilizing their strengths and weaknesses, successful people are able to either adapt to, shape, or select environments that best fit their learning styles
5. On the Sternberg diagram, fill in, as a class, the descriptions of each of the three abilities.
6. Using the Sternberg diagram, have students place an X on the line of the triangle that represents their preferred areas of strength. Remind them that the lines between lettered corners are a continuum between the different abilities. For example, if a student feels more creative than analytical, she or he would place the X closer to the C corner than the A corner. If the student feels more practical than analytical, he or she would place the X closer to the P than the A. If the student feels an equal balance between creative and practical, she or he would place the X on the line midway between P and C.
7. Define three areas of your classroom to be A (analytical), C (creative), and P (practical) areas. Ask students to move to the part of the room that would best represent their area of strength. If students have balances between areas, they should choose one area over the others.

Discussion

Have the students discuss the similarities and differences between the three groups. Ask: Which groups have more students, and why? Which groups have fewer students, and why? Why do you think some people have balances or imbalances between the three areas? How might we use the strengths of the (A, C, or P) group to assist us in the classroom? How could we organize the classroom setting to best meet the learning needs of each of the three groups? How might we do group work differently now that we've identified these abilities? How could someone with a different (or similar) learning style help you work on a project?

Closure

Have students write or draw a reflection on the need for all students to work with differing styles of learning. Or make suggestions for classroom arrangements, group work, or project assignments.

continued ➡

From *Advancing Differentiation: Thinking and Learning for the 21st Century* by Richard M. Cash, Ed.D., copyright © 2011. Free Spirit Publishing Inc., Minneapolis, MN; 800-735-7323; www.freespirit.com. This page may be reproduced for use within an individual school or district. For all other uses, contact www.freespirit.com/company/permissions.cfm.

Sternberg Model of Abilities: Learning Styles Activity (continued)

People with **analytical** ability can:

People with **practical** ability can:

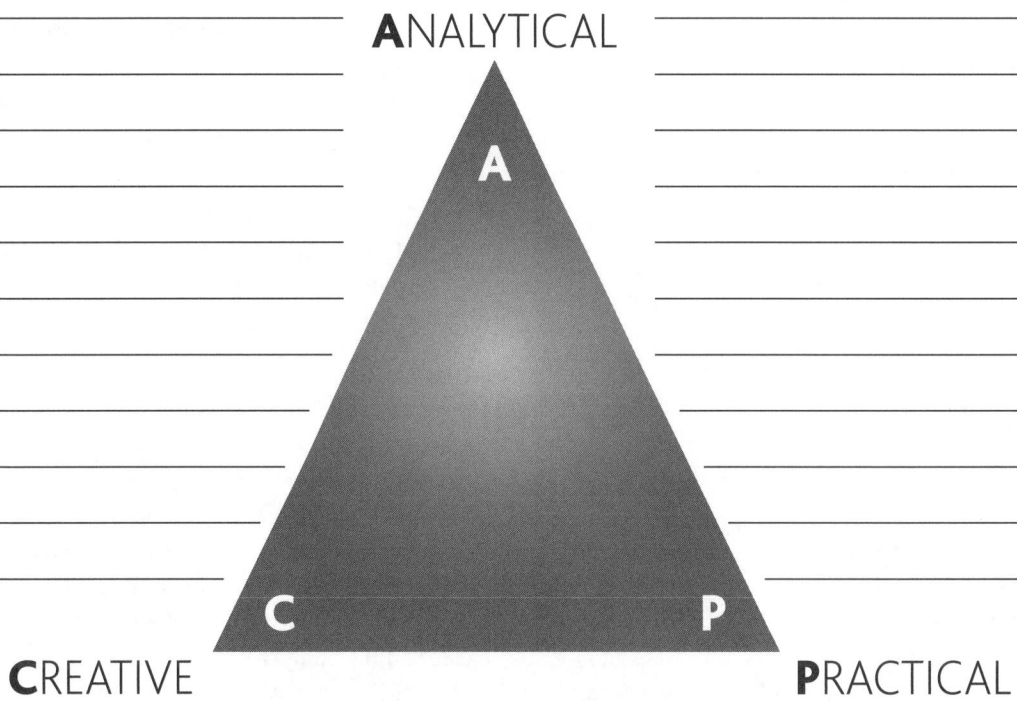

People with **creative** ability can:

From *Advancing Differentiation: Thinking and Learning for the 21st Century* by Richard M. Cash, Ed.D., copyright © 2011. Free Spirit Publishing Inc., Minneapolis, MN; 800-735-7323; www.freespirit.com. This page may be reproduced for use within an individual school or district. For all other uses, contact www.freespirit.com/company/permissions.cfm.

Motivation Strategies Based on Student Learning Preferences

The following activities engage and stretch students in both their preferred and nonpreferred domains of learning.

- **Present information in multiple ways**, including kinesthetic, to encourage learners to branch out of their preferred styles. Many learners tend to prefer specific domains of learning information—often verbal/linguistic for girls and visual/spatial for boys.
- **Use student models and examples** when introducing the learning to be accomplished. Seeing the work of other students who are like them will encourage students to explore beyond their comfort zones to master new subjects and materials.
- **Use wait-time** to allow students to process, connect, and reflect on information. Some learners are deep introspective thinkers, and thus will take longer to respond to in-class questions.
- **Use journaling** as a method of reflection on and development of content knowledge. Having students record each day something new they have learned or something at which they excelled helps them recognize their learning growth. Metacognition may be difficult for some learners who have not been stretched to think beyond the basics.
- **Provide multiple options for students to complete assignments**, ranging from artistic representations to three-dimensional constructions to physical performances. Some learners think outside the box and prefer to do things their own way.
- **Ensure ample opportunities for learners to work in balanced groups as well as individually.** Some students are strong independent learners and need assistance in developing collaboration skills. A developed process to move them from individualistic (possessing only some of the skills needed to accomplish a task) to group-oriented (where a collection of individual skills creates a better product) will assist them in building positive social skills. You might also allow students to develop social networking accounts to network with other learners of like skill or style.
- **Have students take a variety of learning styles instruments** to help them understand all their unique abilities and preferences. Many students have a good understanding of their abilities and preferred learning style based on Howard Gardner's Theory of Multiple Intelligences, but may not be familiar with others, such as Anthony Gregorc's Model (Concrete, Abstract, Random, Sequential), Hemispheric Dominance Theory, VARK (Visual, Aural, Read/Write, Kinesthetic), and Sternberg's Successful Intelligence Theory (Analytical, Creative, Practical), to name a few. A simple Internet search of "learning styles" will produce numerous websites of inventories and instruments. Be clear on your purpose and which styles you are willing to work with and through.
- **Use elaborate rehearsal.** Elaborate rehearsal (ER) is the active process of relating new material to something the learner already knows. ER focuses on the meaning of information through authentic practice and blurring the lines between content areas. When using ER, students are required to actively use all of their senses to encode information into long-term memory. Activities that are considered elaborative rehearsals are:
  - clustering a series of numbers to resemble a phone number (1.8422384943 = 1-842-238-4943)
  - using acronyms or mnemonics to remember sequential or serial information (red, orange, yellow, green, blue, indigo, violet = ROY G BIV)
  - creating analogies, metaphors, or similes to summarize information
  - using mind maps, graphic organizers, or other diagrammatic representations of the information
  - engaging in reenactment of an event, role play, or simulations

From *Advancing Differentiation: Thinking and Learning for the 21st Century* by Richard M. Cash, Ed.D., copyright © 2011. Free Spirit Publishing Inc., Minneapolis, MN; 800-735-7323; www.freespirit.com. This page may be reproduced for use within an individual school or district. For all other uses, contact www.freespirit.com/company/permissions.cfm.

Using Assessment to Motivate and Engage

In the past, assessment and evaluation was often used to rank students or to keep some students in or out of certain programs, especially gifted programs. Today, assessment has three primary uses: to gather information about how students are learning; to determine where students are in the learning process; and to provide feedback to the teacher on the success of methodology and practice, which then guides changes needed in the instruction. A fourth use for assessment that is sometimes overlooked is to motivate and stimulate students to learn. When students are aware of how they're doing and what new knowledge they're acquiring at all points in the learning process, they are more likely to engage in and take ownership of the learning, as well as experience several other benefits. See **Figure 4.10.**

"If the wrong kinds of praise lead kids down the path of entitlement, dependence, and fragility, maybe the right kinds of praise can lead them down the path of hard work and greater hardiness."

—*Carol Dweck, author and educator*

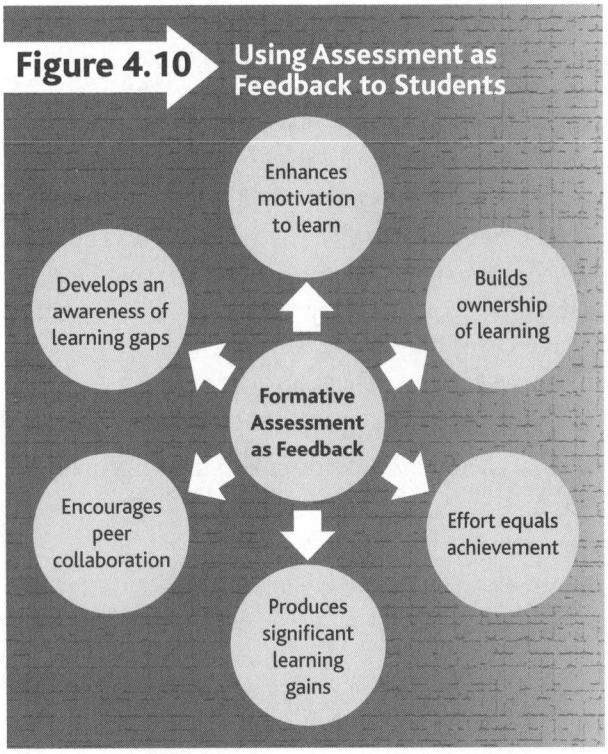

Assessment should be used to inform students how close they came to meeting the learning goal. It should also represent a valuation of the students' application, demonstration, and understandings of newly acquired knowledge. Above all, assessment should be *flexible* (it is implemented differently for different students), *meaningful* (both the student and teacher can use the information to make changes), and *customizable* (some may need more assessments and some may need fewer).

Three Types of Assessment

There are three main types of assessment used in the classroom: **preassessment** (also called diagnostic), **formative** assessment, and **summative** assessment. Preassessment, as the name suggests, is used prior to the learning process. Formative assessment occurs during the learning process. Summative assessment is a summation of what the learner has learned and is used at the end of the learning process.

When teachers are fully aware of where their students are in the learning process, how they are learning, and what strategies and techniques are working, they are better able to meet the learners' needs. Many strategies exist for assessing student learning. Following is a review of a few of those ideas that determine if your students are ready for instruction and also motivate students to engage in new learning.

Preassessment

Using assessment *before* the learning helps you find out what students know and don't know, recognize their strengths and weaknesses, detect errors or holes in their learning, and gather data for remediation, enrichment, and extensions. Preassessments are also wonderful for piquing students' interest in the topic.

Preassessments are generally not graded. When students have the burden of a grade lifted in the assessment process they are more likely to show you what they do and don't know.

Examples of Preassessments

- Pretests
- Open-ended discussions
- KQI charts (see page 51)
- Four square concept maps (page 63 and **Figure 4.11**)

The four square concept map uses multiple forms of representation, so you can assess learners' understanding of conceptual knowledge. Students should keep this preassessment throughout the learning and do another map at the end of the learning to compare their growth and advancing sophistication.

Four Square Concept Map

Directions:

1. Write the concept in the middle circle.
2. In the upper left box, write a definition of the concept.
3. In the upper right box, draw a picture of what the concept looks like.
4. In the lower left box, give examples of the concept.
5. In the lower right box, write or draw examples of what the concept is *not*.

Four Square Concept Map

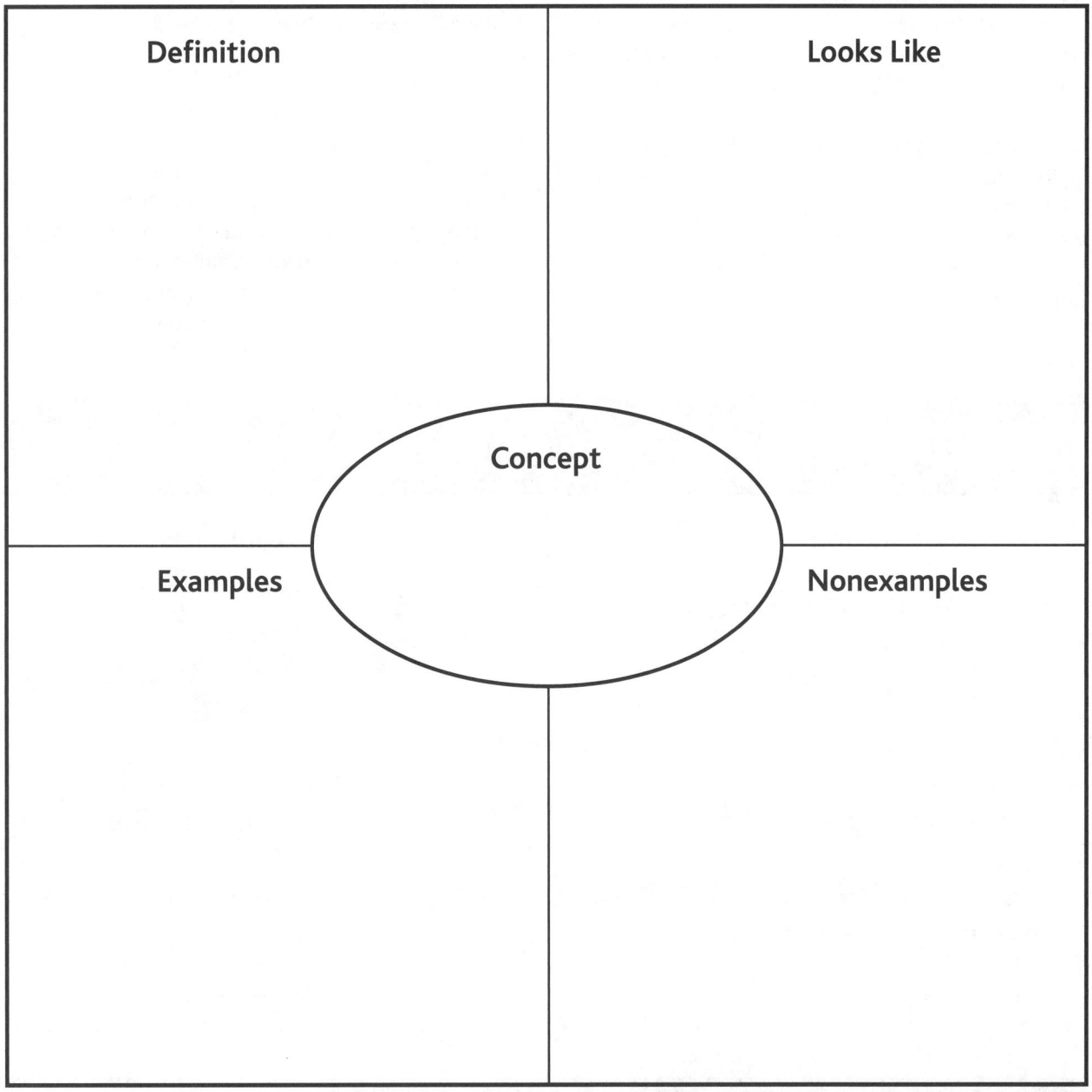

From *Advancing Differentiation: Thinking and Learning for the 21st Century* by Richard M. Cash, Ed.D., copyright © 2011. Free Spirit Publishing Inc., Minneapolis, MN; 800-735-7323; www.freespirit.com. This page may be reproduced for use within an individual school or district. For all other uses, contact www.freespirit.com/company/permissions.cfm.

Formative Assessment

Formative assessment is assessment *for* learning. This includes strategies for finding out where students are in the learning process, and in what ways the learner is approaching the goal. It provides the student with an understanding of his or her own proficiency regarding the benchmarks of a learning goal. This ongoing assessment also gives teachers guidance on adjusting and modifying instruction to move the learner closer to the benchmark and goal.

Grades on formative assessments are generally used to inform learners of individual progress. You may sometimes use these assessments to inform both students and parents about the learner's effort or attention to detail. Formative assessment grades should not be combined or averaged with a final evaluation grade; practice should be practice *only* and should not affect the final grade. If necessary, separate out the formative assessment grade as a stand-alone grade to inform parents and the student how much effort they put forth during the practice and to show growth during the learning process.

Examples of Formative Assessment:

- Student reflection log
- Quizzes
- Homework
- Teacher/peer/parent observations
- Daily work
- Discussion
- Read-Write-Pair-Share and Think-Pair-Share **(Figure 4.12)**
- 3-2-1 Exit Slip/Entrance Ticket (see page 67)
- 1–3 Minute Coaching/Consultation **(Figure 4.13)**
- Tiered Review/Practice **(Figure 4.14)**
- Roundtable Review (see pages 68–69)

Summative Assessment

Summative assessment, or assessment *of* learning, is conducted after a unit of instruction to determine where the learners are relative to the goal. Summative assessment gathers information on the students' factual knowledge, provides a way for students to demonstrate proficiency in skill development, and shows the students' ability to transfer their understanding of concepts. It is a culmination of the entire learning process.

Figure 4.11 Four Square Concept Map: Example

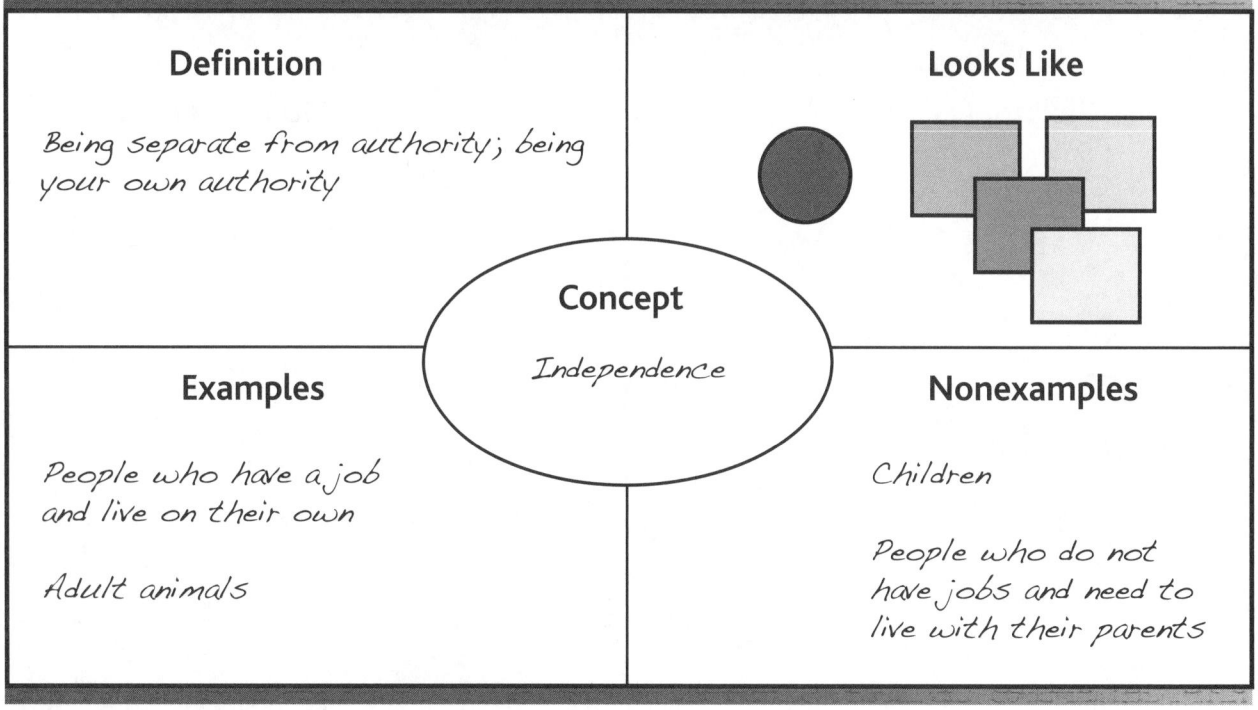

Grading a summative assessment generally defines a learner's proficiency and goal attainment. It can also inform where and how to begin the next unit of study. In this way, summative assessment can be used as a preassessment of an upcoming unit, for example, does the student have enough prior knowledge from the previous unit? It can also be used as formative assessment, for example, what do I need to reteach or enrich so the students are engaged and successful in the next unit?

Examples of Summative Assessment:

- Final exams
- Authentic projects
- Self/peer assessments
- Standardized tests

Page 70 provides a listing of additional strategies that can assist you in motivating students based on assessment. See Chapter 6 (pages 88–89) for a discussion of how assessment can build learner autonomy.

Figure 4.12 Read-Write-Pair-Share and Think-Pair-Share

READ-WRITE-PAIR-SHARE

Directions:

1. Have students individually read a passage of written text. The entire class can read the same passage, or members can all read different passages.
2. Ask students to write about their passage, either answering guiding questions or summarizing what they read.
3. Have students work with partners to share their written work and discuss the guiding questions.
4. Have each pair or selected pairs share with the class what they discussed and the outcome. Post responses from all groups for the class to view.

THINK-PAIR-SHARE

Directions:

1. Ask students a provocative question, present information requiring discussion, or suggest a scenario worth pondering.
2. Use a guided thinking question (see Chapter 7, page 97) to frame the students' think time.
3. Allow students to spend no more than two minutes thinking about how they might respond to the guiding question.
4. Have students pair with another student to discuss and compare each of their answers to the guiding question. During this time students should decide which of their answers is most convincing or answers the question most completely. Or they may decide to form a new answer based on the shared discussion.
5. Have each pair or selected pairs share what they discussed and the outcome. Post responses from all groups for the class to view.

Figure 4.13 1–3 Minute Coaching/Consultation

Directions:

- Select a different small number of students with whom you will meet individually each day. You should be able to cover your entire class within one to two weeks of instruction.
- Near the end of class or during work time, invite individual students to meet with you for a few minutes to discuss how the learning is going.
- Coach the learner on strategies or techniques to improve learning, or praise the student on specific achievements in the learning.
- Invite the student to consult with you on individual learning matters, such as extended projects, enrichment, needs for remediation, or on other matters related to teacher-student relationships.

Figure 4.14 Tiered Review/Practice

Directions:

One way to ensure your students have addressed the three levels of objectives for a unit of study is to create a tiered system of review. Divide students into three groups (factual, procedural, and conceptual). Base groups on students' levels of readiness in each of the three domains, or use mixed-ability groups. Have groups spend up to 10 minutes at each of the tables to complete the activities. Then, groups either move to another table or present to the class what they created at each table. If students rotate between tables without reporting to the class, be sure you have created three separate activities at each table and that groups leave behind what they created so the other groups can review, assess, or interpret preceding groups' work.

Table One
Factual Knowledge

Students will *list (recall)* significant dates, times, elements, vocabulary involved in the unit of study. Use mirrored[10] questions or expectations to assist students in the review of factual knowledge.

Table Two
Procedural Knowledge

Students will *demonstrate (application)* the skills and/or strategies used in the unit of study.
Provide mirrored processes used on the unit exam.

Table Three
Conceptual Knowledge

Students will *discuss/debate/examine/argue/interpret/offer new ideas for (analysis, synthesis, and evaluation)* related major concepts or topics covered in the unit. Provide mirrored essay questions that will appear on the unit exam.

10 Mirrored: questions, examples, or processes that are similar to those that will appear on the exam. Providing students with mirrored examples will tune them in to the language of the exam and allow them to test their answering abilities without the risk of failure.

3–2–1 Exit Slip/Entrance Ticket

Directions:

Prior to the end of a class session (as an exit slip) or as homework (as an entrance ticket), have students write in the boxes:

3 ideas or things you know or remember from the class session
2 connections you can make to other subject areas or topics you know something about
1 question that you still have or would like to ask in the next class session

3 Things you know about this topic			
2 Ways this topic connects to other topics			
1 Question you have about this topic			

From *Advancing Differentiation: Thinking and Learning for the 21st Century* by Richard M. Cash, Ed.D., copyright © 2011. Free Spirit Publishing Inc., Minneapolis, MN; 800-735-7323; www.freespirit.com. This page may be reproduced for use within an individual school or district. For all other uses, contact www.freespirit.com/company/permissions.cfm.

Roundtable Review

Directions:

1. On selected days throughout the unit or at the end of a unit of study, rearrange the classroom in table groupings. There should be as many tables as major topics in the unit of study.
2. At each table, place a placard with the topic listed. Choose discussion topics about which students either know a lot or need to review. You may also want to put highlighted notes or important bits of information that students must know, be able to do, and understand at each table.
3. Students select at least four tables to visit throughout the class period.
4. Students will visit each table for up to five minutes to share information about the table's topic.
5. After each round, students spend two minutes debriefing, writing notes, and finding answers. (Use the attached Roundtable Reflection form.)
6. At the end of the four cycles, do a walk-through with students of all the topics covered.

Topics Covered in This Unit

continued ➡

From *Advancing Differentiation: Thinking and Learning for the 21st Century* by Richard M. Cash, Ed.D., copyright © 2011. Free Spirit Publishing Inc., Minneapolis, MN; 800-735-7323; www.freespirit.com. This page may be reproduced for use within an individual school or district. For all other uses, contact www.freespirit.com/company/permissions.cfm.

Roundtable Reflection

TOPIC	WHAT I REMEMBER	WHAT I LEARNED

Additional Thoughts:

_____

_____

_____

_____

From *Advancing Differentiation: Thinking and Learning for the 21st Century* by Richard M. Cash, Ed.D., copyright © 2011. Free Spirit Publishing Inc., Minneapolis, MN; 800-735-7323; www.freespirit.com. This page may be reproduced for use within an individual school or district. For all other uses, contact www.freespirit.com/company/permissions.cfm.

Motivation Strategies Based on Assessment

The following activities acknowledge and respect what students already know and their need to know more.

- **Provide mini-lessons on facts and procedures** students will encounter in the unit of study. For advanced learners who require less time to learn facts and procedures this allows them to "buy" time for advanced levels of activities. For all other learners, this provides a warm-up or additional exposure to the material that will be covered.
- **Provide varied levels of reading materials**, from elementary to college-level texts and trade books and professional journals from the field of study. These materials will expose the learners to the professional language of the field of discipline, as well as provide a wider range of subject diversity. The students can then develop a professional vocabulary list.
- **Flexibly group students by ability or comprehension of content.** In these smaller groups, students can collaboratively work on authentic issues related to the content, develop questions they would like to explore, debate ethical ramifications, and investigate, interview, or contact experts from the field of study.
- **Have learning materials available other than text.** Not all learners enjoy or acquire knowledge from text, therefore use other materials such as audio recordings, videos/DVDs/CDs, websites, or computer simulations that will allow students to digest the required information.
- **Highlight key points in the text.** Some learners read text and believe all the material is highly relevant. Highlighting helps them focus on the most relevant and important notes.
- **Use creative activities** to assist learners in stretching beyond the basics in math and science. The experiences must require the practice of novelty, originality, and creating new ideas.
- **Use graphic organizers** to help learners organize their knowledge and connect prior learning to new ideas.
- **Adjust questioning practices** for the varied levels of learners in the classroom. Questions should encourage students to elaborate on points of discussion. All learners are able to think at higher levels, but advanced learners require a more complex degree of analysis, synthesis, and justification.
- **Encourage reciprocal teaching.** Reciprocal teaching occurs when a student is secure in the knowledge and is willing to share or assist others in a greater sense of understanding. To teach requires a deep understanding of the material, therefore allowing students to become reciprocal teachers who can provide other students assistance in learning and guidance in understanding the material. Being a reciprocal teacher can build learners' confidence as well as their knowledge of the subject.
- **Develop discovery-based lessons and content** that uses the Internet so students can access any piece of information at any time and in any sequence. This process must teach the learner how to discern and critically analyze information for bias, opinion, or irrelevance.

From *Advancing Differentiation: Thinking and Learning for the 21st Century* by Richard M. Cash, Ed.D., copyright © 2011. Free Spirit Publishing Inc., Minneapolis, MN; 800-735-7323; www.freespirit.com. This page may be reproduced for use within an individual school or district. For all other uses, contact www.freespirit.com/company/permissions.cfm.

Chapter 5

Developing Student Self-Regulation

> Acquiring higher mental functions allows children to make a critical transition from being "slaves to the environment" to becoming "masters of their own behavior."[1]
>
> *—Dr. Deborah J. Leong and Dr. Elena Bodrova, psychologists*

The role of schooling in a child's life is to expose him or her to the common knowledge we hold true as a society. The teacher's role is to provide this information in compatible ways for the child's brain to retain and use for future success. The student's role in school is to become self-regulated and develop new knowledge for future generations. The theory of self-regulation is based on the interaction of knowledge, emotion, and actions toward the formation of new knowledge, ideas, and products. Teachers provide those interactions when they offer students opportunities that encourage them to think and take authentic action.

Self-Regulation Theory

For over four decades, the idea of self-regulating has been an important area of educational and psychological research. The ideas behind how humans learn, both in academic and social settings, suggest that the competent, successful people believe that most things can be accomplished as long as one puts effort forward, has a goal in mind, knows how to deal with conflict, avoids distraction and impulsivity, stays focused on the task at hand, and acknowledges both success and failure.

Based on studies done by leading research scientists in the field of motivation and competence, Berry Zimmerman and Anastasia Kitsantas: "There is evidence that the attainment of peak levels of academic and athletic competence requires more than basic talent and high-quality instruction; it also involves self-belief, diligence, and self-discipline."[2] This development is completed in the four phases of self-regulation **(Figure 5.1).**

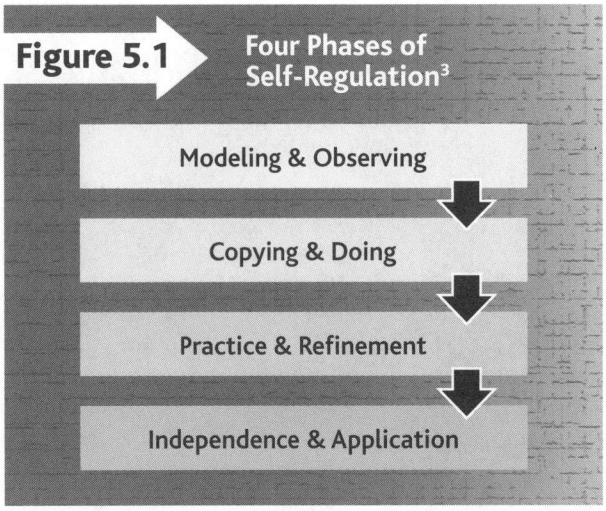

Figure 5.1 Four Phases of Self-Regulation[3]

1 From Leong, Deborah J. and Elena Bodrova. "Developing Self-Regulation: The Vygotskian View." *Academic Exchange Quarterly,* Winter 2006.

2 Zimmerman, B. J. and A. Kitsantas. "The Hidden Dimension of Personal Competence: Self-Regulated Learning and Practice." In *Handbook of Competence and Motivation.* New York: The Gilford Press, 2005, p. 509.

3 Zimmerman, B. J., S. Bonner, and R. Kovach. *Developing Self-Regulated Learners: Beyond Achievement to Self-Efficacy.* Washington DC: American Psychological Association, 1996. Zimmerman, B. J. and A. Kitsantas. "Developmental Phases in Self-Regulation: Shifting from Process Goals to Outcome Goals. *Journal of Educational Psychology,* 89, 1997, pp. 29–36.

Students have the capacity to learn how to self-regulate when the learning is effectively modeled for them, they can emulate or practice the modeled learning with others, they can use the learning during independent practice to employ it automatically, and they can transfer the learning to other learning activities.

The following skills guide learners in developing self-regulation:

- goal setting
- task strategies
- visual imagery
- self-instruction
- time management
- self-monitoring
- self-evaluation
- selecting and creating learning environments
- help-seeking

Zimmerman also proposed that the developmental process of how people acquire skills for success is cyclical in nature. As you can see in **Figure 5.2**, learning to develop self-regulation involves three cyclical phases.

In phase one, *pre-learning*, students set the stage for learning to occur. They examine the task to be completed and then set a plan of action to complete the task. Students must also evaluate the meaningfulness behind the task, as well as their own intrinsic beliefs about the task. At this point, students may want to use the Student Perception Questionnaire (Chapter 7, page 108) and also complete a Work Plan (Chapter 7, page 109).

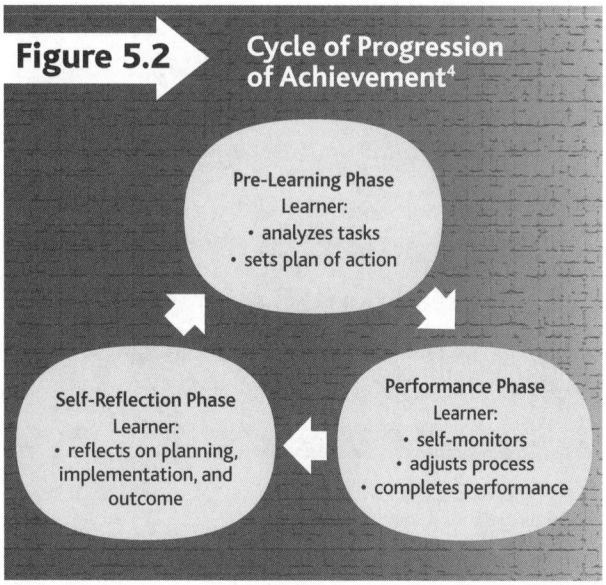

In the *performance phase*, students monitor their attention and focus on completing the task. After reviewing their work plans, students may find that they need additional support and guidance, or that they are on track to reach their goals. When the performance has been completed, the *self-reflection phase* follows, where students reflect upon the earlier phases of planning and performance. Students should review the work plan, looking back on the effectiveness of the goal setting, the availability of resources, whether they had the skills necessary to complete the task, and to what extent they accomplished the goal. Key to the success at each phase of this model is the student's sense of self-efficacy. *Self-efficacy* is the personal understanding one has about his or her skills and abilities to perform tasks, as well as a sense of commitment to complete a given task. Students with high self-efficacy are more willing to take on challenges, put forth effort to complete tasks when faced with temptations or distractions, and can effectively self-evaluate. Students with low self-efficacy display more learning and test anxiety, are more distractible, posses less intrinsic motivation, and are often disengaged from learning. You can help students develop and maintain a healthy level of self-efficacy by setting up a classroom that fosters thinking, encourages risk taking, and provides opportunities for students to develop autonomy.

Building Self-Regulation Through Goal Setting

An effective strategy to build self-regulation is through helping students set a goal, manage their progress toward the goal, and assess their attainment of the goal. Begin with short-term goal setting at the beginning of each day or lesson.

Steps in Short-Term Goal Setting

1. Model for students the writing of three goals at the beginning of class.
2. Have students write their own goals for the class session or the day.
3. Midway through instruction, pause class to monitor and reflect on your goals, thinking aloud.
4. Have students do the same with their own goals, either with a partner or alone.

4 Zimmerman, B. J. "Becoming a Self-Regulated Learner: An Overview." *Theory Into Practice, 41, No. 2* (Spring 2002), pp. 64–70.

Questions to ask:
- Have I met any of my goals?
- Why or why not?
- What should I do for the remainder of the class or day to make sure I meet my goals?

5. At the end of the class or day, repeat a verbalization of goal reflection, and have students do the same.

Questions to ask:
- Did I meet my goals?
- Why or why not?
- How will I celebrate my success?
- What will I do differently next time to meet my goals?

To effectively help students build autonomy in goal setting, begin with very short-term goals, such as lesson-by-lesson, class-by-class, or day-by-day. Then move to a weekly goal that is reviewed midway through the week. Build the students up to long-term goals of monthly, quarterly, or yearly. Goal setting should be practiced every day, made a part of instruction, and become an expectation of every student and teacher.

Building Self-Regulation Through Mindset

Another way to look at self-regulation is through the "mindset" work of Dr. Carol Dweck. Dweck defines mindset as one that is either fixed or growth. In a *fixed mindset,* a person believes their intelligence and talents are a fixed trait that cannot be changed or enhanced. We maintain the fixed mindset through reliance on documentations, such as IQ tests and achievement tests, to tell us that a person can or cannot do something. When people have a fixed mindset, they measure success by the amount of intelligence or talent a person possesses. Failure is measured the same way.

Students with a fixed mindset have a difficult time admitting to or correcting mistakes. Advanced learners who spend many years in under-challenging courses don't develop an understanding of or a need for effort. When they hit challenging courses, they believe they shouldn't need to put forth effort, so they think of themselves as not gifted. Failure threatens their sense of ability and therefore threatens their giftedness. Students who have not been challenged sufficiently do not develop important life skills such as patience, perseverance, or persistence (P^3).

A person with a *growth mindset* believes that most skills and abilities can be learned. We begin with what we have and build from there. It is through dedication, hard work, and effort that we gain success. "When people believe their basic qualities can be developed, failures may still hurt, but failures don't define them."[5] In other words, intensity as a learner is a far more useful trait than tested or perceived ability. Having a growth mindset encourages the development of self-regulation and valuable life skills. Students who develop a growth mindset learn useful tools for overcoming negative labels or stereotyping, learn how to mitigate difficult situations, and learn how to overcome perceived or real barriers to learning. These strategies can be most effective for students who are culturally or linguistically diverse. See Chapter 11, pages 169–170 for a suggested list of growth mindset questions, compliments, and strategies that are helpful for parents in developing self-confidence and a growth mindset in their children.

> Having a growth mindset encourages the development of self-regulation and valuable life skills.

To help students shift from a fixed mindset to one of a growth mindset, we need to employ strategies that build their self-regulation. This can be done by creating classroom settings that are stimulating and that allow students to develop the skills of monitoring their actions, thoughts, feelings, and behaviors in order to be academically and personally successful—in other words, by creating a *student-centered classroom.* The next section provides an overview of a student-centered classroom, along with numerous strategies and techniques for increasing student self-regulation.

The Student-Centered Classroom

A student-centered classroom is one where students are actively engaged in the discovery of information and are responsible for the learning. As you will see in Chapter 6, the roles of teaching and learning shift in a student-centered classroom from teacher-directed to learner-directed. The transitioning of the roles of teacher and student build learner autonomy by developing an intrinsic desire to think and learn.

5 Dweck, Carol S. *Mindset: The New Psychology of Success.* New York: Ballantine Books, 2006. p. 39.

Students develop the following critical elements in a student-centered classroom: (See student checklist on page 78.)

- responsibility for learning
- self-efficacy
- an intrinsic desire to succeed
- persistence, patience, and perseverance (P^3)
- metacognitive skills
- critical thinking skills
- problem-solving skills
- creative abilities and production
- a growth mindset

Teachers in a student-centered classroom have the following responsibilities (see teacher checklist on page 79):

- facilitate learning
- guide students to success
- understand and encourage student differences
- employ a variety of instructional practices, interventions, and assessments
- know content essentials and curriculum standards
- set high expectations for all students

Five Keys for Creating a Student-Centered Classroom

1. Establish a Community of Scholars

Students learn best when they feel safe and are not threatened. Following this first rule of brain-compatible learning can also help students feel welcomed and connected to others through a sense of belonging. You can do this by making your classroom a "community of scholars." In a community of scholars, all participants are expected not only to act as learners, but as learners who develop a knowledge base in order to produce new knowledge. Being able to build upon prior knowledge and be innovative in developing new ideas are keys to students' success in the twenty-first century. In a community of scholars, students build a common understanding of the reason they are there, the shared responsibility of all class members, and the ways they can hold each other accountable.

Ideas for Establishing a Community of Scholars:

- **Create a bill of rights.** Have students construct a constitution or bill of rights in which the roles and responsibilities of each participant in the classroom are spelled out. An example of a classroom bill of rights might include:

  All participants in the classroom have the right to:
  - A safe and welcoming learning environment
  - Active and engaging learning experiences
  - Meaningful instruction and curriculum
  - Knowledge that is represented in a format most appropriate to the learning experience
  - Accurate, effective, and immediate feedback that can lead toward success
- **Develop classroom conventions.** Have students collectively develop conventions for the classroom. Different from rules, conventions are agreements, compacts, or standards of practice. Examples of classroom conventions might include:
  - All skills and processes are presented and approached as learnable.
  - Patience, persistence, and perseverance are valued, modeled, and expected.
  - All feedback will be constructive to inspire future success.
- **Form an oversight council.** Have students elect members of the class to form a council that oversees the implementation of the Bill of Rights or Classroom Conventions.
- **Use restorative justice.** Use the method of restorative justice to manage classroom conflicts and grievances. Restorative justice is a process that repairs the harm caused by infractions or offenses. It brings together the victim, offender, and other members of the classroom community to meet and decide how to repair and transform the situation from one that is negative toward one that is positive. Through the use of sequential questioning justice is restored. Harms are repaired, wrongdoers are held accountable for their actions, victims feel empowered, agreements are negotiated, participants take ownership or responsibility for their actions, and closure is attained.

  Sequential Questioning:

  What happened?
  How did it happen?
  What part did you play in it?
  How were you affected?
  Who else was affected?
  What do you need to make it right?
  How can we repair the harm?

2. Build Students' Empathy and Wisdom

Dr. Ben Dean states, "Wisdom is the product of knowledge and experience, but it is more than the accumulation of information. It is the coordination of this information and its deliberate use to improve well-being. In a social context, wisdom allows the individual to listen to others, evaluate what they say, and then offer them good (sage) advice."[6] Likewise, Robert Sternberg claims that people are wise when they use their intelligence to seek the common good and have an understanding of how their actions can affect others.[7] In essence, when a person is able to balance their personal needs with the needs of other individuals and of a greater community, they are more likely to be happy, healthy, and successful.

Ideas for Building Empathy and Wisdom:

- **Assign Roles.** To build cooperative learning skills, give each student a role within the group and have them report on how well they performed their duty. Also, ask other students in the group to give positive critique to each other on their performance within the group.
- **Use service learning** projects in which students help others less fortunate than they are.
- **Use a buddy system.** Help students develop a classroom, lunchtime, or playground buddy system. Older students buddy with younger students at least once per month. Activities could include a conversation; reading a book together; working on a project, game, or puzzle together; or helping with a homework assignment.
- **Hold a fundraiser.** Have students investigate charities or other organizations that help people, and then hold a fundraising event.
- **Partner with an organization.** Partner your class with a nursing home, homeless shelter, or other social service organization. Students then develop plans to offer the partner assistance or volunteer work throughout the school year.

3. Develop a Supportive Classroom Environment

In a supportive environment, both you and your students understand people's fundamental needs to feel safe, welcome, and wanted. As the teacher, you ensure that the curriculum is rigorous and holds relevance for all students. Class members forge supportive relationships that can lead to individual student success.

Ideas for Developing a Supportive Classroom:

- **Mobilize resources.** Help students develop an understanding of how to mobilize their resources. Post the following list in your classroom to encourage students to take on the responsibility for learning and to become more autonomous:
  - Use what you have (believe in yourself).
  - Draw on the expertise of those around you (teachers, classmates, parents, and other adults).
  - Use the materials available.
  - Ask questions, or ask for help.
  - Request more support, information, or resources, if needed.
- **Express yourself.** You and all of your students represent yourselves as individuals through an introductory display, poster, or performance.
- **Know names.** You and all of your students know each other's names.
- **Know interests.** You know quality information about your students that can inform instruction. Interest surveys are a wonderful way to gather this information.
- **Know abilities.** You know the differing abilities of each student and respect those differences through tiered instruction and activities.

4. Develop Students' Metacognitive Skills

Metacognition is basically "thinking about your own thinking." In a student-centered classroom, you routinely focus students on how they are thinking, processing, and relating to the material being taught. Students also develop an awareness of their strengths and weaknesses. Gear activities and lessons toward helping students construct meaning, and use tools to help them solve problems, make decisions, and evaluate their productivity. Developing skills to think about how and what they are thinking can improve students' learning and increase intelligent behavior. (See Chapter 7 for more information about metacognition.)

Ideas for developing metacognitive skills:

- **Use KQI charts.** Start each lesson with a "What do you know?" and "What do you have questions about?" activity that focuses learners on what needs to be learned. Use a KQI, KWL, or KWI chart (see page 51 for an example).

---

6 "Wisdom" by Ben Dean, Ph.D., www.authentichappiness.sas.upenn.edu/newsletter.aspx?id=78.

7 Sternberg, R. J. "Schools Should Nurture Wisdom." In B. Z. Presseisen (Ed.), *Teaching for Intelligence*. Arlington Heights, IL: Skylight Training and Publishing, 1999.

- **Use verbal repetition.** Learning happens best when students can verbalize what they have learned. We store and process our memories through repeating information verbally. Think about the last time you tried to remember a phone number. You likely said the number over and over again. This type of rehearsal helps set the information into short-term memory. For the information to be stored into long-term memory, we must use the information repeatedly before it become automatic. For example, use this partner problem-solving strategy: one partner verbalizes the problem while the other partner listens and asks clarifying questions.
- **Keep thinking journals.** Have students create a "thinking journal" to take notes on their ideas or thoughts throughout lessons. The journal can be used during study time, conferences, or end-of-unit reflection on what the student has learned. The "I Chart" can be incorporated into this journal. (See page 48.)
- **Encourage reflection.** Allow students to reflect on their learning continually throughout the day. Provide time in each lesson for students to debrief, discuss, debate, and digest new ideas and information. Reflection should be done at least every 20 minutes. The reflection can be writing, oral, or graphic.
- **Require self-evaluations.** Have students do self-evaluations at the end of every unit. Provide them with a checklist and rubric of the objectives and unit outcomes.
- **Use the 10:2/20:2 Rule** to help students remember information, stay focused, and remain active. (See **Figure 5.3**.)

5. Develop Persistence, Patience, and Perseverance (P^3)

Life is a series of problem-solving actions. When faced with a problem, either major or minor, we are unlikely to successfully solve it without useful and effective strategies. In today's world, situations occur at an accelerated pace, so our students must be prepared with key skills to nimbly work through problems and find solutions. When developing persistence, patience, and perseverance (or P^3), students learn to reduce impulsivity and review their work to ensure accuracy.

Ideas for Developing P^3:

- Focus feedback and praise on the amount of effort students put forth rather than on their level of ability.
- Give students a pad of sticky notes so they can write down their thoughts rather than verbally interrupt a lesson.
- Establish and maintain a daily class routine so that students are aware of what is to come and when breaks or changes in activities will happen.
- To practice impulse control, provide students with games in the classroom that build patience and persistence.
- Model how students should take turns, ask questions, wait in line, and listen to others.
- For students who are impulsive, give them tactile fidgets or stress toys, such as squeeze balls, to use when they are most likely to interrupt or be impatient.
- Teach students proofreading and answer-checking skills, such as working backwards in math to check answers, reviewing their writing for spelling errors, or asking a friend to review their work.
- Give students a list of commonly misspelled words, common punctuation errors, common grammatical errors, or common math computational errors.

Figure 5.3 10:2/20:2 Rule

10:2 (ten to two)
or
20:2 (twenty to two)

The brain learns information best when allowed time to process and connect new ideas. This rule takes into account the amount of time and information the brain can handle before it needs to download or use the information.

Elementary grades: For every 10 minutes of instruction, allow up to two minutes of discussion, application, movement, or restating what was just stated.

Secondary grades: For every 20 minutes of instruction, allow up to two minutes of discussion, application, movement, or restating what was just stated.

- Before students hand in assignments, give them the grading criteria or scoring rubric so they can check over their work to ensure they have addressed all objectives.
- Give students a list of questions to ask before they turn in work, such as:
  - Did I do what was asked?
  - How can I be sure I met the objective?
  - Have I reviewed my work?
  - Have I had someone else review my work?
- Give students logic problems (from easy to difficult) to solve over a period of time.
- Have students explain each of the steps they take when solving a problem.
- Encourage students to try several different ways to solve a problem.
- Have multi-piece puzzles in the room for students to work on over a period of time.
- Provide ample wait-time. Counting to 10 in your head is a handy technique to help you offer students wait-time.
- Expect students to redo assignments that do not show proficiency.

Student Checklist for a Student-Centered Classroom

AS A STUDENT:	NEVER	SOMETIMES	OFTEN	ALWAYS
I'm responsible for my own learning.				
I'm capable of doing most anything I put my mind to, as long as I work hard.				
I'm patient with myself and others when I/they don't get it.				
I persist and persevere until I do get it.				
I think about what I'm going to do before I do it.				
I think about what I'm doing while I'm doing it.				
I think about what I've done when I've done it.				
I know and use several different strategies to solve problems.				
I think "outside" the box to come up with new ideas, thoughts, and products.				

From *Advancing Differentiation: Thinking and Learning for the 21st Century* by Richard M. Cash, Ed.D., copyright © 2011. Free Spirit Publishing Inc., Minneapolis, MN; 800-735-7323; www.freespirit.com. This page may be reproduced for use within an individual school or district. For all other uses, contact www.freespirit.com/company/permissions.cfm.

Teacher Checklist for a Student-Centered Classroom

AS A TEACHER:	NEVER	SOMETIMES	OFTEN	ALWAYS
I facilitate learning rather than direct it.				
I guide students to success rather than lead them.				
I understand and encourage student differences rather than expect all students to learn the same way at the same time.				
I use a variety of instructional practices, interventions, and assessments to ensure my students are successful.				
I know the content essentials and curriculum standards so my students can achieve to their highest potential.				
I set high expectations for *all* students.				

From *Advancing Differentiation: Thinking and Learning for the 21st Century* by Richard M. Cash, Ed.D., copyright © 2011. Free Spirit Publishing Inc., Minneapolis, MN; 800-735-7323; www.freespirit.com. This page may be reproduced for use within an individual school or district. For all other uses, contact www.freespirit.com/company/permissions.cfm.

Chapter 6

The Teaching and Learning Continuum: Building Success Through Autonomy

> Success is about being your best self, not about being better than others; failure is an opportunity, not a condemnation; effort is the key to success.
>
> *—Carol Dweck, author and educator*

The ultimate outcome of differentiated curriculum and instruction is to cultivate the passion for learning in your students. As you differentiate, you must be knowledgeable about what turns a learner on to new information and stimulates a desire to investigate a topic further. Learning becomes autonomous when students are driven to gain greater knowledge in any study without the prodding of a teacher. This is what we envision when we say "lifelong learners." You build learning autonomy by guiding your students to take responsibility for and control of their learning. Autonomous learners find more relevance in the material, are more intrinsically motivated, and show greater gains in achievement.

All people want to be competent at meaningful tasks; it is part of our nature. Our competencies define who we are, promote our self-esteem, and help make us valuable to others. When individuals feel competent and understand the relevance of information, they are more likely to be motivated toward autonomy in future pursuits. This autonomy is what propels us to success. Robert Sternberg states that people most efficiently achieve success when they have engaged in purposeful and meaningful tasks. Your students' attitudes toward learning are enhanced when you provide them with learner-centered situations that build toward student independence. Through this, students are taught skills for self-directed learning. Ultimately, the learner builds an attachment to the content and is able to initiate his or her own true learning.

Learner autonomy is sometimes misinterpreted as self-guided instruction, independent study, or self-initiated learning. While these are all strategies that can and should be used when building learner autonomy, autonomy goes beyond a set of strategies. To develop learner autonomy, students need to gradually build toward independence through stages in the teaching and learning process. Dr. Diane Heacox and I have created a teaching and learning continuum to assist you in guiding your students toward greater learning autonomy. This chapter presents the conceptual model of the Teaching and Learning Continuum (TLC) (pages 82–83), the frameworks supporting it, and the various teacher/student activities and assessments within each level.

What Is the TLC?

The TLC is intended to be a guiding framework to assist you and your students in developing learner autonomy. Students may progress through this model at different times and varied paces based on their need for challenge and complexity. Additionally, students may move up through the model and then back to lower levels as new skills or content are introduced.

For example, using the TLC model, in a high school civics lesson on racial disparity in the court systems, you would begin instruction to the entire class by directly teaching the structure, systems, and vocabulary of the court network *(didactic instruction)*. You would then ask students to work in groups to research the number of court cases in a particular county, the outcomes of the cases, and the racial statistics of all the cases *(facilitated instruction)*. Next, you would ask the student groups to report on their findings and derive conclusions *(coached instruction)*. As an extension to this activity, some students, who may choose to pursue an independent study based on the findings of the class, will look to you as an advisor *(consultative instruction)*. Finally, these students will present their independent study results to an authentic audience suggesting actions for change. Authentic audiences consist of people who either are practicing professionals in the discipline, invested in the use of the information, or participants who can offer purpose or direction to the work. For each project, the audience will change based on the work and the level of feedback needed.

Examples of Presentations to Authentic Audiences:

- Presenting to professionals in the field
- Presenting to professional organizations
- Writing for publications (both electronic and print)
- Participating in contests and competitions
- Creating a public display outside the classroom or school

The TLC model shares ideas for how you and your students design learning goals, adjust instructional methods, and construct and enact assessments. Learning goals, modes of instruction, and assessment will vary through each of the levels of the model. Teachers and students are not restricted to any of the specific strategies or ideas presented. These ideas are intended to act as guides for moving students toward learning autonomy.

Why Build Autonomy?

Developing learner autonomy not only helps your students learn, it also helps you develop as a teacher.

Autonomy Is Essential for Student Learning

Learners in the twenty-first century will either be passive receptacles and storehouses of rote information or they will manipulate knowledge and ideas to create new ideas and products. Learning does not occur as a response to teaching, but *through* the authentic engagement in and application of this knowledge. Today's learners need to have the skills, attitudes, and confidence that come with learning autonomy to be successful in this century.

Self-confidence is an essential life skill. Students who lack self-confidence as learners rarely find success. In many cases, they have not developed the necessary skills, such as planning, organizing, and monitoring progress of learning, which can lead them to success. Many students lack self-confidence because they lack the opportunity to develop self-direction. As you guide students through the framework of the TLC model, they gain self-confidence through gradually taking control of and becoming responsible for their own learning.

As learners build self-confidence in learning, they also develop the following:

- greater desire for academic challenges
- awareness of their learning strengths
- abilities for planning and monitoring progress toward a goal
- increased usage of critical reasoning skills, problem-solving strategies, and creative idea generation
- deeper curiosity for further investigations
- significant motivation toward achievement

Autonomy Is Essential for Teacher Development

Leading motivation researchers Richard Ryan and Edward Deci suggest, "teachers who are autonomy supportive (in contrast to controlling) catalyze in their students greater intrinsic motivation, curiosity, and desire for challenge."[1] Teachers who facilitate and guide, who are supportive and caring, and who construct an environment that encourages learners to flourish, can develop autonomous learners. These learners continue

1 Ryan, Richard M. and Edward L. Deci. "Self-Determination Theory and the Facilitation of Intrinsic Motivation, Social Development, and Well-Being." *American Psychologist*, January 2000, pp. 70–71.

Teaching and Learning Continuum (TLC)

CONSULTATIVE			
TEACHER ROLE	STUDENT ROLE	LEVEL OF INDEPENDENCE	LEARNING FOCUS
Advisement on learning plan	Conduct self-guided learning	Autonomous	Metacognition Self-awareness
• Provide consultation and feedback as needed	• Develop, implement, and complete a learning plan • Seek advisement as necessary and appropriate • Produce, present, and evaluate • Develop self-efficacy	Student independently: • Develops a learning plan • Monitors progress • Documents process and progress • Seeks advisement as necessary and appropriate • Concludes learning • Presents results authentically • Evaluates process and results	Students: • Evaluate • Critique • Create By: Innovating, designing, and creating new authentic plans, ideas, and products

COACHED			
TEACHER ROLE	STUDENT ROLE	LEVEL OF INDEPENDENCE	LEARNING FOCUS
Monitor and support learning progress	Refine skills and deepen understanding	Collaborative	Conceptual
• Feedback/ Conferencing • Guided practice • Resource channel	• Listen, consider, practice, retry • Rethink, revise, reflect, refine, recycle • Develop self-regulation	Student poses and teacher refines: • Problem • Design • Timelines • Process • Evaluation criteria	Students: • Apply • Analyze • Create By: Applying analyzed information to formulate or compile to make new ideas

continued ➡

Based on work by Richard Cash and Diane Heacox, 2008.

From *Advancing Differentiation: Thinking and Learning for the 21st Century* by Richard M. Cash, Ed.D., copyright © 2011. Free Spirit Publishing Inc., Minneapolis, MN; 800-735-7323; www.freespirit.com. This page may be reproduced for use within an individual school or district. For all other uses, contact www.freespirit.com/company/permissions.cfm.

Teaching and Learning Continuum (TLC) (continued)

FACILITATED			
TEACHER ROLE	**STUDENT ROLE**	**LEVEL OF INDEPENDENCE**	**LEARNING FOCUS**
Provide structure for and facilitation of learning	Actively participate in constructing, examining, and extending meaning	Guided	Procedural
Examples include: • Discussion • Problem-based learning • Questions (open-ended) • Socratic seminar	Examples include: • Listen, question, consider, explain • Pose/define problems, solve, evaluate • Answer and explain, reflect, rethink • Consider, explain, challenge, justify	Teacher provides options and student: • Selects from among topics • Completes open-ended assignments • Poses and answers questions • Follows preset timelines • Performs self-evaluation according to prepared criteria • Develops skills of problem solving • Documents stages in the process	Students: • Understand • Apply By: Translating, interpreting, reorganizing, and applying information

DIDACTIC			
TEACHER ROLE	**STUDENT ROLE**	**LEVEL OF INDEPENDENCE**	**LEARNING FOCUS**
Provide direct instruction	Passive participant who receives, takes in, and responds	Directed	Factual
Examples include: • Demonstration/ modeling • Lecture • Questions (focused on convergent thinking)	Examples include: • Observe, attempt, practice, refine • Listen, watch, take notes, question • Answer, give responses	Teacher constructs and student: • Makes choices • Finds answers • Uses resources • Plans time • Uses basic elements of critical and creative thinking • Sets goals • Follows through • Discusses goal attainment	Students: • Remember • Recall By: Verifying factual knowledge

Based on work by Richard Cash and Diane Heacox, 2008.

From *Advancing Differentiation: Thinking and Learning for the 21st Century* by Richard M. Cash, Ed.D., copyright © 2011. Free Spirit Publishing Inc., Minneapolis, MN; 800-735-7323; www.freespirit.com. This page may be reproduced for use within an individual school or district. For all other uses, contact www.freespirit.com/company/permissions.cfm.

to learn beyond the classroom, through alternative learning methods, and with a greater degree of creativity. Crafting this kind of environment requires you as a teacher to use more expansive skills beyond didactic/direct instruction.

A classroom that encourages learner autonomy requires you to hone pedagogical skills that advance differentiated instruction. The true goal of differentiated instruction is to guide students toward greater levels of success and competency. The Response to Intervention (RTI) model also utilizes these strategies and interventions to move all students to greater levels of independence and autonomy. By focusing on the needs of the individual learner to become more autonomous in learning, you take on a new role as coach, guide, and consultant.

Framework Supporting the Teaching and Learning Continuum (TLC)

The TLC model builds on decades of research on how teachers teach and students learn. It was developed to synthesize the most effective strategies of instruction, learning, and assessment. The following three theories provide a framework that grounds the TLC.

The Gradual Release of Responsibility Model

A model that has informed the TLC is the Gradual Release of Responsibility Model (**Figure 6.1**). This model is most often associated with the teaching of literacy and scaffolds student learning in the following steps:

1. The teacher demonstrates or models a strategy.
2. The teacher offers guided practice in a large group setting.
3. Students practice independently in small groups.
4. Students apply the strategy independently.

The Gradual Release of Responsibility Model has been used successfully for many years. Optimal learning is achieved when supports and scaffolds are gradually removed. Students also shape responsibility to learn.

Figure 6.1 Gradual Release of Responsibility Model[2]

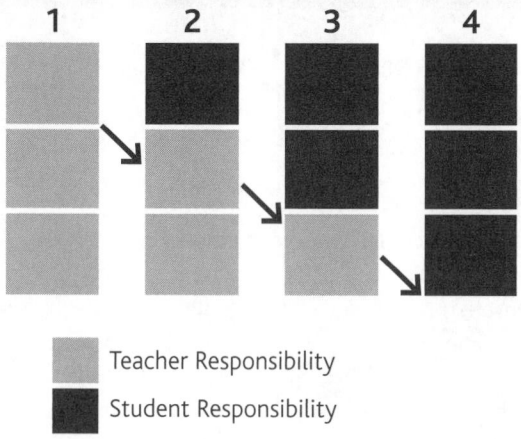

Self-Determination Theory

Self-determination is a theory of human motivation based on the psychological needs of survival, relatedness, and competence.[3] In a natural process of growth and development, individuals use life experiences to construct a sense of self. When people are more self-determined, they are more confident, perform better, develop greater persistence, display greater creativity, have stronger self-esteem, and maintain an overall healthier well-being.

Student Competence and Self-Regulation

Students feel empowered to learn when they have experiences and competence with skills that support new learning. When students recognize how new skills and knowledge can increase their quality of life, they build what is called *intrinsic achievement motivation*. Intrinsic achievement motivation is a personal desire or need for success or excellence. Additionally, students gain power when they can collaboratively work together with others to achieve success. (See Chapter 4 for an in-depth discussion of motivation.)

2 Based on Pearson, P. D. and M. C. Gallagher. "The Instruction of Reading Comprehension." *Contemporary Educational Psychology, 8,* 1983, pp. 317–344. Adapted by Richard Cash and Diane Heacox, 2008.

3 Ryan and Deci, 2000.

Each of the self-regulating skills listed in Chapter 5 on page 72 can be seen as a cyclical progression of achieving academic competence (see Figure 5.2 on page 72). This design is naturally embedded within the TLC model and can act as a guide in developing learner autonomy.

As learners move upward in the TLC model, they acquire skill development, practice, reinforcement, and application of these self-regulating strategies and progress toward competency and autonomy.

Mindset Theory

As discussed in Chapter 5 on page 73, Carol Dweck has defined the mindset with which people view their own abilities as either *fixed* or *growth*. People who believe their abilities to be fixed often describe these traits as either "you have it or you don't." Those with a growth, or malleable, mindset believe that you can achieve almost anything you put your mind to with effort.

Using a Growth Mindset

Learners develop mastery of a skill through the awareness of their progress and success, which is communicated through descriptive, constructive feedback. When you use a growth mindset with learners, you do the following:

- develop a wholeness of learning
- spark innovative thinking
- strengthen a sense of belonging through partnership with others
- focus on a self-definition rather than an "others" definition
- put learners in charge of their own learning

The TLC model develops this growth mindset in both teachers and students by progressively building learner competence through relevant and meaningful tasks, descriptive and constructive feedback, and learning activities that gradually demand greater degrees of authenticity (real-world application).

The Four Levels of the TLC Model

The TLC model provides a framework for you to identify the progression of teaching, learning, and assessment systems from a teacher-controlled level to student autonomy. It is helpful to know that as a teacher you have control over your students' progress through the levels. Below are insights into how you might encourage this progression.

TLC Level 1: Didactic Instruction—Teacher Prescribed, Student Acted

At the didactic level, you are in charge of the learning process by controlling the content and the activities to build understanding. Student participation is limited based on the direction you offer. At this, the broadest level, students acquire information for recall, deliver and rehearse factual and procedural skills, and build a ground of conceptual knowledge.

Many would suggest that at this level you are enacting "direct instruction." The term "direct instruction," however, should not indicate that the learner is passively participating in the learning. On the contrary, the student is actively building an accurate understanding of the ideas and concepts at the heart of the content. You are also helping the student do the following:

- learn a common language within the discipline
- know the vocabulary of the lessons
- gather the skills and processes

For instance, when you want to introduce a new skill, you would model the skill for the students showing them exactly the process to follow. Or, if you are introducing a unit on the Renaissance, for example, you might share artifacts and music to ground the students in the "sense" of the time period.

Through didactic instruction the student is able to build an understanding of the ideas and concepts to be covered in a unit of study. Students begin to make connections to prior learning experience, build awareness of topics, and establish what is unique or common about the new information. At this level you, as a teacher, directly instruct, infuse, and prescribe specific self-regulating skills and development.

This is a very important phase of learning, especially for students from a language background other than English or for students who live in poverty. Students are developing the academic language and building the foundation for further learning. **Figure 6.2** shows how the learning is structured at this level from goal setting to instruction to assessment.

TLC Level 2: Facilitated Instruction—Teacher Differentiated, Student Acted

The facilitated level begins to see students more actively involved and teachers less dominating in the learning process (see **Figure 6.3**). You still maintain a range of control as the instructional manager of the curriculum and of the instructional and assessment processes.

You establish learning goals based on standards and allow students varied opportunities for addressing the standards through units that provide interdisciplinary connections. Learning at this level includes greater student participation through open-ended questioning and discussion. This interaction encourages students to share thoughts and ideas and to challenge beliefs and opinions. Additionally, students build listening, questioning, and thinking skills, which are essential for the more advanced levels of the TLC.

The importance of this level cannot be stressed enough. At the facilitated level, the student gains a greater degree of independence, but with your support and guidance. Learners engage in intellectual risk taking and practice self-regulation skills to stretch and grow toward autonomy. Students start to believe they have the means to learn and perform effectively on their own.

TLC Level 3: Coached Instruction—Teacher Differentiated with Student Input

The coached level of the TLC has teacher and student roles significantly changing (see **Figure 6.4**). Coaching is a learning technique, in which you observe the student at work and provide feedback to enhance performance or correct deficiencies. Effective feedback to enhance performance is the essential component at this level.

Your role as a teacher shifts from control of what and how students learn to mediation and support of student learning. During coached instruction, you engage in the students' learning by guiding their thinking, communication, data gathering and sharing, grouping configurations, and thinking techniques and strategies. You provide descriptive feedback to sustain your students' self-directed learning, and you monitor and reinforce students' self-regulating strategies for greater development of self-efficacy.

Your primary goals at the coached level are to build learners' sense of purpose, ownership, and meaning through activities and tasks that accomplish the following:

- anchor to larger authentic problems or issues
- involve emotional engagement
- challenge and test learners' beliefs and opinions

Figure 6.2 TLC Level 1: Didactic Instruction

LEARNING GOALS	INSTRUCTION	ASSESSMENT
Teacher: • Establishes learning goals based on state/provincial standards • Uses state/provincial standards to determine student needs • Plans for the group • Plans instruction so students cover same or similar goals • Defines and prescribes for class or groups of students	• Teacher presents lessons, provides exercises, arranges and supervises student applications (guided practice) • Teacher provides structure, direction, specificity, and clearly established purpose for learning • Teacher focuses on explicit, systematic, relevant teaching points • Teacher demonstrates explicit, deliberate, meaningful instruction • Teacher explains and models "what, how, why" prior to student independent work • Students may select activities from options provided by the teacher	• Teacher conducts evaluation and reports to students • Teacher uses established criteria • Teacher provides feedback on specified procedures as well as performance • Teacher provides students with information on their goal attainment • Students may self-evaluate based on teacher developed criteria

- reflect the complexity of the "real world"
- offer ambiguity
- require learners to cultivate and use advanced thinking tools
- encourage alternative methods of assessment
- provide opportunities for reflection on both the content and learning processes

TLC Level 4: Consultative Instruction—Teacher Managed, Student Designed and Guided

As students guide their own learning process, they have entered the consultative level of the TLC model (see **Figure 6.5**). At this level the teacher and student roles change dramatically. Students now become the initiators and designers of their own learning, while you provide recommendations and advice. You no longer facilitate from the position of expert, but move to the position of skilled feedback provider and advisor.

Throughout this level, you act as a consultant to assist learners in applying the strategies of self-regulation and autonomy developed in the lower levels. Learners are now in charge and responsible for constructing, implementing, and evaluating learning plans.

Figure 6.3 TLC Level 2: Facilitated Instruction

LEARNING GOALS	INSTRUCTION	ASSESSMENT
• Teacher plans for specific goals based on state/provincial standards • Teacher uses diagnostic data to determine student specific goals	• Student paced • Open-ended tasks • Flexible instructional groups • Simulations • Problem solving and decision making • Choice in content, process, or product • Problem-based learning • Critical thinking and reasoning • Socratic seminars	• Teacher evaluates student performance based on shared criteria • Teacher provides feedback on content/process/product • Student and peer evaluation using shared criteria • Student and peer evaluation are reported to the teacher

Figure 6.4 TLC Level 3: Coached Instruction

LEARNING GOALS	INSTRUCTION	ASSESSMENT
• State/provincial standards and teacher- and student-developed goals • Teacher provides students with information related to their strengths and needs and identifies individual learning goals • Students are given opportunity to pursue additional goals related to their learning preference and/or interests • Student assumes primary responsibility for particular goals	• Students assume primary responsibility for pursuit of particular learning goals • Teacher as "encourager" • Teacher provides resources, instruction in necessary skills and processes, feedback, and guidance. • Student self-selection • Guided inquiry • Open choice and options • Compacting and acceleration • Active experiential learning	• Teacher and students confer regularly to monitor progress, evaluate work in progress, identify necessary improvements, and to make modifications • Teacher and student evaluation based upon agreed criteria

Figure 6.5 TLC Level 4: Consultative Instruction

LEARNING GOALS	INSTRUCTION	ASSESSMENT
• Students determine goals based on needs and interests with teacher advice and consultation • Teacher works with the student to plan the course of action but student assumes ownership, responsibility for the goal • Student-based goals	• Student initiates the tasks, identifies and solves problems that arise, and faces challenges independently • Teacher as counselor and consultant • Resources/mentors beyond the classroom and school • Producers of knowledge • Innovation, transformation, ingenuity are exhibited • Self-awareness, self-advocacy, self-determination, and resilience are at the core for success • Task analysis • Hypothetical thinking • Personal critique • Need to defend thinking and work • Acceptance of personal responsibility for talent development and roles as learners	• Student involvement in determining explicit criteria and evaluating their performance • Teacher advises on criteria and provides feedback • Critical reflection

Assessment That Builds Autonomy

Teachers can build learning autonomy by offering appropriate intervention and assessment strategies. Students gain greater responsibility for learning when they do the following:

- set, monitor, manage, and evaluate their own goals
- develop choice and voice (for example, What do I need? How can I get it?)
- negotiate the learning process
- utilize technology skills and competence

Inherent in the TLC is a model of assessment that can build learner autonomy (see **Figure 6.6**). As the learner moves upward toward the consultative level, the assessments naturally change from being based on a single discipline to being based on multidisciplinary projects and performances. Assessment also shifts from imitational (regenerative tests of factual knowledge) to authentic performances (useful original products). Thinking expands from bilateral/convergent (yes/no questions) to multi-lateral/divergent (questions that have more than one correct answer). Learners also start to develop social interactions from collaborative production versus solo performances and move from passive recitation to social action.

By using the TLC model, you can ensure you are differentiating to build learning autonomy. Figure 6.6 gives you many examples and ideas at each stage of the model. The model can be used as a guide when reviewing your entire year's curriculum, as a pacing guide toward autonomy, or to plot units of study that can develop student autonomy. In some cases, you may find there will be overlaps from stage to stage in the model. There is no clear delineation between stages; ascending to autonomy and self-regulation is a process along a spectrum of learning.

In addition, the TLC's design includes the three forms of assessment outlined in Chapter 4, from diagnostic (preassessments) to formative (assessment to guide the learner) to summative (assessment of completion).

Figure 6.6 Assessment That Builds Autonomy

TLC LEVEL	KNOWLEDGE LEVEL	TYPE OF ASSESSMENT		
		DIAGNOSTIC	FORMATIVE	SUMMATIVE
Consultative • Student designs assessment to develop, monitor, and evaluate own learning process	**Self-Regulatory*** • Create • Produce • Hypothesize • Build • Compose • Critique • Extend • Invent • Originate • Transform	• Student-directed investigation to find problems • Personal goal setting • Proposal development	• Case study • Hypothesis development • Personal goal-setting update • Website • Progress report • Expert feedback	• Student-designed rubric • Student-designed product • Assessment by audience/expert
Coached • Teacher and student collaborate to design assessment	**Conceptual** • Evaluate • Design • Support • Adapt • Discriminate • Analyze • Connect • Deconstruct • Differentiate • Examine • Infer • Integrate • Test for	• Interest survey • Contract • Self-preassessment	• Lab/experiment • Thesis statement • Self-assessment/progress report • Discussion forum • Simulation • Wiki • Reciprocal teaching	• Student- and teacher-negotiated rubric • Teacher- and student-negotiated product • Self-assessment • Peer review • Portfolio • Research report • Contract completion
Facilitated • Teacher constructs assessment with options for individual learners or groups	**Procedural** • Construct • Perform • Solve • Reason • Understand • Analogize • Redesign • Predict • Map • Relate • Show • Examine • Inspect • Categorize • Classify • Clarify • Compare • Conclude • Contrast • Demonstrate • Distinguish • Explain • Illustrate • Interpret • Paraphrase • Predict • Represent • Reorganize • Summarize • Translate • Apply • Develop • Display • Execute • Implement • Model • Solve • Use	• KWL • Guided questioning • Group discussion • Mind map • Inventory of learning styles/modes/preferences	• Discussions • Reflections • Demonstration • Homework • Research • Exit cards • Oral presentation • Games • Check-ins • E-bulletin boards/e-chats	• Subjective assessment (open-ended essay) • Poster • Research paper • Teacher-designed rubric • Debate • Group project • Assessment stations
Didactic • Teacher constructs assessment based on whole-group learning	**Factual** • Recall • Remember • Verify • Respond • Match • Choose • Define • Describe • Identify • Label • List • Locate/Find • Name • Recite • Say • Tell	• Teacher-constructed pretest	• Quizzes • Homework • Practice exams • Class participation • Performance assessments	• Objective assessment (multiple choice, true/false) • Standardized tests

MULTIPLE DISCIPLINES ↑ SINGLE DISCIPLINE

AUTHENTIC ↑ IMITATION

*Note: Self-regulatory replaces metacogntive as the fourth knowledge dimension in this chart.

Part Two
Putting Thinking Skills to Use in the Classroom

When you differentiate instruction, you provide students with avenues to own their learning. Students accomplish this by thinking critically and creatively about the content and by solving problems that are meaningful and relevant to their lives. The following five chapters supply an understanding of the essential thinking skills and offer tools to help your students develop these skills.

Chapter 7

The Thinking Classroom

> I like a teacher who gives you something to take home to think about besides homework.
>
> —*Edith Ann (played by Lily Tomlin)*

As we continue into the second decade of the twenty-first century, the need for our students to be active thinkers becomes more apparent. New problems arise every day that require more complex solutions. The flattening and shrinking of the world necessitates a greater need for collaboration and cooperation.

Unfortunately, automation and new technologies have made it more convenient for us to rely on a machine to do our thinking, which creates a concern I call "intellectual laziness." Students who rely on technology to solve their problems, plan and organize their days, or simply tell them what to eat, are, in essence, letting the technology think for them. Over time, the practice of thinking atrophies to a point where students are reluctant to think on their feet or think for themselves. To guard against intellectual laziness, we teachers must infuse thinking into our everyday instructional practices.

How many times have we said to our students, *"Now think about this . . ."*? Sometimes we may have been amazed by what they came up with, while other times we were frustrated because they did not think deep enough or generate any new information. What may be lacking in our teaching and instructional process is the art of constructing a framework, or context, for students to do their thinking. This chapter will define what thinking is, share some characteristics of a thinking student, and suggest how you might frame your curriculum to encourage students to do a better job of thinking.

What Is Thinking?

Thinking is the mental process of using information to reach a conclusion. For students to do a good job of thinking, they must be presented with frameworks that can assist them in being more proficient at the act of thinking. Students can be at least four different types of thinkers at any given time.

Four Types of Thinkers

Receivers are those who ingest information at face value. They don't seek to analyze or validate the information. They simply take it "as is."

Intuitive thinkers use their gut feelings to validate thoughts. Based on past experiences, they evaluate what they are receiving and then make a decision based on that information. This type of thinker will often be critical of authority.

Sequential thinkers hold information to a set of criteria to interpret, such as rules or procedures. The sequential thinker takes time to think things through in a step-by-step manner. They then form opinions based on the information. This type of thinker may over-think information or spend too much time thinking about solutions and find it difficult to reach a conclusion.

Finally, **connected thinkers** are able to connect what is learned in one discipline to another. These thinkers take into account the views of others, and are open and fair-minded. They stretch to look beyond the facts to find new perspectives that may explain the implications of actions. Connected thinkers are the thinkers we should be developing in our classrooms.

Divergent Thinking vs. Convergent Thinking

In addition to different types of thinkers, there are different types of thinking. The two main types are divergent thinking and convergent thinking. Both are useful and necessary, depending on the situation.

Divergent thinking is the process of generating and creating new and imaginative ideas. When you "diverge" from the usual pathways of thinking and attempt to find more than one right answer, you are using divergent thinking.

Guiding principles to keep in mind for divergent thinking are:

- **Keep an open mind.** Don't critique or judge ideas until all ideas have been considered.
- **Come up with many ideas.** The more ideas you have to choose from the better the outcome.
- **Be accepting of all ideas.** You never know when and if something will work.
- **Use all of your senses.** Think with your eyes, ears, nose, mouth, and skin. The brain acquires information through your senses; using all of them opens up multiple avenues of thought.
- **Sleep on it!** Sometimes the best solutions come after a good night's sleep.
- **Take risks.** Break out of your comfort zone and boldly go where you've never gone before.
- **Hitchhike on others' ideas.** Listen to other people's ideas and add to them, elaborate on them, or attach your own ideas to them.

Convergent thinking is thinking through a set of logical steps to come up with one right answer. Convergent thinking is not necessarily in opposition to divergent thinking. Whereas divergent thinking seeks multiple answers, you will eventually need to settle on the one answer that will solve the problem (convergent thinking).

Principles to keep in mind for convergent thinking are:

- **Clarify the problem.** Find out exactly what needs to be solved or resolved.
- **Evaluate the solution.** Just finding a solution is not enough. You must know if the solution is working or not.
- **Look at all options.** Problems may require different solutions than those that were tried in the past.
- **Be reflective.** Keep asking yourself, "Is this working? Am I getting to resolution?"
- **Sleep on it!** Again, sometimes the best solutions come after a good night's sleep.
- **Be positive.** Don't be critical of your ideas or others' ideas. Look for the strengths and positive aspects of all ideas.

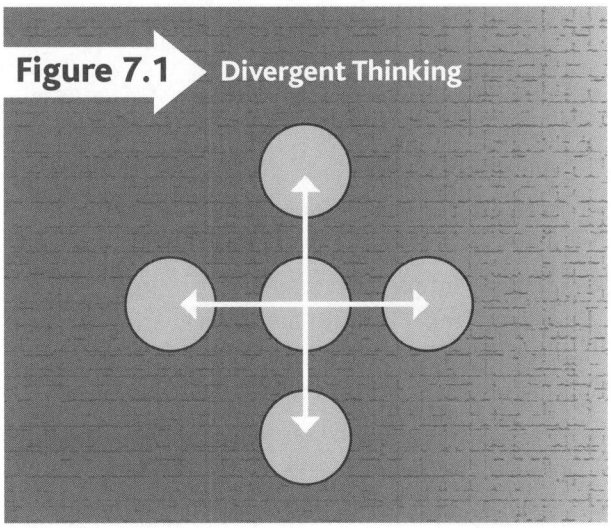

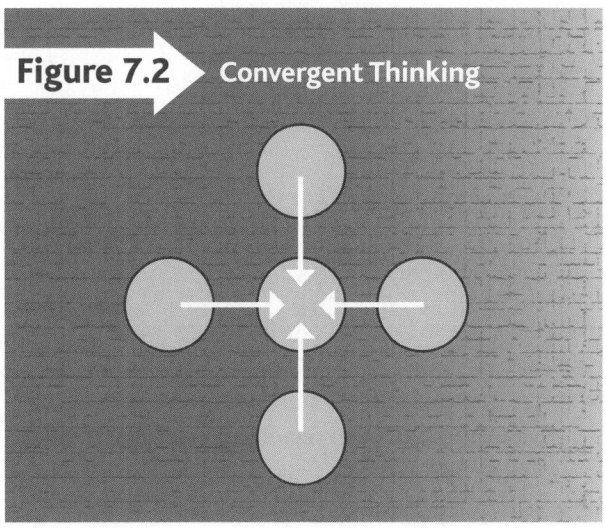

Characteristics of a Thinking Student

For students to do well in the act of thinking, they must possess several characteristics (see checklist on page 100).

Thinking students have the following capacities:

- **Openness.** They have an active imagination, are alert to their own and others' feelings, are curious, and enjoy variety.
- **Ego-control.** They are able to look both inside and outside themselves for solutions and understand that there are limitless ideas.
- **Spontaneity.** They are free from the constraints of their feelings and are willing to trust their own instincts.

Thinking students have a willingness to be:

- **Flexible.** Like athletes, thinkers are able to bend and think of things in new and different ways.
- **Adaptable.** They can take what was learned in one setting and apply it to a new setting or problem.
- **Intellectual risk takers.** They are open to trying new lines of thinking or doing.

Thinking students have a tolerance for:

- **Ambiguity.** They can appreciate the uncertainty of problems and situations.
- **Complexity.** They realize there are many different layers, perspectives, and points of view in any given situation or problem.
- **Disorder.** They understand, respect, and anticipate the unpredictable nature of life.

Finally, thinking students must be:

- Task and learning motivated.
- Persevering.
- Not expecting immediate gratification or closure.

Characteristics of a Thinking Classroom

For a classroom to be conducive to effective thinking, it must have the following traits (see checklist on page 101).

- **Encourages intellectual independence.** Students are encouraged and expected to think beyond what is delivered in the curriculum.
- **Recognizes and nurtures brain development.** All aspects of the classroom support and care for the basic needs of the students as well as provide for greater cognitive growth.
- **Allows and encourages intellectual risk taking.** Students are encouraged to stretch intellectually and explore new fields of study.
- **Eliminates stereotyping, bias, oppression, and bullying.** Students feel safe being themselves.
- **Delays gratification.** The emphasis in a thinking classroom is on hard work and effort, not on immediate reward.
- **Nurtures social relationships and community.** All students feel part of the classroom and school community. Each person has something to offer the group.
- **Fosters a supportive environment where all learners have choices and a sense of control.** Choices are meaningful to learners, and learners must feel as though they have control over making those choices.
- **Builds learners' responsibility for the learning.** Your job is to teach; the learner's job is to learn.
- **Is enjoyable and fun!** Students must want to be in the classroom. That can be accomplished with an environment that includes humor as well as pleasurable activities.

Characteristics of a Thinking Curriculum

For a curriculum to promote thinking skills, it must include the following characteristics (see checklist on page 102).

- **Focused on learning goals.** Students are clear as to where they are going and what they will learn in each lesson.
- **Presents essential questions.** The unit is designed around essential questions worth investigating (see Chapter 2).
- **Is concept-based.** The unit has a focus on the "big picture" concepts.
- **Scaffolds intellectual readiness toward independence.** Students are provided with sufficient modeling, practice, and independence to become autonomous in their learning (see Chapter 6).
- **Provides interrelated learning.** Units are interdisciplinary or provide cross-curricular connections.

- **Inspires emotional engagement.** Students find emotional reasons (joy, trust, surprise, anticipation, and excitement) to engage in learning tasks or discussions.
- **Offers ambiguity.** There are times when all the answers are not available, and students will be expected to do further investigation to unravel the mysteries.
- **Introduces provocative issues that challenge students' beliefs, understanding, or prior knowledge.** The content stimulates conversations that arouse feelings and move students to action.
- **Contains room for further questioning and investigation.** Some students may be interested in seeking out additional information within a unit of study. Resources and materials should be made available for such studies.
- **Is relevant to the learner and encourages personal connections.** Students find the content personally meaningful and relevant to their current lives.
- **Provides authentic learning opportunities that require authentic products.** The best learning and outcomes occur when the products are useful and are reviewed by the audience who will use them or by a professional in that field of study.
- **Challenges all students and builds competence.** Building competence is building confidence. All learners want to be competent at meaningful tasks.
- **Includes assessment and evaluation that are focused on student learning development.** For quality student growth, students must be informed about what they don't know, where they are in the learning, and how close they are to meeting the goal.
- **Builds reflective practices into every learning experience.** All students need time to reflect on what they are learning. You must provide time within the lessons for students to stop, make notes, discuss with others, and document what they have learned.

The following checklists (pages 100–102) of characteristics of a thinking student, classroom, and curriculum can be used as guides before, during, and after instruction. They can also be used and posted as general guidelines of what is expected in a thinking classroom. Students can use the student checklist to monitor their own thinking. You can use the curriculum checklist as a reminder when developing units, lessons, and activities. The thinking classroom checklist can also be shared with parents to show them the expectations in the classroom.

Methods for Developing Intellectually Disciplined Thinkers

Just like the skill of walking, thinking is a natural process that begins with small baby steps (everyday thinking, such as which shirt to wear, what to eat for lunch, and when to go to bed) and develops to running (advanced levels of thinking, such as which route to take when a road is closed or what to do about the 2010 oil spill in the Gulf of Mexico).

Though our brains are designed to think, advanced levels of thinking take place in a relatively newer area of our brain. Our brains have evolved in such a way that we have moved from simply solving problems of daily survival to more advanced levels of thinking and problem solving. The advanced levels of thought take place in the neocortex or "new brain" (frontal lobe and prefrontal cortex).

All of your students are capable of advanced levels of thinking, not only your gifted students. Just as learning to walk takes practice, so does the art of thinking. And just as learning to be a good runner requires stamina and endurance to continually run faster and farther, so does developing techniques for advanced thinking. As a teacher, your job is to coach students in achieving these advanced levels of thinking.

Method #1: Explicitly Teach Thinking Skills

Students cannot learn to think critically or creatively on their own or by simply being asked to think. There must be direct, systematic instruction of thinking skills and creativity-building activities, through introduction and development of the skills and repeated practice in application. Each skill must be labeled as it is being taught so that students are aware that the skill is a specific tool that they own and can use whenever appropriate—at school, at home, at work—throughout life. Students need to be made aware of when each skill is best employed. Students also need practice and guidance with the skill and they must be directly shown how it can be used in a variety of settings and ways.

The Teaching Thinking Skills: Lesson Format Template on pages 103–104 can help you directly teach a thinking skill or strategy. See **Figure 7.3** for an example.

Figure 7.3 Teaching Thinking Skills Lesson Format: Example

Thinking Skill: SCAMPER

Focus Activity
Display a handheld computer (such as an iPhone or Blackberry), a telephone, and two tin cans connected with a piece of string. Ask students:

"What do all these items have in common?"

"How did we get from the tin cans to the telephone to the handheld computer?"

"What do you think will be the next great invention in communication?"

Objective
Students will be able to use the technique of SCAMPER to come up with innovative ideas.

Modeling
Definition of the skill: SCAMPER is a thinking technique to help you come up with new ideas by using seven different strategies: substitute, combine, adapt, modify, put to other uses, eliminate, and revise.

Explain how and when to use: SCAMPER can be used when you are asked to create a novel idea or project, or you are trying to solve a common everyday problem. Come up with a new idea for each of the seven strategies.

Ways to remember the skill: The word SCAMPER is an acronym that stands for each of the seven strategies: **S**ubstitute, **C**ombine, **A**dapt, **M**odify, **P**ut to other uses, **E**liminate, **R**evise.

Practice Activity
Ask students: "How could you improve upon a pen?"

"What could you **substitute** on a pen to make it better?"

"What could you **combine** with a pen to improve upon it?"

"How could you **adapt** a pen for use in various situations?"

"In what ways could you **modify** a pen to meet your needs?"

"How might you **put it to other uses** than writing?"

"What characteristics of a pen could you **eliminate** to make it better?"

"What characteristics of a pen could you **revise**, reorder, or rearrange to make it better?"

Reflection/Metacognition
Ask students:

"When might you use SCAMPER in your school or personal lives?"

"Can you think of products that may have been designed using the SCAMPER method?"

"How could you use the SCAMPER method to help you be more successful?"

Method #2: Use Guided Thinking

Guided thinking is the practice of helping students improve their thinking by engaging them in knowing what they are thinking at the beginning of a study, monitoring their thinking throughout the study, and understanding what they have accomplished at the end of a study. Using formative assessment (see Chapter 4, page 64) is an excellent way of keeping students in tune with where they are in the thinking process from the beginning to the end of the unit. Activities within the unit should also be designed to engage students in actively thinking about and processing important ideas, topics, and issues. See page 105 for a blank Guided Thinking Template, and **Figures 7.4 and 7.5** (pages 106 and 107) for partially completed subject-specific examples.

Method #3: Teach Students to Think *About* Thinking: Metacognition

All great thinkers spend time thinking about the process of thinking. We should also be teaching our students this process as well. When René Descartes, the renowned French philosopher said, "I think, therefore I am," he was not only speaking about existing as a human, but about what makes us human: the profound ability to think about our actions, thoughts and ideas. Thinking is a process that helps us develop our "self," the person who we are or want to become.

Students must learn the process of metacognition in order to achieve greater success in learning. Metacognition assists in the development of self-regulation (described more completely in Chapter 5). When students are able to think through all steps of the learning process, from beginning to end, they can better judge what their outcome will be. During the learning process it is very important that students monitor their efficacy—their capacity to produce the required effect. This capacity to produce comes from the effort the learner is willing to put forward. Students achieve because of working hard and using effort, not from innate ability.

Students sometimes fail or do not achieve success due to low self-esteem. Self-esteem is a primary key to well-being and happiness. Building self-esteem is about recognizing what you are good at and what strengths you possess. Knowing these abilities, putting them to use, and then identifying how those abilities and strengths propelled you toward success is a major factor in developing self-esteem. Learners must also understand that mistakes or failures may be signals to put forth more effort next time. Remember, success without failure or effort is pure luck!

Student Perception Questionnaire

Page 108 provides a questionnaire teachers can administer to their students to help them guide their own metacognition and self-regulation. First, students need to identify their level of motivation or attention for the upcoming activity, because how they feel about a learning situation will determine how much focus they give to the learning. Students should find ways to monitor, control, or adjust their attitude throughout the activity (**efficacy**). Secondly, students should be openly aware of all the tasks involved in the activity and the skills required (**regulation**). If they don't understand any component of the activity they should know who to ask questions and how to ask, or they should have the resources available to them to find the answers. Students also need to have an understanding of how they will use previously learned skills and processes within the new learning, and how to apply those skills and processes. Thirdly, students should build their support network and strengths as a learner by building their own confidence (**self-esteem**). They should know who to ask for emotional or moral support throughout the learning, recognize their strengths, and celebrate their accomplishments. Finally, students must be able to reflect on what they learned, how they felt about the learning process, and what changes they might make in the next round of learning (**metacognition**).

Method #4: Create Work Plans

Another strategy for assisting students in building self-regulation and metacognition is to have them create a work plan before a project begins. Page 109 includes a work plan template that students can use to set their direction, maintain and monitor their progress, and evaluate how effective they were in completing a project.

Set a SMART Goal

The work plan begins with students setting a SMART goal. SMART is an acronym used as a planning device to help students focus their efforts on what they want to accomplish. The goal is formatted to define *what* the student will do, *how* they will do it, and *why* it's important. The more precise the goal, the better the goal can be measured and students can realize their learning.

SMART Goals

S = Specific: In plain language, students spell out exactly what it is they must accomplish. Tell them to avoid general statements such as "Get an A on this assignment." A more specific goal would be "Achieve at least 90% of the total points on this project."

M = Measurable: Students set a time line and criteria for measuring their progress toward the goal. This will help them stay on track, see their progress, make adjustments when needed, and feel the satisfaction of their efforts. Measurable goals answer the questions of "Where?" "When?" "For how long?" and "By how much?"

A = Achievable: Have students set goals they can truly achieve. Setting unattainable goals will only hinder their growth. Instruct them to set the goal high enough to be challenging, but within reach.

R = Realistic: Similar to achievable, students should make the goal something they want, are willing to work toward, and have the skills and support to get there. Tell students to avoid being overly aggressive or under achieving. They must believe in themselves and be willing to stretch to reach the goal.

T = Timely: Related to measurable, students must set an end point for the goal. They should keep the timeline reasonable and short-term, and plan to meet the goal within six weeks.

Once students set a SMART goal, they must decide what work habits they need to employ to achieve their goal. For example, if the goal is: "Achieve at least 90% of the total points by the end of this project," work habits might include:

- **Attendance and punctuality:** be in school and on time every day
- **Productivity:** get motivated to work hard
- **Initiative:** get started doing the work without being reminded or prodded
- **Cooperative:** get along with, listen to, and support my class members
- **Accurate:** pay attention to details and ensure I am working through mistakes
- **Diligent:** put forth effort and work until the work gets done
- **Open-minded:** be willing to try new ideas, graciously accept constructive criticism, and embrace creativity
- **Honest, fair, and trustworthy:** be a good person, do unto others as I would have them do to me

Everyone needs support from time to time. Ask students: Who or what will be your supports? Support can be people who can assist them when they make mistakes, have questions, or need a shoulder to cry on. Or it may be a place they can go for quiet, reflection, time alone, or to rejuvenate their thinking. It can even be an item such as a lucky hat that brings them ideas, joy, or strength. Ask students: Do you believe yourself to be "someone who can do it" or do you believe yourself to be "someone who can't"? Tell them to decide which frame of mind they are in and make sure that it is one that supports them in achieving their goal.

Use Check-Ins

While students are working toward their goal, they can use check-ins to help them stay on task. When they check in with you, encourage them to ask guiding questions such as:

- How can I make my project better?
- Am I getting close to what is required?
- Are there things I could be doing that can help me go above and beyond what is required?

When checking in with a peer, students can ask questions such as:

- What suggestions do you have that could improve my project?
- How might I enhance the components I've included so far?
- What part of my project stands out for you?

Students can also check in with a parent or other adult as a way to inform them of what is occurring in the classroom. In this case, students may want to start a discussion in the following ways:

- The part of my project that I am most proud of is . . .
- The most difficult aspect of this project has been . . .
- I have worked the hardest on . . .

Finally, encourage students to check in with themselves and reflect on the effort they put forth. They can ask themselves questions such as:

- If I were to do a project like this again, I might . . .
- The most time-consuming part of this project was . . . Therefore, I will need to . . .
- Because of this project, I have come to understand that I am good at . . .

Method #5: Reflection Logs

When the work is complete, have students reflect on how they did. They should truthfully evaluate their initial estimation of what they wanted to accomplish, how they felt working on the project, how much effort they put forth throughout the process, how close they came to meeting the goal, and how they feel about their accomplishment. As with every accomplishment, students should take time to celebrate the good work they did and reflect on what they might do better next time.

The Student Reflection Log (page 110) can be used to assist learners in building reflection and metacognitive skills. At the beginning of the lesson or unit of study, students fill in the top part of the form that seeks information about what the student already knows about the topic and what they wonder about the topic. At the end of the unit of study, students document what they have learned about the topic and what they would like to know more about related to the topic. There is also space for students to let you know what they liked about the unit, what they didn't like, what they didn't understand, and what suggestions they have for improvements for future teaching of the unit.

General Strategies to Improve Student Thinking

- Use thinking skills every day and all the time—both you and your students.
- Use broad, open-ended questions.
- Use wait-time. Before asking students to respond to a question, allow at least 10 seconds for students to process their ideas and answers.
- Use follow-up statements or questions for deeper thinking, such as:
  - "Tell me more."
  - "Can you clarify your answer?"
  - "Provide me with evidence to support your answer."
  - "Tell me how you got to that answer."
- Use focused, directed thinking strategies in every lesson.
- Plan instruction that incorporates and uses Higher Order Thinking Skills (HOTS) and expect students to use HOTS in questioning, product work, and group work every day.
- Make students aware of their thinking process.
- Model thinking and share your own metacognition on thinking with students.
- Always encourage students to ask questions.

Checklist of Characteristics of a Thinking Student

CHARACTERISTIC	NOT YET	JUST BEGINNING	I'M TRYING	ALMOST THERE	THIS IS ME!
Open to new ideas					
Able to see from others' points of view					
Spontaneous					
Flexible					
Adaptable					
Intellectual risk taker					
Enjoys ambiguity					
Likes complexity					
Understands disorder					
Motivated to complete a task					
Will persevere until an answer is found					

From *Advancing Differentiation: Thinking and Learning for the 21st Century* by Richard M. Cash, Ed.D., copyright © 2011. Free Spirit Publishing Inc., Minneapolis, MN; 800-735-7323; www.freespirit.com. This page may be reproduced for use within an individual school or district. For all other uses, contact www.freespirit.com/company/permissions.cfm.

Checklist of Characteristics of a Thinking Classroom

CHARACTERISTIC	NOT YET	JUST BEGINNING	WE'RE TRYING	ALMOST THERE	THIS IS US!
Encourages intellectual independence					
Recognizes and nurtures brain development					
Allows and encourages intellectual risk taking					
Eliminates stereotyping, bias, oppression, and bullying					
Focuses on hard work, not instant gratification					
Fosters relationships and community					
Provides all students with choices and empowerment					
Builds students' responsibility for learning					
Understands disorder					
Creates a fun and enjoyable environment					

From *Advancing Differentiation: Thinking and Learning for the 21st Century* by Richard M. Cash, Ed.D., copyright © 2011. Free Spirit Publishing Inc., Minneapolis, MN; 800-735-7323; www.freespirit.com. This page may be reproduced for use within an individual school or district. For all other uses, contact www.freespirit.com/company/permissions.cfm.

Checklist of Characteristics of a Thinking Curriculum

CHARACTERISTIC	NOT YET	JUST BEGINNING	WE'RE TRYING	ALMOST THERE	THIS IS US!
Learning goals are well articulated					
Essential questions are worth investigating					
Concepts are clearly defined					
Activities are designed to move the learner toward independence					
Activities build student confidence					
Content is interdisciplinary					
Activities are emotionally engaging					
Situations involve ambiguity					
Provocative issues are raised					
There is room for additional questions and deeper investigations					
The content is relevant to the learners					
Activities and projects are authentic					
Assessments and evaluations are designed to provide learners with quality feedback					
All lessons involve some form of student reflection					

From *Advancing Differentiation: Thinking and Learning for the 21st Century* by Richard M. Cash, Ed.D., copyright © 2011. Free Spirit Publishing Inc., Minneapolis, MN; 800-735-7323; www.freespirit.com. This page may be reproduced for use within an individual school or district. For all other uses, contact www.freespirit.com/company/permissions.cfm.

Teaching Thinking Skills: Lesson Format Template

Instructions

Thinking Skill: Identify the thinking skill that will be introduced to the students. Clearly articulate what the skill is and when it may be most efficient to use that skill.

Focus Activity: This is your "anticipatory set." Do something that will grab the students' attention in regards to the skill and will help them concentrate on what will come next.

Objective: Inform students what they will learn in this lesson and why it's relevant. Give examples of when the skill can be used. Communicate the objective of the skill before, during, and after the lesson.

Modeling: Demonstrate the skill with the students. Provide information regarding this thinking skill including:

- A clear definition (add synonyms where relevant)
- An explanation of how and when the thinking skill is used
- An easy way to remember the mental operations used in the thinking process (mnemonics)

Students who have a working knowledge of the thinking skill may benefit more from an inductive approach. Instead of giving a definition and description of operations try posing a problem to solve. Use questions to help the class generalize a definition and list the operations they used. Are there any rules to be followed?

Practice Activity: Allow students time to practice the skill in context. You will act as a guide or facilitator while the student builds independence with the skill.

Reflection/Metacognition: Give students time to debrief, discuss, or reflect on the use of the skill and how it can help them achieve learning goals. You might use journal writing, PMI, Think-Pair-Share, or other activities.

continued ➡

From *Advancing Differentiation: Thinking and Learning for the 21st Century* by Richard M. Cash, Ed.D., copyright © 2011. Free Spirit Publishing Inc., Minneapolis, MN; 800-735-7323; www.freespirit.com. This page may be reproduced for use within an individual school or district. For all other uses, contact www.freespirit.com/company/permissions.cfm.

Teaching Thinking Skills: Lesson Format Template (continued)

Thinking Skill: _____

Focus Activity: _____

_____

_____

_____

_____

Objective: _____

_____

_____

_____

_____

Modeling

Definition of the skill: _____

_____

_____

Explain how and when to use: _____

_____

_____

Ways to remember the skill: _____

_____

_____

Practice Activity: _____

_____

_____

Reflection/Metacognition: _____

_____

_____

From *Advancing Differentiation: Thinking and Learning for the 21st Century* by Richard M. Cash, Ed.D., copyright © 2011. Free Spirit Publishing Inc., Minneapolis, MN; 800-735-7323; www.freespirit.com. This page may be reproduced for use within an individual school or district. For all other uses, contact www.freespirit.com/company/permissions.cfm.

Guided Thinking Template

GUIDED QUESTION	PRIOR TO INSTRUCTION	DURING INSTRUCTION	AFTER INSTRUCTION
Question related to the CONCEPT			
Question related to the PROCESS			
Question related to the FACTS			

From *Advancing Differentiation: Thinking and Learning for the 21st Century* by Richard M. Cash, Ed.D., copyright © 2011. Free Spirit Publishing Inc., Minneapolis, MN; 800-735-7323; www.freespirit.com. This page may be reproduced for use within an individual school or district. For all other uses, contact www.freespirit.com/company/permissions.cfm.

Figure 7.4 Guided Thinking: Math Example

GUIDED QUESTION	PRIOR TO INSTRUCTION	DURING INSTRUCTION	AFTER INSTRUCTION
What is an unknown?	I'm not sure what an "unknown" is.	I learned that the "unknown" is a number we are looking for and it is represented by the letter X.	When I see a problem with a bunch of letters in it rather than numbers, I know that I can use math to figure out all the unknowns.
Describe the process of finding an unknown.	In most of my math, I have either added or subtracted to find the answer.		
How does working backwards help identify missing numbers?	I'm not sure.	When I work backwards I can use the opposite operation to make sure I have the right answer.	

Figure 7.5 Guided Thinking: History Example

GUIDED QUESTION	PRIOR TO INSTRUCTION	DURING INSTRUCTION	AFTER INSTRUCTION
Describe independence.	It's when I do things on my own.	In this unit independence is about a city, state, or country being self-governed.	
In what ways did the colonists work toward building their own government?	I learned in my elementary classes that the colonists tried several different types of governments that failed before they decided upon the democracy structure we now have.		
List the colonies in order.	I only remember: Connecticut Delaware Massachusetts Pennsylvania Rhode Island Virginia		

Student Perception Questionnaire

ATTITUDE/Efficacy

How do I feel about this learning activity? _____

_____

What issues am I dealing with that may be distracting my attention? _____

_____

What can I do to adjust my attitude toward this learning activity? _____

_____

What do I need in order to make this a more successful experience? _____

_____

SKILL/Regulation

Do I completely understand the tasks involved in this activity? _____

Do I have the skills required to complete the tasks? _____

Do I have all the resources I need? _____

Do I have the time to complete the tasks? _____

Do I have the support to complete the tasks? _____

CONFIDENCE/Self-Esteem

Who can I ask for help if I need it? _____

Who can I ask for support if I need it? _____

What skills do I possess that will help me do well on these tasks? _____

_____

What will I do to celebrate my accomplishment? _____

_____

REFLECTION/Metacognition

This was my best work because: _____

_____

I could have worked harder on: _____

_____

Next time I will: _____

_____

From *Advancing Differentiation: Thinking and Learning for the 21st Century* by Richard M. Cash, Ed.D., copyright © 2011. Free Spirit Publishing Inc., Minneapolis, MN; 800-735-7323; www.freespirit.com. This page may be reproduced for use within an individual school or district. For all other uses, contact www.freespirit.com/company/permissions.cfm.

Work Plan

Before You Begin Work

Set a SMART goal

SPECIFIC MEASURABLE ACHIEVABLE REALISTIC TIMELY

At the end of this unit I will: _____

_____

_____

_____

How do you plan on achieving the goal?

Work habits I need: _____

_____

Support I will need: _____

_____

Mindset for achievement: _____

_____

While You Are Working

How is the work progressing?	DATE	NOTES
Check in with a teacher	_____	_____
Check in with a peer	_____	_____
Check in with a parent or other adult	_____	_____
Check in with self	_____	_____

After the Work Is Complete

How close to your goal did you come?

- ☐ I did better than I thought I would do.
- ☐ I accomplished my goal.
- ☐ I didn't accomplish everything I wanted to, but I learned some new things.
- ☐ I tried but didn't really learn much.
- ☐ I didn't really try to accomplish my goal.

What specifically can you work on next time to improve your performance? _____

_____

_____

_____

From *Advancing Differentiation: Thinking and Learning for the 21st Century* by Richard M. Cash, Ed.D., copyright © 2011. Free Spirit Publishing Inc., Minneapolis, MN; 800-735-7323; www.freespirit.com. This page may be reproduced for use within an individual school or district. For all other uses, contact www.freespirit.com/company/permissions.cfm.

Student Reflection Log

Name: _____

Date: _____

Topic: _____

What I **know** about this topic: _____

_____

_____

What I **wonder** about this topic: _____

_____

_____

What I **learned** about this topic: _____

_____

_____

What I **want to learn more** about related to this topic: _____

_____

_____

I liked: _____

_____

_____

I did not like: _____

_____

_____

I did not understand: _____

_____

_____

I'd like the lesson more if: _____

_____

_____

From *Advancing Differentiation: Thinking and Learning for the 21st Century* by Richard M. Cash, Ed.D., copyright © 2011. Free Spirit Publishing Inc., Minneapolis, MN; 800-735-7323; www.freespirit.com. This page may be reproduced for use within an individual school or district. For all other uses, contact www.freespirit.com/company/permissions.cfm.

Chapter 8

A Framework for Thinking: Digging Deeper into Bloom's Taxonomy

> I cannot teach anybody anything, I can only make them think.
>
> —*Socrates, philosopher*

All students have the right to think at high levels. Some need more scaffolding to reach those high levels, while others require greater degrees of sophistication when working in the highest levels. When differentiating the thinking process for students, you need to pay attention to the variances in students' abilities to work in high levels of thinking.

Teaching our students to think more deeply and with more complexity means we need to provide them with a thinking framework. The process of structuring deep levels of thinking must be connected to classroom curriculum and standards. Most prepared curriculum and textbooks do not offer activities that can systematically guide students into the deep thoughtful process of learning. This chapter will explain a sequential method, built on Bloom's Taxonomy, for moving students into greater depths of learning.

A Brief Introduction to Bloom's Taxonomy

In 1956, Benjamin Bloom and his colleagues published the *Taxonomy of Educational Objectives, The Classification of Educational Goals, Handbook I: Cognitive Domain*[1]. The main purpose of this text was to define a taxonomy (a classification system) to help educators design hierarchic learning objectives and deal with curricular and evaluation issues. The taxonomy became known simply as Bloom's Taxonomy (see **Figure 8.1**). It provided teachers and curriculum designers with a framework for advancing student thinking through a hierarchy of learning objectives. Beginning with the recall of information, the knowledge base of all disciplines, the taxonomy provided a common language educators could use in the development of more precise objectives that would lead students through increasingly complex learning activities that required them to apply, dissect, and appraise learned content.

Bloom's Taxonomy was one of the most influential educational tools of the twentieth century. It continues to be a standard reference in defining quality curriculum, instruction, and assessments. Virtually every administrator and teacher at all levels of education is familiar with this tool and has applied it in one form or another. Bloom's Taxonomy has had a significant influence on helping teachers translate educational theory into effective practice. The enduring power of the taxonomy may be linked to its sequential intellectual scaffolding to higher levels of thought. Cognitive science suggests that the brain learns best when information is connected, richly practiced, and then reflected upon.

1 Bloom, Benjamin S., ed. *Taxonomy of Educational Objectives, The Classification of Educational Goals, Handbook I: Cognitive Domain.* New York: McKay, 1956.

The taxonomy provides a logical structure for students to build both learning and thinking. To most effectively use the taxonomy, you should be aware of how each level interacts with and supports the succeeding levels. This chapter discusses the levels of the taxonomy, offers a broad framework for each level, and then makes suggestions for how you can apply the taxonomy in a meaningful way for students. Finally, the chapter provides a structure for constructing advancing levels of tiered assignments by delving more deeply into Bloom's Taxonomy.

Performing Automatically to Performing Consciously

The base levels of Bloom's Taxonomy are intended to assist learners in constructing a solid foundation of content knowledge in order to support more advanced cognitive processes. As stated in Chapter 4, the function of automatic performance is situated in the lower levels of the brain (cerebellum). This automaticity is very important in allowing energy to be concentrated in the higher levels of the brain (the cerebral cortex). This higher level of brain activity is called *conscious performance;* because we don't have to think about the basic processes, we can focus our attention instead on more mindful, sophisticated thoughts. For example, when students have achieved automaticity of multiplication facts, they can more rapidly and fluently complete advanced algorithms without pausing to think about the basics. Having proficiency at the basic skill level is an important step toward internalizing the content (metacognition) and then realizing the benefit of learning (self-regulation).

Figure 8.1 Bloom's Taxonomy 1956[2]

Building on Bloom's

With each generation of educators, Bloom's Taxonomy has been refined to adhere to the needs of the marketplace students will be entering, which speaks to the valuable contribution this taxonomy has sustained. In 2001, researchers Lorin Anderson and David Krathwohl revised the taxonomy to realign the upper two levels and include a second dimension. Anderson and Krathwohl, students of Dr. Bloom's, suggest that the mental activity of creativity (synthesis) is more complex than that of evaluation, thus moving synthesis to the highest level. The original taxonomy was developed within a single dimension of cognitive processes. The second interrelated dimension added by Anderson and Krathwohl is the knowledge dimension, which includes the three main types of knowledge: factual, procedural, and conceptual, as well as metacognitive knowledge.

The addition of the knowledge dimension to the taxonomy provides for more flexibility in constructing more complex tasks and for moving students to greater degrees of autonomy. The knowledge levels progress students from basic tasks to more sophisticated undertakings. As previously discussed in Chapter 2, curriculum is framed in factual, procedural, and conceptual knowledge. Cognitively, learners are also storing memories in the same three ways: factually, procedurally, and conceptually. Therefore, including this second dimension to the taxonomy is supported both within a quality curriculum and by effective brain learning strategies.

As we continue into the twenty-first century, I have built on the work of Anderson and Krathwohl by including suggestions for tiering to deeper and more complex activities. I have also added a frame for assessment options to consider at each of the stages in the learning process. Since the passage of the No Child Left Behind (NCLB) legislation, classroom assessment has taken on a much more prominent role. Many highly regarded assessment experts suggest that

2 Bloom, 1956.

formative assessment/assessment *for* learning be used to identify the comprehensive understanding of student learning throughout the process and the effectiveness of instructional strategies.[3] This is why I suggest that assessment should be implemented at *each* stage of the taxonomy, not just at the end of the process (see **Figure 8.2** on page 116). Assessment in this context is more about understanding where students are in the learning process, how close they are coming to reaching the academic goals, and to what degree the instructional activities and procedures are affecting their learning.

Accordingly, **Figure 8.3** on pages 114–115 shows the additional three main knowledge levels (minus metacognitive knowledge) along with general statements for each of the corresponding cognitive processes in the taxonomy. Assessments are also displayed for each of the corresponding cognitive process dimensions. Notice that the assessment technique becomes more sophisticated and performance-oriented as students progress up the taxonomy.

Another modification I have made to Anderson and Krathwohl's work is to consider the metacognitive domain *within* both the assessment level and throughout the learning process as a self-regulation strategy toward autonomy (see Chapters 5 and 6). This does not require the teacher to prepare separate activities to help students build self-regulation. As stated in Chapter 5, self-regulation and metacognition develop when students are provided with supportive descriptive feedback and encouraged to take intellectual risks to stretch through their zone of proximal development.

The next section will describe each of the six cognitive process dimensions of the revised Bloom's Taxonomy (with my new suggestions for implementation) and share ideas of how to dig deeper into those dimensions. Two example units of study are used to demonstrate how to apply the revised taxonomy (see **Figures 8.4** and **8.5** on pages 117 and 118) and a planning tool called the Digging Deeper Matrix (DDM) is provided on page 124.

Recall: Retrieving Information and Developing a Knowledge Base

At the lowest level of the learning continuum is Recall, or sometimes denoted as Remember. Simply, the learner is to recall or recite previously learned material. At the first level (factual knowledge) of Recall, the student may recite vocabulary, facts, names, dates, or terms within the discipline or unit of study. Having this basic level of knowledge is important for students to support higher levels of cognition. As they move into level two of Recall (procedural knowledge), students define the steps in a process; learn problem solving and thinking skills; are trained in algorithms, models, and structures; and learn the steps in experiments, how to write reports, or how to list events in a sequence or on a timeline. At level three of Recall (conceptual knowledge), students are able to outline or define theories, taxonomies, periods of time, laws, and principles or generalizations.

In the American Revolution example (see Figure 8.5) students reinforce their knowledge base by listing important dates sequentially, giving the students a broad understanding of when the Revolutionary War took place and how long the events unfolded. Moving into Level 2, students describe methods of warfare that were used by the different armies. This helps them recognize the organizational structures of the two governments and how they each approached conflict. Finally, students define the concept of a revolution either from their personal experience or through the context of the introductory material.

Assessment at the Recall Level

Assessment at the Recall level is intended to validate that the students have acquired the fundamental factual information and are able to recite or recall it correctly.

Types of assessment at the Recall level include:

- Objective exams/tests/quizzes
- True/false questions
- Matching
- Fill in the blank
- Multiple choice
- Short answer
- One right answer
- Standardized tests
- Checklists
- Vocabulary recitation
- Question and answer period

3 Fisher and Frey, 2007; Gusky, T., 2009; Marzano, R. J., 2000; O'Connor, K., 2002; Reeves, D. B., 2004.

Figure 8.3 Bloom's Revised Taxonomy with Additional Assessment Layer[4]

KNOWLEDGE DIMENSION	COGNITIVE PROCESS DIMENSION			
	RECALL	UNDERSTAND	APPLY	
FACTUAL KNOWLEDGE	**Specific/Concrete** Recall specific concrete information **Key words:** *vocabulary, names, symbols, facts, dates, sources of information, basic elements*	**Translate** **WHAT?** Translate the facts into one's own words **Key words:** *retell, recap, repeat*	**Original Way** Apply the information in the original context **Key words:** *apply, use, utilize*	
PROCEDURAL KNOWLEDGE	**Tools/Skills** Remember procedural definitions, tools, and skills **Key words:** *problem solving, process, algorithm, structure, method, steps, model, parts, organization, action, criteria, technique*	**Interpret** **SO WHAT?** Interpret the meaning of the information **Key words:** *paraphrase, restate, summarize, reword, explain, construe, clarify, give details, describe, represent*	**Practical Way** Apply the information in a practical, authentic way **Key words:** *implement, employ*	
CONCEPTUAL KNOWLEDGE	**Abstract Information** Retrieve abstract knowledge **Key words:** *theory, theorem, classification, taxonomy, periods, laws, principles, generalization, relationships, understandings*	**Extrapolate** **NOW WHAT?** Extrapolate the information into another context **Key words:** *illustrate, model, exemplar, paradigm*	**Creative Way** Apply in a creative way **Key words:** *execute, relate, perform, stage*	
ASSESSMENT: EXAMPLES	Objective tests True/false Matching Fill in the blank Multiple choice Short answer One right answer Standardized tests Checklists Vocabulary recitations Q&A periods	Subject tests Open-ended questions Essays Constructed responses Selected responses Journals/reflections Short answer Q&A periods Discussions Oral reports Posters/displays/dioramas	Performances Re-creation of product Demonstrations/ presentations Games/ simulations Open-ended essays Experiments Projects Research reports	

4 Based on Anderson, Lorin W., and David R. Krathwohl, eds. *A Taxonomy for Learning, Teaching, and Assessing: A Revision of Bloom's Taxonomy of Educational Objectives.* New York: Addison Wesley Longman, 2001.

ANALYZE	EVALUATE	CREATE
Individual Elements Analyze the individual elements **Key words:** *observe, examine, survey, organize, find*	**Check Clarity** Check information for clarity **Key words:** *check, test, assess, question, evaluate, monitor*	**Reorganize** Reorganize elements of the original information **Key words:** *reorder, rearrange, restructure, change, alter, fashion, form, craft, generate*
Relationship Among Elements Analyze the relationship among elements **Key words:** *determine, establish, ascertain, differentiate, distinguish*	**Judge Accuracy** Judge information for accuracy **Key words:** *judge, ensure, confirm, review, authorize, decide*	**Formulate** Formulate designs for new uses for the information **Key words:** *design, devise, plan, express, articulate*
Principles Governing Elements Analyze the principles that govern the elements **Key words:** *appraise,connect, dissect, probe*	**Critique Validity** Critique information for validity **Key words:** *critique, validate, verify, scrutinize*	**Innovate** Create innovative and original ideas or products **Key words:** *create new, produce, build, invent, deconstruct, originate, initiate*
Compare/contrast charts Hierarchical diagrams Research reports/papers Essays Open-ended/subjective tests	Criterion-referenced assessments Surveys Research reports Experiments	Speeches/debates Research proposals Graphic representations Designs Research proposals Performance-based productions

Figure 8.2 Implementing Bloom's Revised Taxonomy[5]

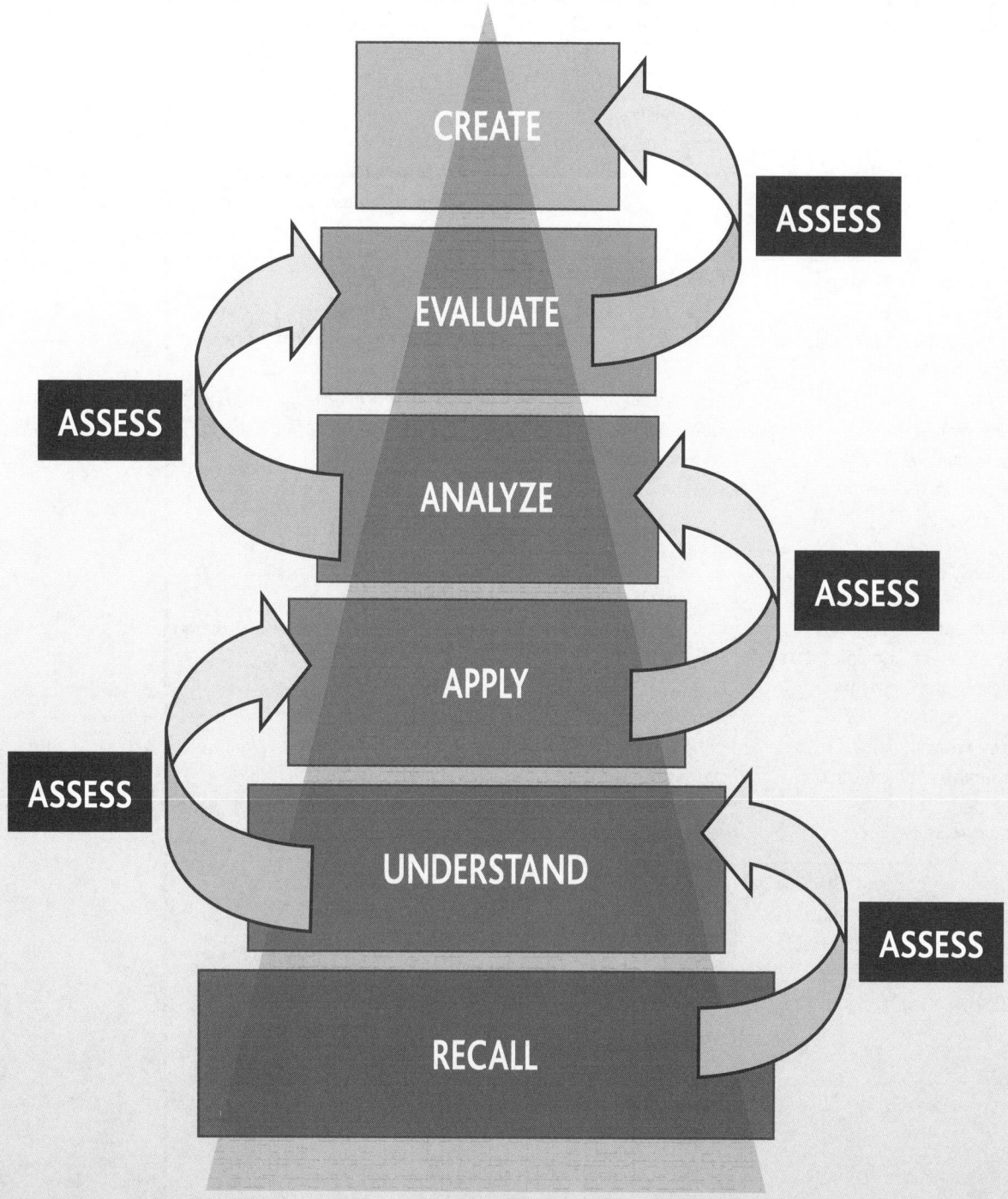

5 Based on Anderson, et al., 2001.

Figure 8.4 Digging Deeper into Bloom's: Science Example (Lower Grades)[6]

Unit: Health/Nutrition
Standard: Students will understand how healthy behaviors lead to a healthy life.[7]
Students will know: vocabulary related to healthy eating and the Food Guide Pyramid
Students will be able to: explain how the body uses nutrients and design a healthy eating and living plan
Students will understand: healthy eating leads to a healthy life

	RECALL	UNDERSTAND	APPLY	ANALYZE	EVALUATE	CREATE
Level 1 Factual	**Specific/Concrete** List vocabulary words related to healthy eating and living.	**Translate WHAT?** Describe the Food Guide Pyramid.	**Original Way** Keep a journal of the foods you eat for one week.	**Individual Elements** Review your journal to calculate the average amount of nutrients you receive each day.	**Check Clarity** Graph how well you did at meeting the daily average nutrients needed by a child like you.	**Reorganize** Create a weeklong menu that would provide a healthy diet for you.
Level 2 Procedural	**Tools/Skills** Describe how nutrients supply our body with energy.	**Interpret SO WHAT?** Define why the Food Guide Pyramid is important for a healthy life.	**Practical Way** Using the school lunch menu for one week, place all items on the Food Guide Pyramid.	**Relationship Among Elements** Analyze the school's lunch menu and calculate the average amount of nutrients students receive each day.	**Judge Accuracy** Graph how well the school does in meeting the daily average needs for nutrients for a child like you.	**Formulate** Using the average amount of nutrients needed for a student your age, create a weeklong healthy school lunch menu.
Level 3 Conceptual	**Abstract Information** Describe how healthy eating and living can lead to a healthy life.	**Extrapolate NOW WHAT?** How might we use the Food Guide Pyramid as a school/class?	**Creative Way** Build a healthy school lunch menu for one week.	**Principles Governing Elements** Evaluate the school's lunch, defining strengths and weaknesses in the menu, and devise suggestions for change.	**Critique Validity** Why do you think the school has strengths or weaknesses in its school lunch menu related to nutrients needed by a child like you?	**Innovate** Create a healthy school lunch menu using only local or organic products.
Assessment: Examples	Vocabulary quiz Poster Short essay	Poster/report Short essay Newspaper article Position statement	Journal/log Poster/report	Report	Graph Editorial	Lunch menu Report

6 Based on Anderson, et al., 2001.
7 Adapted from The Joint Committee on National Health Education Standards. *National Health Education Standards: Achieving Excellence (2nd Edition)*. Atlanta: American Cancer Society, 2007.

Figure 8.5 Digging Deeper into Bloom's: History Example (Upper Grades)[8]

Unit: Revolution and the New Nation 1763–1820

Standard: The student will demonstrate knowledge of how the principles of the American Revolution became the foundation of a new nation.[9]

Students will know:

1. Important vocabulary, dates, and events (such as treaties, battles, political uprisings, and relations with foreign nations and Native Americans) related to the American Revolution
2. Important political, economic, military, and cultural figures related to the American Revolution (such as George Washington, Samuel Adams, John Adams, Paul Revere, Thomas Jefferson, Charles Cornwallis, Marquis de Lafayette, Thomas Paine, Patrick Henry, John Locke, and Baron de Montesquieu)
3. Important debates and facts over slavery; statues of free blacks, women, and Native Americans; migration to Canada; and the westward movement of white settlers

Students will be able to:

1. Analyze major economic, political, and philosophical conflicts leading to the American Revolution
2. Explain how and why the American colonists won the war against the more superior British resources
3. Interpret the impact the Revolutionary War had on groups within American society
4. Infer the impact of revolution on nations and groups of citizens within those nations

Students will understand: the causes, effects, and consequences of revolution

	RECALL	UNDERSTAND	APPLY	ANALYZE	EVALUATE	CREATE
Level 1 Factual	**Specific/ Concrete** List important dates of the Revolutionary War.	**Translate WHAT?** What led to the colonists' revolt against Britain?	**Original Way** How did the Treaty of Paris change the mapping of territories of North America?	**Individual Elements** What were the basic disagreements among the Native Americans, colonists, British, and French?	**Check Clarity** Why did the Native Americans, colonists, British, and French have their disagreements?	**Reorganize** Put yourself in the role of a colonial ambassador. What message would you send to Britain or France?
Level 2 Procedural	**Tools/Skills** Describe how the Red Coats attacked Boston.	**Interpret SO WHAT?** Why was this revolt important?	**Practical Way** How did the change of territories after the Treaty of Paris affect the colonists?	**Relationship Among Elements** How did these disagreements relate to each other?	**Judge Accuracy** In what ways might any or all of the disagreements have been avoided?	**Formulate** Put yourself in the role of a British ambassador. What plans would you make to settle disputes in the colonies?
Level 3 Conceptual	**Abstract Information** Define a revolution.	**Extrapolate NOW WHAT?** What effect has the American Revolution had on our nation and Britain?	**Creative Way** Describe a modern day conflict where map boundaries were redrawn.	**Principles Governing Elements** Why did each group seek control?	**Critique Validity** What made one group's claim more valid than the other group's claims?	**Innovate** Create a position statement that would either support or oppose colonization.
Assessment: Examples	Paper/pencil test	Essay	Performance	Graphic representation	Essay Persuasion speech Role play	Speech/debate Research proposal Graphic representation

8 Based on Anderson, et al., 2001.

9 Adapted from Minnesota Academic Standards in History and Social Studies, United States History Grades 4–8, Minnesota Department of Education, May 15, 2004.

Understand: Grasping the Meaning of the Information

The Understand (or Comprehension) level involves students restating information in their own words to show they understand the information. This level can be thought of as the "What? So What? Now What?" level (see **Figure 8.6**). At stage one, the "What?" stage, the student would restate the words used at the Recall level into their own words or summarize the meaning behind all the words, what was just said, done, or learned. In the example (see Figure 8.5) students identify what led up to the revolution, framing the context for the revolt.

Next is the "So What?" stage, defining what makes this information important. The learners must interpret what the information means to them personally or put it into the context of the study. Students paraphrase, restate, or summarize the information in personally meaningful ways. The example asks students to define why they believed the revolution has importance. This kind of open-endedness forces the students to inductively reason through the content.

Finally, at the "Now What?" stage, students extrapolate the information to hypothesize or theorize how things will change or what will happen next. Students generate examples and illustrations. Notice in the example (see Figure 8.5), students connect a past event to current situations. For an additional example of What? So What? Now What?, see Figure 11.5 on page 176.

Figure 8.6 The Three Stages of the *Understand* Level

WHAT?	SO WHAT?	NOW WHAT?
What led to the colonists' revolt against Britain? *The development of semi-autonomous states that longed for independence from British finances* *Increasing numbers of immigrants from other nations*	Why was this revolt important? *It led to the foundation and formation of the United States.*	What effect has the American Revolution had on the United States and Britain? *Losing the American colonies forced Britain to reevaluate its fiscal and military might and to seek a more collaborative connection to the newly formed United States.* *The United States and Britain have since been very strong allies.*

Assessment at the Understand Level

Assessment at the Understand level is designed to display student comprehension of the content and concepts. Assessing understanding is more complex here than at the Recall level. Students must be able to summarize the information and put it into their own words.

Types of assessment at the Understand level include:

- Subject tests/open-ended questions/essays
- Constructed responses where students supply the answers
- Selected response where students choose the answers
- Journals/reflections
- Short-answer tests/quizzes/exams
- Question and answer periods
- Discussions
- Oral reports
- Posters/displays/dioramas

Apply: Putting It to Use

Once information has been gathered and given meaning, students then put it to use. Students must correctly apply and demonstrate the information learned. Initially, at Level 1 of Apply, the student puts the information to use in the original context (inauthentic practices, such as worksheets or teacher-guided work). In the example (see Figure 8.5) students demonstrate their knowledge of the effect of the application of the Treaty of Paris on changes to mapping the territories of North America. This is an authentic activity, one directly related to the content.

Moving into the next level, students use the information in a more practical way (more authentic practices within the domain of the content, still with the support and coaching of the teacher). In the example, the students must think about the greater effects the Treaty of Paris had on people years later. The students are required to use the content information more broadly.

Finally, at the deepest level of application, the student applies the information or process in a variety of new contexts. This may include applying laws, theories, or principles learned in one content area to another content area. The example has students applying learned information to a new context, such as a modern day conflict that resulted in a similar boundary change to that of the Paris Treaty.

Assessment at the Apply Level

At the Apply level students must be able to perform the skills being learned. These types of assessments require a greater degree of authenticity and practicality.

Types of assessment at the Apply level include:

- Performances
- Re-creation of product
- Demonstrations/presentations
- Games/simulations or other interactive exercises
- Open-ended essays
- Experiments
- Projects
- Research reports

Analyze: Recognizing Relationships of the Parts

The analysis level of Bloom's Taxonomy is one that overlaps with the levels before and after, so it should not be considered a stand-alone level in the process. In fact, it is hard to do analysis without some level of understanding and application. And as in all levels of Bloom's Taxonomy, there is a degree of evaluation involved. Analysis is the beginning of what can be defined as higher levels of thought or learning and is essential to critical reasoning and decision making. The cognitive activity at this level requires a more sophisticated amount of attention paid to both individual parts of the content as well as to the content as a whole.

To dig deeper into the Analyze level, students begin by identifying and classifying the characteristics of the individual elements of the content. The American Revolution example (see Figure 8.5) has students defining the various disagreements that each group held prior to the war. Through this activity students come to understand the complexity of the issues. Next, the students compare and contrast the relationships between the individual characteristics or elements. Once the students have defined the multiple disagreements, they analyze how the issues interrelate. Finally, based on the information gleaned from the previous steps, students make an inference to articulate principles or generalizations that govern the content. At this stage the students are making conjecture as to why each of the groups would want to seek control.

Assessment at the Analyze Level

At the analytical level, students reason through information to form purpose, solve complex problems, and draw conclusions about the importance of the data. Authenticity of assessment is much more significant at this level.

Types of assessment at the Analyze level include:

- Compare/contrast charts with reports
- Hierarchical diagrams
- Research reports/papers
- Essays
- Open-ended/subjective tests

Evaluate: Determining Clarity, Accuracy, and Validity

At the evaluation level students are using critical thinking skills to ensure information is clear, accurate, and valid. Evaluation, in this sense, is not summative as in a final exam. At this stage in the learning, students must be able to look back on how well information has been applied and analyzed. This can be done by using criteria created by the students, by the teacher, or by an expert in the domain. The three tiers of Evaluate begin with students being able to clarify how the facts come together to support or oppose building new ideas. At Level 2 of Evaluate, students determine how accurately a skill has been implemented and in what ways this procedure can be refined to reach the Create level. In the most advanced stage of evaluation, students critique the merits of ideas that have been presented and justify the positive or negative outcomes that have occurred because of these ideas.

Assessment at the Evaluate Level

The evaluation level involves students reflecting back on previously learned information, skills, and ideas and looking forward to how they can construct new thoughts and knowledge.

Types of assessment at the Evaluate level include:

- Criterion-referenced assessments
- Surveys
- Research reports
- Experiments

Create: Generating New Ideas

Building on the previous levels of Understand, Apply, Analyze, and Evaluate, students can then move up to the level of Create (also called Synthesis). Synthesized thoughts and ideas are created from an understanding of the information, knowing how it is put to use in varied and new settings, and being able to take parts and recombine or reconstruct them into entirely new forms. Synthesis is the use of creative thinking skills (see Chapter 10) where students are "putting elements together to form a coherent or functional whole."[10] Thinking and acting creatively is more than a freewheeling practice of making things up. Creating requires constructing ideas or products that address learning objectives or outcomes, offer feasibility of implementation, and can produce the required effects. Creative ideas and products must have practical applications.

Students begin the creative process by reorganizing, restructuring, or rearranging information learned in previous experience to generate ideas to solve problems or develop new products. Most students can manipulate information in some way to generate new ideas or outcomes. This may be done by describing a situation in context that needs resolution and suggesting several alternative solutions. In the American Revolution example (see Figure 8.5) the students put themselves in the role of colonial ambassadors to develop a message for Britain or France. This activity uses information that is in the content, but must be shaped by the student's creativity.

Going deeper into Level 2 of Create, students draw on elements from various sources to articulate and design a viable plan for a unique solution or product. Students use hypothetical predictive and deductive thinking to devise resolutions. Notice in the example, the students are taking on the role of the opposing side, which requires a greater degree of creative thinking, as not all information may be readily available.

In the most advanced stage of Create, the student develops innovative products that are original. In the final activity of the example in Figure 8.5, the students must move beyond the information provided and create their own position statement on the colonization by the British. This requires the student to use all the resources and knowledge built from prior activities. When considering objectives or activities that seek

10 Anderson, et al., 2001, p. 84.

unique or innovative outcomes, originality takes different forms based on the individual or group. Younger children may be taking newly learned information and rearranging it in a way that is new to them, such as designing a new ending to a story or writing it from a different perspective. Older students may develop a new hypothesis as to why certain chemicals interact or react to one another after several experiments and studies. Both outcomes are original, based on the level of the student.

Assessment at the Create Level

Types of assessments at the Create level include:

- Speeches/debates
- Research proposals
- Graphic representations
- Designs
- Performance-based productions

Assessment: Making Judgments About the Knowledge Throughout the Process

As I suggest in Figure 8.3, assesssment is not a final step in the learning process. It is an ongoing integrated practice of using critical reasoning at each stage of Bloom's Taxonomy. At every level of the learning process, students continually contemplate how they are doing, their correctness, and their proficiency or mastery toward a set goal. Forms of assessment move from concrete, inauthentic regeneration of knowledge, to more abstract, authentic representations of acquired knowledge or new thoughts or ideas. As seen in Figures 8.4 and 8.5, the flow of assessment begins with internal reflection out to external reviews by others, progressing from tests or checklists, to essays, performances, or representations, and finally to speeches or debates. This is accomplished through applying both internally defined criteria and externally imposed norms.

Internally defined criteria include such self-evaluative questions as:

- Does this make sense to me?
- How can I more specifically define this topic?
- Does this feel right?

Externally imposed norms offer guidelines that include:

- Teacher-designed objectives
- Teacher-constructed tests, quizzes, or checklists
- State standards and benchmarks

Putting It All Together: The Digging Deeper Matrix (DDM)

The Digging Deeper Matrix (page 124) can assist you in developing unit plans that can move all students into advanced levels of thinking. The model provides a tiered system for creating activities at every level of Bloom's Taxonomy that are rigorous and complex, and respect the varying needs for academic difficulty in a mixed-ability classroom. Every student can think at higher levels, and some students need more sophisticated activities that stretch them into more advanced levels of thinking.

All students can work at Level 1 of the matrix, some students may work to Level 2, and the advanced learner possibly will move deeper into Level 3. The number and letter in the parenthesis in each box are a code for the cognitive process *(recall, understand, apply, analyze, evaluate,* and *create)* and level of knowledge acquisition *(factual, procedural,* and *conceptual)*.

The DDM can be used:

- As a guide for instruction
- To assign activities during lessons or for homework for all students
- As selected activities used during lessons or homework provided to all students in small flexible groupings
- As sequential movement from recalling to creating
- To offer students choices to work at greater degrees of difficulty (*Note:* do not allow students to work at levels below their ability)
- To suggest topics of greater research, investigation, or exploration
- As an assessment tool for curriculum and instructional practices

Steps to Using the DDM:

Use the following six steps as a guide to adding rigor for all students and deeper degrees of complexity for students who require more sophisticated activities.

1. At the top of the model, record the topic and unit title.
2. Using your district, state, or provincial standards, create objectives of what you want students to know (facts), what you want them to be able to do (procedures and processes), and what you want them to understand (concepts).

3. Using a previously prepared unit or a newly developing unit, place activities in the appropriate level of thinking on the matrix. Check the key words from Figure 8.3 to ensure you have placed the activity at the right level.

4. Design activities or assignments that address open boxes. In most cases you will be developing activities and assignments that are more complex and/or difficult. Again, use the key words in each column and level to guide you. Be careful not to create new activities and assignments that are just more work. All activities within the model should be equally engaging, interesting, and have a degree of fun.

5. Activities can be constructed for individual students, small groups, or whole group instruction. The shading on the template (page 124) represents the three ways to use the matrix. The darkest shaded boxes are activities for all students or whole group instruction. The medium shaded boxes are activities for most students or small groups. The lightest shaded boxes are activities for individual students or advanced learners. If students are doing the more advanced level activities they may not need to do the activities in the other boxes.

6. Assess the activities for each of the learning objectives, using the appropriate assessment strategies. Assessment for the learning objectives of *Recall, Understand, Apply, Analyze,* and *Evaluate* should be used formatively to guide the learner to the final learning objective *Create*.

Moving students to higher levels of thinking requires a comprehensive knowledge of Bloom's Taxonomy, an awareness of the varying degrees of sophistication to which students can perform at each of those levels, and the ability to differentiate activities to greater depth and complexity. The DDM provides you with a structured format for ensuring all students are maximizing thinking and learning to its greatest degree.

Digging Deeper Matrix (DDM)

Unit:
Standard:
Students will know:
Students will be able to:
Students will understand:

	RECALL (R)	UNDERSTAND (U)	APPLY (A)	ANALYZE (Z)	EVALUATE (E)	CREATE (C)
LEVEL 1 FACTUAL	*FOR ALL STUDENTS* **Specific/Concrete** (1R)	**Translate** (1U)	**Original Way** (1A)	**Individual Elements** (1Z)	**Check Clarity** (1E)	**Reorganize** (1C)
LEVEL 2 PROCEDURAL	**Tools/Skills** (2R)	**Interpret** (2U)	*FOR SOME STUDENTS* **Practical Way** (2A)	**Relationship Among Elements** (2Z)	**Judge Accuracy** (2E)	**Formulate** (2C)
LEVEL 3 CONCEPTUAL	**Abstract Information** (3R)	**Extrapolate** (3U)	*FOR ADVANCED STUDENTS* **Creative Way** (3A)	**Principles Governing Elements** (3Z)	**Critique Validity** (3E)	**Innovate** (3C)
ASSESSMENT: EXAMPLES						

Based on Anderson, Lorin W., and David R. Krathwohl, eds. *A Taxonomy for Learning, Teaching, and Assessing: A Revision of Bloom's Taxonomy of Educational Objectives.* New York: Addison Wesley Longman, 2001.

From *Advancing Differentiation: Thinking and Learning for the 21st Century* by Richard M. Cash, Ed.D., copyright © 2011. Free Spirit Publishing Inc., Minneapolis, MN; 800-735-7323; www.freespirit.com.
This page may be reproduced for use within an individual school or district. For all other uses, contact www.freespirit.com/company/permissions.cfm.

Chapter 9

Critical Thinking: Developing Reasoned Thought

> Learning without thought is labor lost; thought without learning is perilous.
>
> —*Confucius, philosopher*

The essence of differentiated instruction and the backbone of a quality education is for students to be proficient in understanding concepts, knowing facts, and being able to perform procedures successfully. However, recalling facts and executing procedures does not directly lead students to the understanding of concepts. It is through the critical thinking process that students come to grasp the concepts that link all knowledge together into a coherent and cohesive education.

The nature of human thought is self-serving. It's about getting what we want and need, and supporting what we believe. We don't naturally see the world the way it really is; we filter our thoughts and perceptions of the world through our various lenses of emotion, past experience, culture, ethnic background, gender, social status, history, and so on. Unconsciously we see the world that fits us. We all rely on the unconscious form of thinking to get us through the day. This kind of thinking is innate to us; it's our survival thinking. However, it's the more evolved, conscious form of thinking that will lead us to a productive and successful life. And this kind of conscious thinking is not "natural"; it must be taught.

Unconscious thinking is ill-formed thinking; it is disorganized, biased, narrow, and without clear direction. Effective conscious thinking is organized, open- and fair-minded, well-reasoned, and able to be clearly communicated to others. This conscious thinking is also known as *critical thinking,* or reasoning. This chapter will provide an overview of critical thinking and offer an array of strategies and tools for developing critical thinking.

Students are bombarded by all kinds of information from television to the Internet to their friends. This overload of information may not always be accurate, precise, factual, or correct. Therefore, we must teach our students how to use the skills of critical thinking and reasoning to be able to take command of their own thinking and use their minds for the better of our world.

What Is Critical Thinking?

Critical thinking is in many ways the opposite of creative thinking. Whereas creative thinking is more intuitive, is shaped somewhat randomly, and seeks multiple answers, critical thinking is more ordered, directed, and controlled. Both types of thinking require advanced levels of brain energy and seek to generate reasoned solutions. They each approach the solution in a different and valuable fashion.

Students are often exposed to curriculum that is grounded in facts and issues devoid of a wider context. Progressing from learned facts to concept development may feel disjointed to students because of this lack of context. Facts outside of context are just that: facts.

Additionally, students may disengage from the material since they are not encouraged to question or critique the validity of the curriculum materials. The student is passive in the curriculum.

"Social relations in the classroom that glorify the teacher as the expert, the dispenser of knowledge, end up crippling student imagination and creativity; in addition, such approaches teach students more about the legitimacy of passivity than about the need to examine critically the lives they lead."[1] Students who actively engage in the questioning and critiquing of content validity are developing critical thinking skills. When students review information from different points of view and legitimize arguments and claims, they are constructing a foundation of thinking skills that doesn't presuppose the validity of any facts out of context or promote concepts disjointed from the facts.

Critical thinking is not about raising skeptics; it is about developing autonomous thinkers.

Critical thinking is not about raising skeptics. It is about developing autonomous thinkers who can identify, evaluate, and reason through information in a broader context outside themselves. Critical thinking is about "awaking the student's awareness that the world contains unrealized possibilities for thoughts and action."[2]

Critical Thinking Is Sound Decision Making

Critical thinking is *making good decisions based on evidence and facts*. The thinker has to take on an impersonal or objective stance, limiting their emotions, bias, opinions, assumptions, and perceptions from the process. This does not mean that the decision maker lacks empathy. It means that the decision maker is guarded against information that can lead to a faulty outcome. Gathering and using evidence and factual information will help in making a better decision. Factual information needs to be corroborated through credible sources.

Critical Thinking Is Analysis and Criticism

Discerning the credibility of information is vital in the critical thinking process, therefore, critical thinkers must have the ability to analyze and criticize. They must be able to scrutinize the source of the information and what views the source holds. To criticize is not to belittle or disparage; it is to critique. When the thinker can assess the validity of an argument, appraise a situation from different angles, and even question as the "devil's advocate," he or she is more likely to form solutions that are well reasoned.

Critical Thinking Is Inductive and Deductive Reasoning

Critical thinking, like creative thinking, requires the use of both inductive and deductive reasoning. Basically, inductive reasoning is going with your gut feelings about the information you have received. Deductive reasoning takes into account all the facts presented with the information. To critically think through information, we cannot deny our internal feelings about the information, but we must temper it with the facts. We must come to conclusions based both on what we infer and what we have as factually tested knowledge.

Essential for skillful critical thinking is the ability to guard against bias, fallacies, persuasion, and rumor. Political campaigns, advertisements, newspapers, magazines, websites, music, art, film, and theater all have an agenda: to get a message to the viewer. The message intends to persuade you to agree or disagree with a candidate, buy a product, espouse a line of thinking, and so on. Good critical thinkers listen to the message, analyze the information presented, seek out hidden messages, acknowledge the propaganda, and make decisions about the information using all of these resources.

General Critical Thinking Strategies

To help your students do a better job of critical thinking, you need to provide them with graphic organizers, templates, and designs to frame their thinking. Following are several examples of general critical thinking strategies.

1 Giroux, Henry A. "Toward a Pedagogy of Critical Thinking." In Walters, K. S. (Ed.) *Re-Thinking Reason: New Perspectives on Critical Thinking*. Albany: State University of New York Press, 1994, p. 202.

2 Maxine Greene in *Re-Thinking Reason*, p. 207.

Validate Information

The broadest strategy of critical thinking is validating information. This strategy requires the student to appraise the source of the information, credibility of the source, and validity of the information. When validating information the student must look at such things as the credentials of the author, date, and source of the information. In addition, knowing the intended audience of the original work can help identify:

- point of view
- stereotyping and bias
- propaganda
- assumptions and generalizations

On page 129 is an excellent spider-design graphic organizer to help students substantiate and validate information. When validating information the student is also discovering both relevant and irrelevant information, sorting out fact from opinion, and uncovering reliable and unreliable sources. (See **Figure 9.1** for a partially completed example.)

Compare and Contrast

Comparing and contrasting is an excellent way for students to categorize attributes of similar and dissimilar things and to then analyze the individual parts. Page 130 shows a compare and contrast graphic organizer that can help students discern individual characteristics, plot out significant similarities and differences, and then interpret what those similarities and differences mean.

Figure 9.2 shows two different types of compare and contrast graphics. The T-Chart is designed to provide parameters for the line of thinking required for an assignment or lesson. In the example, the student is asked to list how U.S. President Abraham Lincoln's administration compared to President John F. Kennedy's administration on key issues. The second design takes the basic two-ring Venn diagram to a higher level by providing three rings within which to compare and contrast. The example seeks out broad characteristics of three U.S. presidents (Washington, Lincoln, and Kennedy) to compare and contrast.

A more advanced level graphic organizer for comparing and contrasting is the Cross-Impact Matrix (CIM) (page 132). The CIM analyzes more than three variables or items and the relationships between them. This form of convergent thinking considers multiple interacting situations or issues. Depending on how you would like to use the CIM, columns and rows can be adjusted (see the two different examples in **Figure 9.3** on page 133). Notice in the Three Little Pigs example that Row 1 and Column A are the same, whereas in the American Civil War example, Row 1 and Column A use different variables. The CIM can be used in various ways depending on the line of thinking you are trying to achieve.

Sequence and Prioritize

Sequencing and prioritizing is used when a student must list characteristics or information, which will then be prioritized in order of importance. This skill can be helpful when solving problems, thinking through large amounts of information, setting work plans, understanding cause and effect, or organizing one's life. **Figure 9.4** on pages 134–135 offers several examples of sequencing and prioritizing graphics.

(Text continues on page 136.)

Figure 9.1 Spider Diagram: Example—Biological Systems

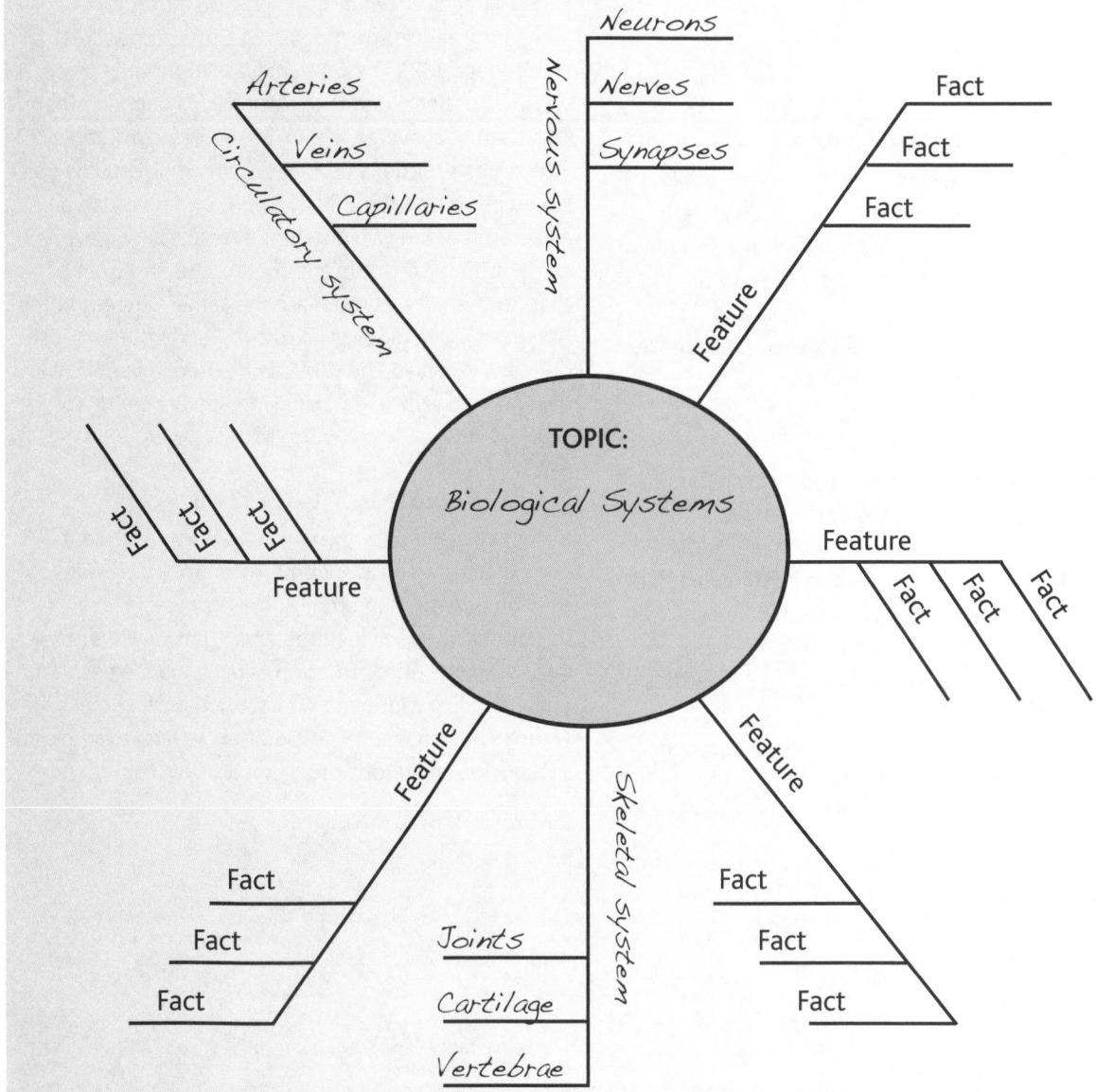

Spider Diagram

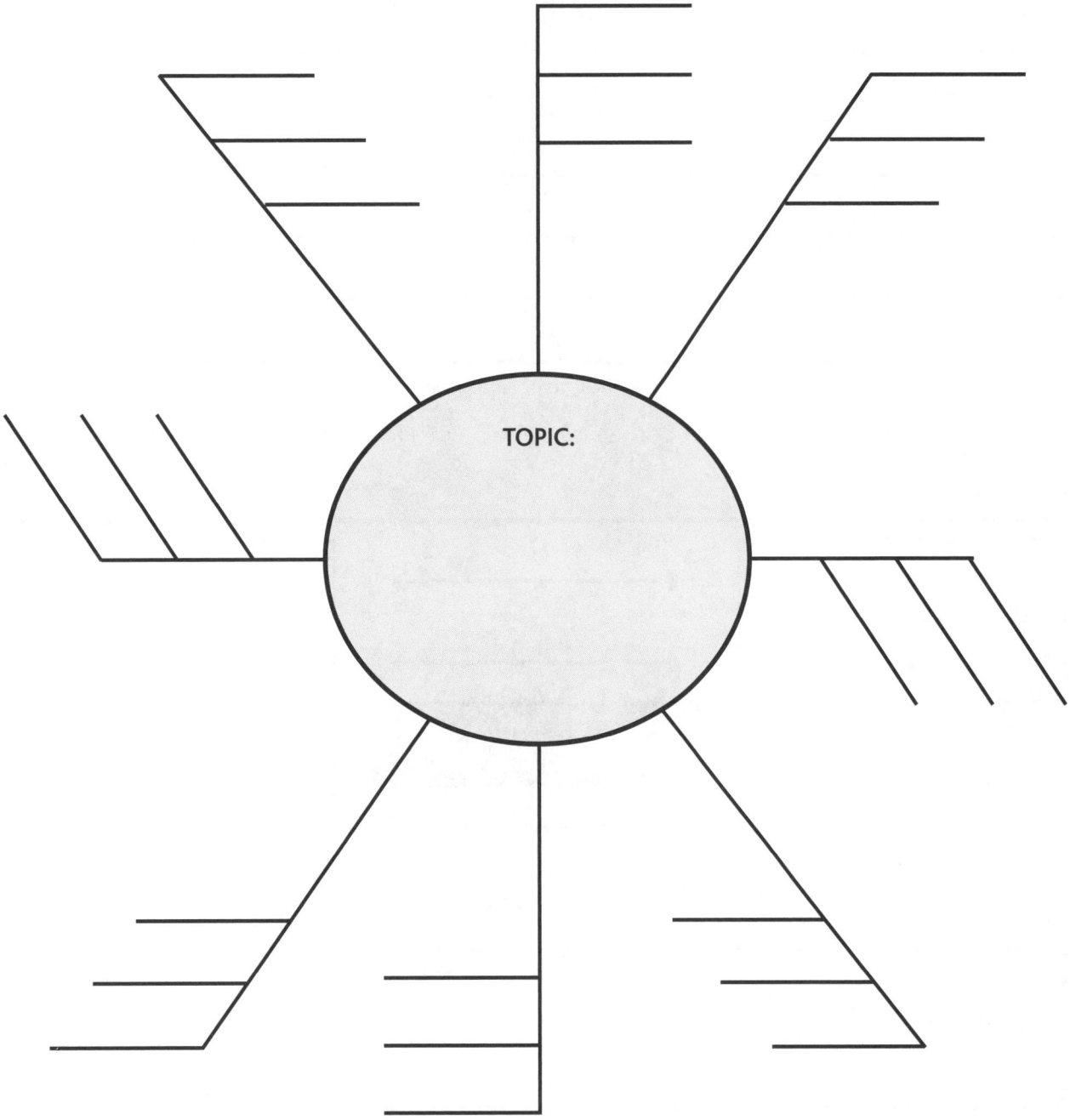

From *Advancing Differentiation: Thinking and Learning for the 21st Century* by Richard M. Cash, Ed.D., copyright © 2011. Free Spirit Publishing Inc., Minneapolis, MN; 800-735-7323; www.freespirit.com. This page may be reproduced for use within an individual school or district. For all other uses, contact www.freespirit.com/company/permissions.cfm.

Compare and Contrast Graphic Organizer

How are they alike?

Significance of Similarities

How are they different?

Significance of Differences

Interpretation

From *Advancing Differentiation: Thinking and Learning for the 21st Century* by Richard M. Cash, Ed.D., copyright © 2011. Free Spirit Publishing Inc., Minneapolis, MN; 800-735-7323; www.freespirit.com. This page may be reproduced for use within an individual school or district. For all other uses, contact www.freespirit.com/company/permissions.cfm.

Figure 9.2 Advanced Compare and Contrast Graphic Organizer: Examples

T-CHART EXAMPLE

Characteristic	Abraham Lincoln	John F. Kennedy
Leadership Qualities	Had the interest of protecting the union over self	Surrounded himself with advisors that were liberals and conservatives
Major Accomplishments	Liberated the slaves Saved the union of the United States	Civil Rights bill passed after his death Sent the U.S. to the moon
Political Skills	Patient, calculated, shrewd	Skillful statesman
Character/ Integrity	Self-made man, humorous, sullen	Intelligent, well-spoken

ADVANCED VENN DIAGRAM EXAMPLE

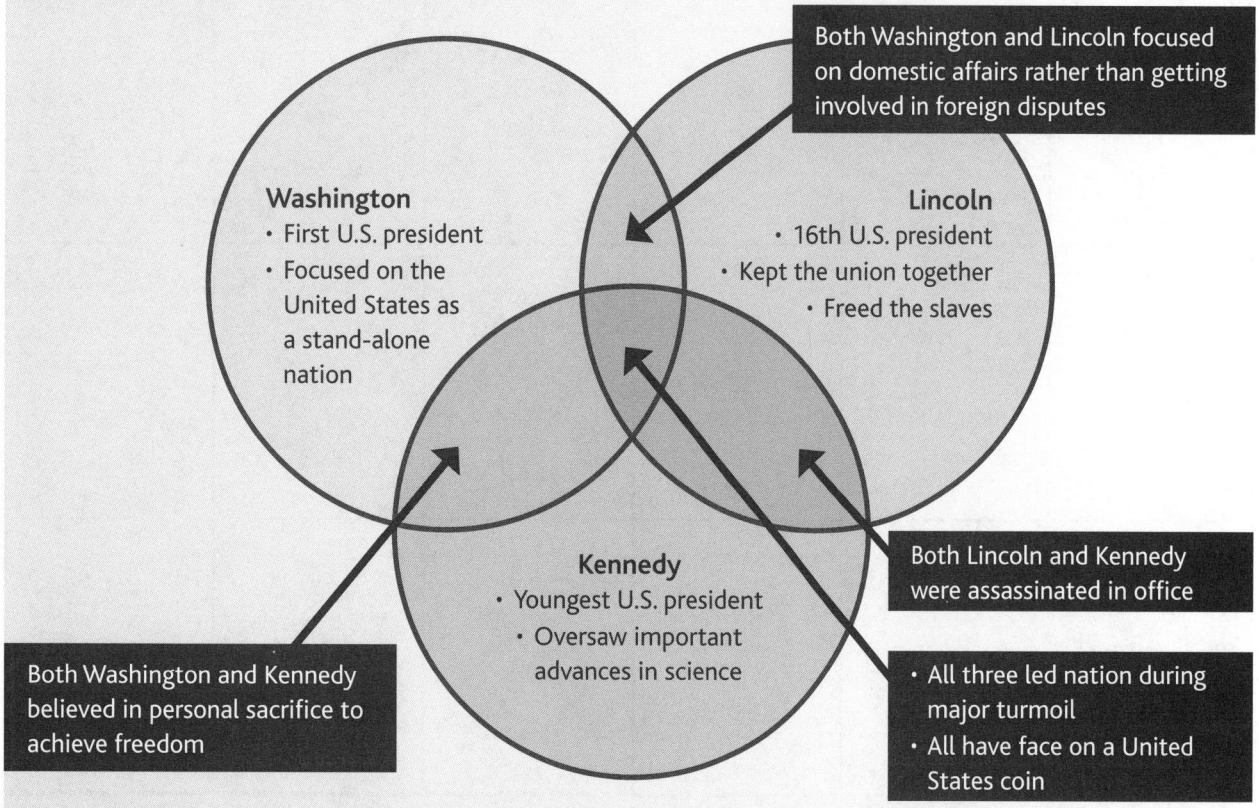

Cross-Impact Matrix (CIM)

What impact does this → have on this? ↓	A	B	C	D	E
1					
2					
3					
4					
5					

From *Advancing Differentiation: Thinking and Learning for the 21st Century* by Richard M. Cash, Ed.D., copyright © 2011. Free Spirit Publishing Inc., Minneapolis, MN; 800-735-7323; www.freespirit.com. This page may be reproduced for use within an individual school or district. For all other uses, contact www.freespirit.com/company/permissions.cfm.

Figure 9.3 CIM: Examples

LOWER GRADES: THREE LITTLE PIGS

What impact does this → have on this? ↓	A Pig 1	B Pig 2	C Pig 3	D Big Bad Wolf (BBW)
1 Pig 1				
2 Pig 2				
3 Pig 3				
4 Big Bad Wolf				

Pig 1 to Pig 1: **N/A**
Pig 1 to Pig 2:
Pig 1 to Pig 3:
Pig 1 to BBW:

Pig 2 to Pig 1:
Pig 2 to Pig 2: **N/A**
Pig 2 to Pig 3:
Pig 2 to BBW:

Pig 3 to Pig 1:
Pig 3 to Pig 2:
Pig 3 to Pig 3: **N/A**
Pig 3 to BBW:

BBW to Pig 1:
BBW to Pig 2:
BBW to Pig 3:
BBW to BBW: **N/A**

UPPER GRADES: THE U.S. CIVIL WAR

What impact does this → have on this? ↓	A The 1860 election of Abraham Lincoln	B The attack on Fort Sumter	C The Emancipation Proclamation	D Lee's Surrender to Grant in 1865
1 Economy				
2 Politics				
3 Race Issues				
4 Social Structure				

Figure 9.4 Sequencing and Prioritizing Graphics

RANK ORDER of facts from most important to least important.

1_____ 2_____ 3_____ 4_____ 5_____

CONTINUUM: Place each fact on the continuum from most important to least important.

Most **Least**

CYCLE: Place the facts in a sequence to show how it represents a cycle.

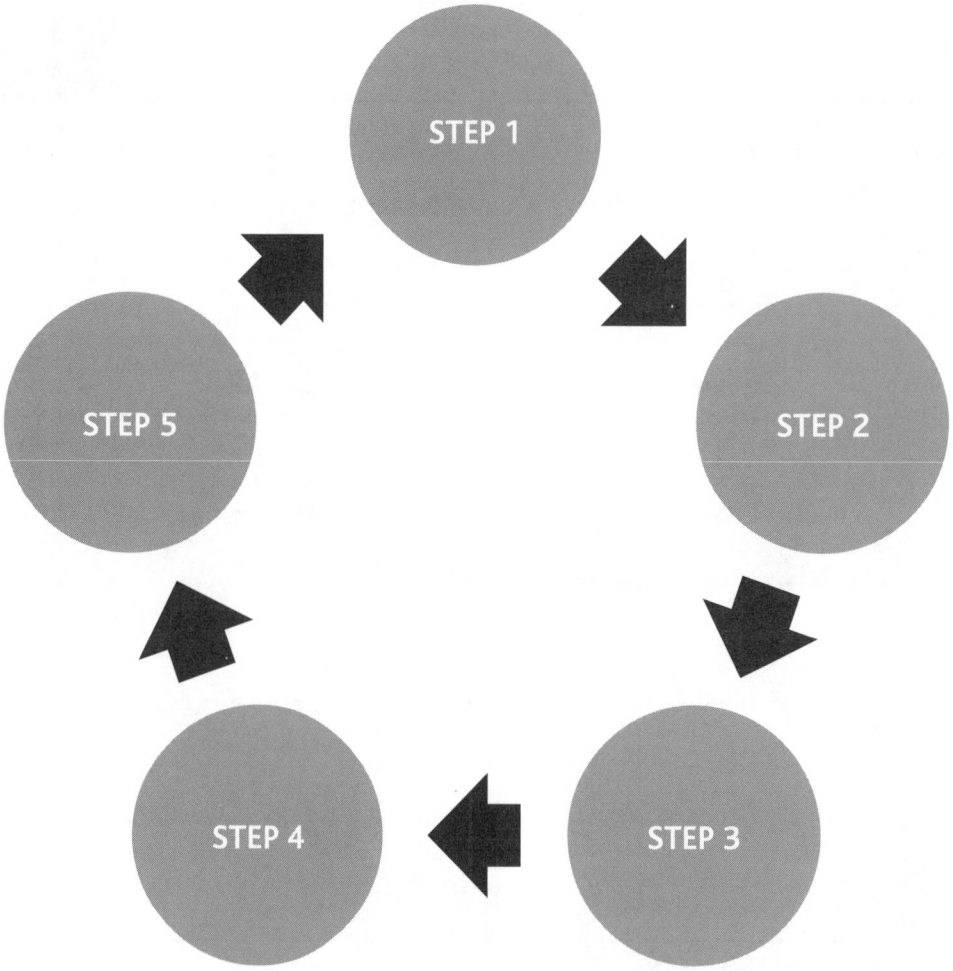

SEQUENCE CHAIN: This tool can be used when trying to solve a problem that may have many types of solutions. It helps students understand that "if at first you don't succeed, try, try again" until you resolve the problem.

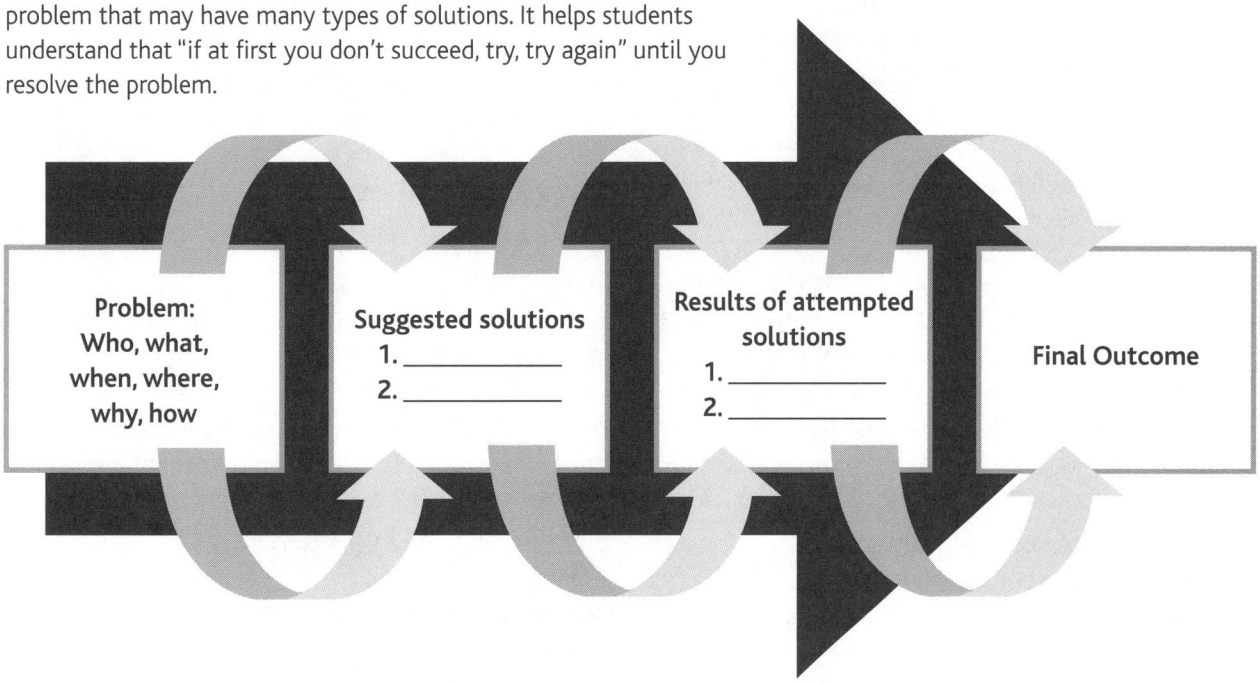

SERIES OF EVENTS: This tool is used when trying to define or describe the stages, steps, or events within a situation that lead to a solution. It can be useful in science (defining the steps in an experiment, or the life cycle of a butterfly), math (how to achieve an answer in a multi-step problem, clarifying a word problem), social studies (historical events that led to an outcome/revolt/new law), language arts (the series of events in a novel, the rise and fall of plot), graphic and performing arts (what led to a particular art style), physical education (how a game is played), or technical education (working on an "if/then" equation).

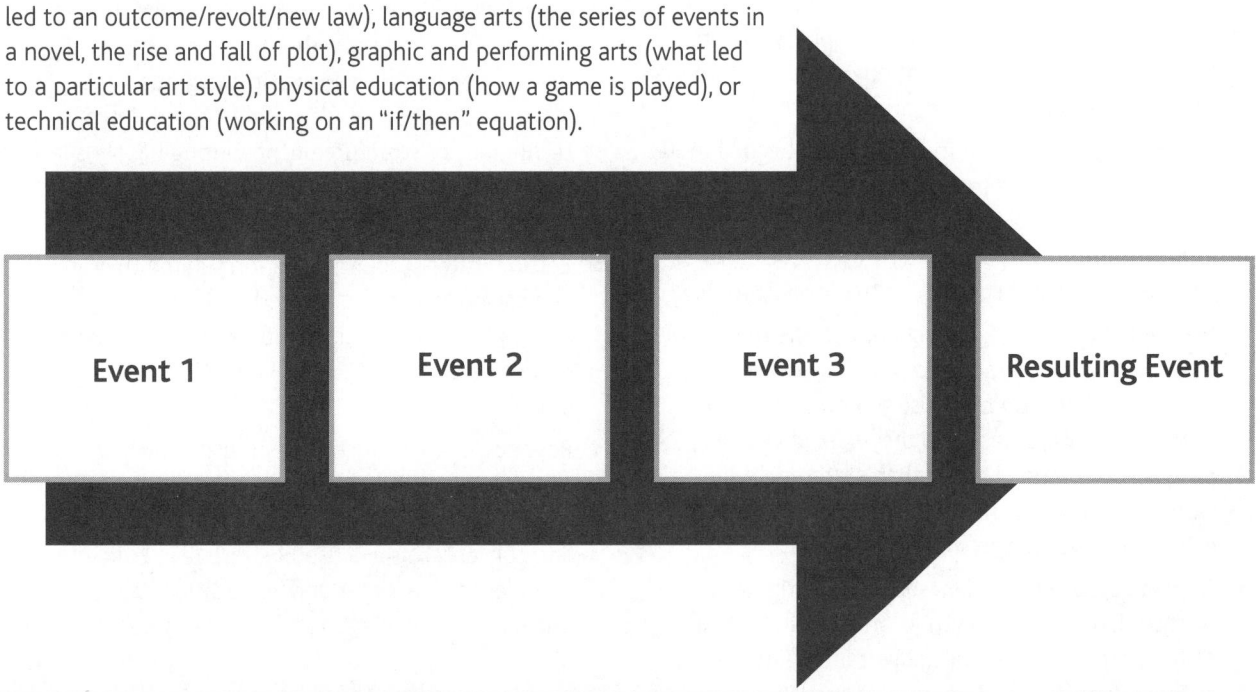

Critical Thinking Strategies in Reading

Reading critically is different from reading for pleasure. Students read critically to discover information. Using critical thinking strategies supports the students' efforts in validating the information. Critical thinking while reading helps students monitor their understanding of the information, recognize the author's point of view, and take into account assumptions and generalizations, all by utilizing their own prior experience with the information. Critical reading requires readers to be active, careful, and reflective about what they are reading. The reader must stand back from the text, distance themselves from the emotions or beliefs it contains, and validate the evidence that supports the author's line of thinking. Critical thinking in reading requires the readers to:

- read for the central idea or purpose of the text
- identify the audience for which the text was written or intended
- understand the historical, political, social, and economic context of the writing
- recognize the discipline within which the text was positioned

Specific critical thinking strategies for reading:

- **Scanning or previewing:** Students look for specific words or repeated words in the table of contents, section or chapter headings, and introduction or conclusion paragraphs. This is also an effective strategy to pique interest in the topic.
- **Skimming:** Students read the text quickly the first time through and focus attention on the main points and ideas for further investigating.
- **Annotating or note taking:** As readers begin a more in-depth or intensive read of the text, they should take notes that succinctly summarize the main ideas in each section. They should also write questions or comments that will suggest further investigation.
- **Highlighting:** Using a highlighter, readers may want to draw attention to specific words or phrases. Be careful students don't overuse this strategy, as not everything is important and they shouldn't end up citing entire sections rather than statements. Key words or sentences that may support or provide evidence for validation should be selected.
- **Contextualizing:** Readers should investigate the historical, political, economic, and social context of the writing for greater understanding of the author's lens.
- **Reflecting:** Students should take notes of their thoughts and reflections on their own beliefs and values and compare and contrast them with the author's.
- **Evaluating arguments:** After substantial reading of the text, students should begin to evaluate the author's arguments or ideas. At this point readers may find other sources that support or oppose the author's point of view.

Critical Thinking Strategies in Writing

The act of critical thinking in writing cannot be isolated from that of critical thinking in reading. As students write they should be aware that the reader will be reading their text with a critical eye. In order to communicate effectively through writing, students must keep in mind that judgments, interpretations, arguments, or opinions will need to be supported not only through quality writing structures but also through effective thinking.

Specific critical thinking strategies for writing:

- **Free writing:** Students write nonstop for a period of time (10–15 minutes) without stopping to make corrections, cross anything out, or critique their thoughts. This type of "stream of consciousness" writing gets students more comfortable with the act of writing, allows for a flow of ideas, and uncovers new ideas.
- **Group discussion:** This technique brings small groups of students together to discuss the writing of either one or all students in the group. Students act as peer editors of ideas only. The editing of techniques or structure of the writing happens later. Students collectively discuss how the ideas are formed, supported, and argued.
- **Editing:** After students have formulated their ideas and structured and supported their arguments, they are ready to have their writing edited. This can be done by a peer or teacher. The editing process is one of collaboration with the editor and the writer.
- **Peer review:** This technique is also known as refereeing. Individual students submit their text to peers to be scrutinized for form, structure, and content. This is a useful strategy in building confidence as a writer and helps students understand how powerful their writing can become.

- **Publication:** Students should have the experience of making their text public. When they subject their writing to publication, they are putting their ideas in view of others for critique and discussion. Publication can take many forms: classroom displays; writing contests; submissions to newspapers, magazines, websites, or professional journals; and submissions to classroom or school publications.

Critical Thinking Strategies in Mathematics

The curricular area of mathematics naturally lends itself to the use and development of critical thinking. During the mathematics process, a student has a need to concisely articulate mathematical meaning, make decisions, solve problems, draw conclusions, use logical/deductive reasoning, and recognize known and unknown facts, among other needs. Some students may use a commonsense approach to solving math problems, while other students need direct attention paid to the appropriate usage of particular critical thinking strategies that are most effective in solving problems. Therefore, you should embed the instruction of critical thinking strategies in mathematics on a consistent basis.

Specific critical thinking strategies for mathematics:

- Justify answers or conclusions
- Check assumptions and facts
- Sort and discard irrelevant facts or information
- Estimate realistic solutions
- Reflect, rethink, and rework
- Comprehend and analyze information
- Do logic and math puzzles
- Decode messages or cryptograms
- Play Sudoku
- Design magic squares
- Work with fractals
- Take part in a math competition
- Join a math team

Critical Thinking Strategies in Science

Like mathematics, science naturally lends itself to critical thinking. Every day, we try to understand the world around us. Scientific thinking *is* critical thinking. The methods used in science—observing, describing, hypothesizing, predicting, testing, experimenting, evaluating, and reporting—all require the use of critical thinking. We also use critical thinking when evaluating scientific claims, such as those in advertisements, opinions, or media.

Specific critical thinking for science:

- Identify problems worth solving
- Use evidence to support claims
- Access relevant data and information
- Be able to control data
- Be able to validate evidence by repetition
- Avoid subjective thinking
- View unreliable information with skepticism
- Be aware of specious arguments
- Use logical reasoning
- Avoid fallacies
- Judge the ethical and moral decisions made with science
- Anticipate the consequences of scientific claims
- Complete science fair projects
- Undertake independent investigations
- Debate controversial issues (for example, evolution, abortion, stem-cell research, etc.)
- Read science mysteries/play Crime Scene Investigations games
- Take part in science competitions

Seven Critical Questioning Strategies to Use Daily

A wonderful strategy to use with students is to offer them critical thinking questions to ponder. This can be done as a sponge activity, before class begins (to get their brains in gear), or during class for those students who finish first, or it can be infused within the content or assessments. Critical thinking questions can even be used on bulletin boards or posters. Students can keep a journal of their responses to the questions and share these responses at conference time or include them in a portfolio assessment of their thinking.

Following are a list of the critical thinking question types and several examples for each type.

1. Analogy

Analogy is the cognitive process of transforming information from one context to another. Developing analogous thinking is an important step in creative production and innovation as well as critical thinking.

Try using a concept (abstract) and a person/place/thing (concrete), as follows.

▶ **Sample questions and activities:**
How is a car (concrete) like an idea (abstract)?

How is a house like a storm?

How is an airplane like a thought?

How is a playground like democracy?

How is a turtle like an education?

How is a bus like awareness?

How is a classroom like indoctrination?

How is a rug like insight?

How is a sidewalk like a paradox?

How is a desk like a perception?

▶ **Or, turn it around:**
How is change like school?

How are systems like a computer?

How is tragedy like a book?

How is joy like a candy bar?

How is conflict like a clock?

How is conversation like a strawberry?

How is migration like a tomato?

How are rituals like a movie?

How is wisdom like a state capital?

How is courage like a cup?

▶ **Or, have students create an analogy** that would explain a novel, a concept, or their state capitol, city, or school.

2. Analysis of Point of View

In the study of historical documents or nonfiction materials, such as reports, research studies, newspaper or magazine articles, or websites, knowing the point of view of the author or creator is critical to the interpretation of the validity or foundation of the information. Knowing the factors that surround the document—how, where, when, why, and for what purpose it was produced—as well as whether the document was meant for public or private consumption, provides the reader multiple lenses through which to view the information.

▶ **Sample questions:**
What biases does the author represent in this article?

How does the author portray his or her point of view?

In what ways can you identify the assumptions of the author?

Why might this author see things the way she or he does?

How might this author's point of view change if he or she were . . . ?

How might someone else see this issue?

What are the various perspectives one could have on this writing?

What economic/cultural/historical/personal context contributed to the author's point of view?

What makes this author's point of view important?

What insights can you gain from this author's point of view?

3. Complete an Incomplete

When not all the facts are in place, the learner must use prior knowledge and other resources to complete the problem-solving process. Questioning an incompletion is a sophisticated level of questioning, as the learner must have a solid foundation of both experiential and factual information.

▶ **Sample questions and activities:**
Find the missing numbers in this sequence: 20, __, 16, __, 12, __.

Fill in the missing word in this sentence: George Read, Benjamin Rush, and John Adams were all____.

The Scientific Method:

1. Ask a question

2. _____

3. Construct a hypothesis

4. _____

5. Analyze your data

6. Communicate your results

Name the two missing steps and tell why they are important.

4. Webbing

Webbing is an excellent tool that can help students see the "ripple effect" of an issue or conflict. Students can also use webbing as an analysis tool to uncover and mine into the complex interrelated causes and effects that develop from one source. This questioning strategy is useful for visual/spatial learners and for those students needing assistance in "unpacking" their thinking.

▶ Sample questions and activities:

Graphically represent the effects of Hurricane Katrina, the recession, the gun laws in your state, etc.

Map out the relationships of all the characters in a particular novel.

Create a graphic organizer or thinking map to show where your lunch comes from.

Create a social web to represent your connections to all students in the classroom. (Social webs are similar to webbing in that students place themselves at the center of the web and connect themselves to others in the classroom.)

Create a drawing to show the impact of global warming on your school.

Diagram the effects of the war in Iraq.

Diagram how technology has changed your life.

5. Hypothetical Thinking

This is a sophisticated level of thinking that requires the learner to use logical questioning and abstract thinking. When thinking hypothetically, the student learns to investigate problems in a careful and systematic fashion.

▶ Sample questions and activities:

What if there is no rain this summer?

What would happen if the schools ran out of money?

What would be the outcome if school ran all year long?

How might this experiment come out?

What if all modes of transportation were limited to bicycles?

How would life change if you had three legs?

What if a gallon of milk cost $10?

In what ways would society change if immigration were not allowed?

What would your life be like if you had a choice whether or not to attend school?

6. Reversal of Thinking

This is an effective strategy to stimulate new thinking or when a student is "stuck in a rut." The process reframes the information and allows the student to look at the problem from a different point of view.

▶ Sample questions and activities:

Suppose the loser of the political race actually won. In what ways would legislation change?

From the perspective of a parent, what are the important factors to consider when sending your child to school?

How is life different in countries where an education is not a legal right?

How has life changed in Afghanistan since 2001?

7. Application of Different Symbol Systems

This strategy is effective when working with learners who think in a more visual manner, especially boys. It also forces learners to step outside their comfort zones to transform information in more than just a written symbol system. Students may transform an arithmetic problem into musical notes, the theme of a poem into chemical elements, a historical event into a mathematical equation, or a scientific theory into an editorial cartoon.

▶ Sample questions and activities:

Act out a math problem.

Draw a picture without words that represents the Gettysburg Address.

Sketch the ideas in your essay.

Use movement to show your understanding of gravity.

Use vectors (line segments with directional arrows) to represent all forces acting on a car traveling at constant velocity.

Make sounds or music to depict a character, situation, or theme in a novel.

Critical Thinking Tools

Following are several specific tools that help build critical thinking skills. The idea behind these tools is that critical thinking is a fluid activity and requires students to think beyond themselves and consider multiple factors when forming responses. After using any of these tools, students should debrief the process they followed and reflect on the thinking that occurred.

PNI: Positive, Negative, Interesting

The PNI (page 142) helps students frame their thinking by asking them to think of positive, negative, and interesting or intriguing ideas about a statement or item. Using the PNI (sometimes called the PMI: plus, minus, interesting) can ferret out students' points of view on a subject, reveal their own assumptions and generalizations, incorporate cause and effect logic, and separate fact from opinion. The PNI also requires students to use both deductive and inductive reasoning.

Figure 9.5 on page 143 shows how the tool can be introduced to lower grade students. For very young students, have them use simple shapes to develop an understanding of positive/negative and interesting characteristics of each shape. Start with a circle. Using a large sheet of paper, have students divide the paper into three columns and three rows, creating nine boxes. Next, have the students label the far left column with a plus sign (+), the middle column with a minus sign (-), and the far right column with a question mark (?).

- Focusing the students' attention on the left-hand column, ask them: "What are some examples of positive (good) circles?" The students should then draw in examples of those things that make a circle positive, such as a smiley face, lollipop, or the planet Earth.
- Turning to the middle column, ask students: "What are some examples of negative (bad) circles?" Students can then draw in examples such as a sad face, pothole, or an ink stain.
- Moving to the far right column, ask students: "What are some examples of what makes a circle interesting?" Students may come up with ideas such as, "A circle has no corners to hide in," "It's hard to draw an exact circle," or "Circles are used to represent life."

Expand from simple shapes in the first chart (with circles) to ideas generated by the curriculum in the second chart (with statements generated from a Frog and Toad book).

Figure 9.6 on page 144 shows an example of how this tool can be used for upper grades as a note-taking device regarding a statement from the curriculum (*December 18, 1865: Slavery was abolished in the United States*). You may also consider using this tool to discuss current events.

The PNI can be used as an individual thinking tool, sponge activity, brain warmup, or whole class activity. You may also think about using this design as a bulletin board in your classroom. I suggest placing the bulletin board near your classroom door, so students can write on it while waiting in line to leave class. Write a statement on the board that gets students actively engaged in serious discussions. You can leave the statement up for several days or weeks to see how students' thinking, opinions, and ideas on one statement can change over time.

CAI: Consider All the Issues

A more advanced level of the PNI is the Consider All the Issues (CAI) tool (see page 145). With this tool, students not only are using the PNI method, they are adding in specific facts to consider in relation to a particular issue. CAI can be a useful tool to help students consider all the relevant factors that can inform their decision making. It can be used when the students need to decide an action, plan an event, or predict an outcome. To develop students' abilities to use the CAI effectively, begin by offering them a practice scenario.

Sample CAI Scenario

After much financial planning, the school district has to cut $1 million from its budget. To balance the budget for the coming school year, the school board has decided to close one elementary school. This would mean that students from the closed school would be sent to at least three different school buildings in the next year. Many families are opposed to this option. A senior organization has agreed to buy the school building once it has closed to use as a senior center. What factors should be taken into consideration when deciding which school to close?

Another possible scenario:

A major pharmaceutical company has developed a pill that can increase intelligence. Your school is considering testing the pill. What should be considered?

Students can work on this issue either individually or in groups. Or, students can work individually on the CAI, then meet with a partner to compare ideas, and continue to meet with up to four new partners to share ideas. After the students have shared their CAI with at least five partners, reunite the class to create a class CAI on the scenario.

PL: Priority Ladder

We are often confronted with issues that are complex and have multiple causes. The Priority Ladder is a useful tool in helping students align their thinking about complex issues and put the multiple causes into a sequence of least to most relevant. This tool may be useful when using the CAI, in that the students must justify the order of factors and the amount of attention or weight each factor should receive. As with the CAI, students can use this tool individually, with partners, in small groups, or as a class.

Sample PL Activities

Students examine the contents of their desk and rank the contents from least to most valuable in solving the following problems.

- math problem
- homework problem
- an issue with a classmate
- being stranded on a desert island
- being called to the principal's office

Another way to practice using the PL is to put students in small groups and have them use the following list of items to accomplish one of the following activities:

Items:

- battery
- paper clips
- pens/pencils
- notepaper
- rubber band
- ruler
- permanent markers
- string
- pushpins
- scissors

Activities:

- solve a math problem
- find your way home
- help you do your homework
- survive on a deserted island

Each team will share how they organized their list and why they put items in the list the way they did. Students will see many creative ways to use everyday items.

To develop your own activity like the previous one, open your junk drawer at home and list 10 items in the drawer. Create four to five distinctly different scenarios for which the students can prioritize the list.

Figure 9.7 on page 146 shows an example of a Priority Ladder. A blank template is included on page 147.

Synthesis 3+1

This tool takes the common 3-2-1 Exit/Entrance Ticket to the next level (see page 148). Students complete the 3-2-1 portion of the graphic, but also add their creative thinking by coming up with one analogy, metaphor, or simile to summarize what they learned in the unit or lesson.

Structured Thinking Organizer (STO)

This tool will help students organize information in multiple formats for easier memorizing (see page 149). You can use the STO as an exit ticket or an additional component in a formative or summative assessment. Students should use this tool as a note-taking device throughout a unit or lesson. The follow-up questions can be used as homework, test preparation, or questions on the final exam.

No Easy Answers

Students often assume that there are answers for everything, which is obviously not true. One way to show students that we (and they) don't have all the answers, that knowing everything is impossible, and that finding solutions can be difficult, is to provide a wall space in your classroom for a bulletin board titled, "Things We Don't Know" or "No Easy Answers."

Students can place sticky notes on the board containing their ideas, thoughts, and questions, or they can write directly on a large sheet of paper. This bulletin board can be directly related to a subject matter or to general daily life. Subject matter questions may be framed around controversial issues (such as stem-cell research, abortion, medical use of marijuana, or assisted suicide) or information the students have an interest in knowing. For daily life issues, students may ask questions such as "When will the recession end?" "How much will college cost by the time I graduate?" or "What is the best field of study for the future?" The bulletin board can be changed weekly, monthly, or kept up all year to see what kinds of questions and ideas students generate. If a question is answered, it is removed from the board.

Your students will vary in their degrees of sophistication when using any of the thinking tools and strategies listed in this chapter. Hence, it is essential for you to know where students are in the learning process, develop differentiated activities to scaffold students to higher levels of thinking, and provide students with differing avenues to show what they know. When students are skilled in critical thinking, they form meaningful questions, develop self-regulation, and can think for themselves.

Positive, Negative, Interesting (PNI)

Topic:

POSITIVE	NEGATIVE	INTERESTING

From *Advancing Differentiation: Thinking and Learning for the 21st Century* by Richard M. Cash, Ed.D., copyright © 2011. Free Spirit Publishing Inc., Minneapolis, MN; 800-735-7323; www.freespirit.com. This page may be reproduced for use within an individual school or district. For all other uses, contact www.freespirit.com/company/permissions.cfm.

Figure 9.5 PNI: Examples (Lower Grades)

What Makes a Circle Positive, Negative, or Interesting?

+	-	?

Toad wants to wait until tomorrow to clean his messy house.

POSITIVE	NEGATIVE	INTERESTING
He will not have to clean today.	His house will be messy.	What will happen if he puts off cleaning his house again tomorrow?
He won't have to spend all day inside the house.	He won't have clean dishes to eat from or a clean sofa to sit on.	What if Toad has company?
He can do other things that he wants to do.	His house will be even dirtier tomorrow, so it will take him longer to clean it.	Why does Toad procrastinate?

Figure 9.6 PNI: Example (Upper Grades)

December 18, 1865: Slavery was abolished in the United States.

POSITIVE	NEGATIVE	INTERESTING
Involuntary servitude was outlawed.	It resulted in a loss of income for those who made a living trafficking humans.	The 13th Amendment was the first constitutional amendment in 60 years.
The 13th Amendment led to the 14th and 15th Amendments (civil rights in the states & ban on racial restrictions of voting).	Social structures were not put in place to support freed slaves. Not much changed in the South for them and the Union Army could not offer much protection.	The abolishment of slavery was mainly associated with the Republican party.
This began the Era of Reconstruction.	Andrew Johnson, Lincoln's successor, had little interest in helping freed slaves.	Laws were passed after the 13th Amendment that actually kept slaves in poverty.

Consider All the Issues (CAI)

ISSUE	PLUS	MINUS	INTERESTING

From *Advancing Differentiation: Thinking and Learning for the 21st Century* by Richard M. Cash, Ed.D., copyright © 2011. Free Spirit Publishing Inc., Minneapolis, MN; 800-735-7323; www.freespirit.com. This page may be reproduced for use within an individual school or district. For all other uses, contact www.freespirit.com/company/permissions.cfm.

Figure 9.7 Priority Ladder: Example

Issue: The school board has decided to close one elementary school in the community.

MOST IMPORTANT

Savings of up to $1,000,000 each year

No teacher lay-offs

Goodwill in the community

Students may have to be bused to new school site

School community is disrupted

Parents upset with board's decision and won't vote for board members

The building to be closed needs many repairs

The building may be needed in the future if community grows

Negative impact on neighborhood home values

What to do with all of the fixtures in the building?

Neighbors of the school like having the children present

Local residents would have to go to another site to vote

LEAST IMPORTANT

Priority Ladder

Issue:	MOST IMPORTANT
	LEAST IMPORTANT

From *Advancing Differentiation: Thinking and Learning for the 21st Century* by Richard M. Cash, Ed.D., copyright © 2011. Free Spirit Publishing Inc., Minneapolis, MN; 800-735-7323; www.freespirit.com. This page may be reproduced for use within an individual school or district. For all other uses, contact www.freespirit.com/company/permissions.cfm.

Synthesis 3 +1

1 Analogy, Metaphor, or Simile for Topic

1 Question

2 Connections

3 New Bits of Learning

From *Advancing Differentiation: Thinking and Learning for the 21st Century* by Richard M. Cash, Ed.D., copyright © 2011. Free Spirit Publishing Inc., Minneapolis, MN; 800-735-7323; www.freespirit.com. This page may be reproduced for use within an individual school or district. For all other uses, contact www.freespirit.com/company/permissions.cfm.

Structured Thinking Organizer (STO)

Directions:

1. On the left side of the triangle, write an analogy for the information presented.
   Then, explain why you chose this analogy.
2. On the right side of the triangle, write an analogy to define the *opposite* of the information presented. Explain why you chose this analogy.
3. Inside the triangle, draw a picture to represent the information presented. (The picture should *not* be an exact replica of the information.)
4. At the end of the unit of study, answer the five follow-up questions beneath the triangle.

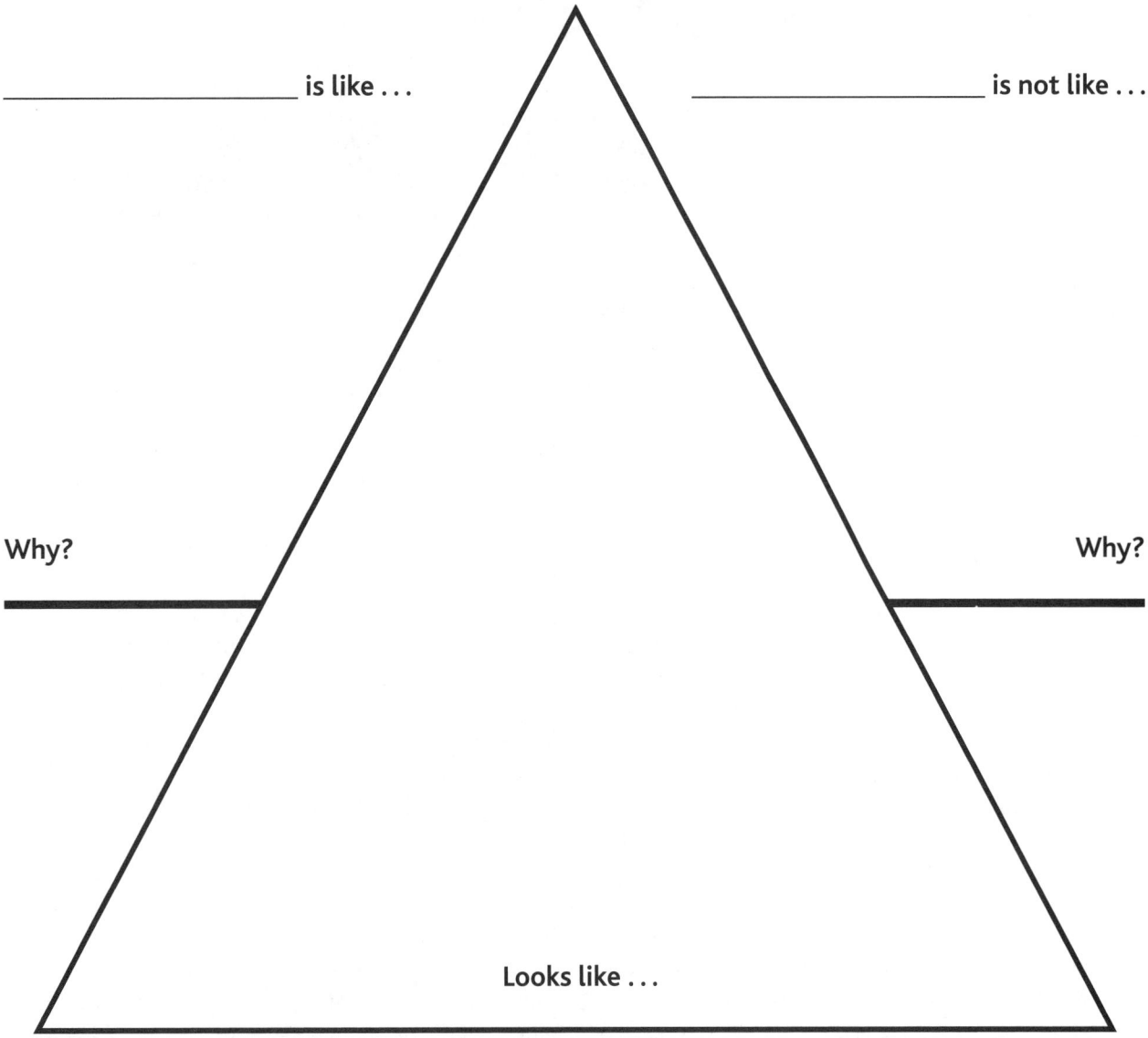

Follow-Up Questions

1. What did you already know about this topic?
2. How can you connect this topic to your everyday life?
3. How would you explain this topic to another person?
4. What patterns do you see?
5. What new ideas did you come up with?

From *Advancing Differentiation: Thinking and Learning for the 21st Century* by Richard M. Cash, Ed.D., copyright © 2011. Free Spirit Publishing Inc., Minneapolis, MN; 800-735-7323; www.freespirit.com. This page may be reproduced for use within an individual school or district. For all other uses, contact www.freespirit.com/company/permissions.cfm.

Chapter 10

Creative Thinking: Stepping Outside the Box

> We are all creative, but by the time we are three or four years old, someone has knocked the creativity out of us. Some people shut up the kids who start to tell stories. Kids dance in their cribs, but someone will insist they sit still. By the time the creative people are 10 or 12, they want to be like everyone else.
>
> —*Maya Angelou, author*

Recent studies suggest that levels of creativity have declined in the United States.[1] The reasons for this decline may be related to schools being overwhelmed by the mandating of standards and assessments, making it difficult for teachers to efficiently infuse creativity into curriculum and instruction. Additionally, some feel that the skills of creativity are limited to art and music classes, which are being eliminated in many schools in these hard financial times.

Creativity, the act of producing something original and useful, is an essential skill for the twenty-first century and considered to be the number-one competency for leadership. Europe and Asia have placed substantial emphasis on idea generation and creative thinking in order to position themselves as world leaders economically, politically, and culturally. As we consider our students' futures, it is critical that we view creativity not only as a vital learning tool, but also as a crucial component in national confidence and success.

Brilliant researchers have authored many books on creativity—where it comes from and how to develop it. There are also substantial resources available to teachers that directly teach the art of creativity. My intent in this book is to offer a general overview of the idea of creativity; characteristics of creative individuals; general strategies of creativity; and how creativity can be infused within your daily routine, lessons, and curriculum. Creativity is natural to every person, but for many, this natural inclination toward creativity gets suppressed throughout their years in school. When we ask students for that one right answer, or we test them on reaching the correct solution, we may be inadvertently stifling the creative process. I am not suggesting that finding the right answer is not important, but that our heavy reliance on close-ended solutions is not reflective of thinking for the twenty-first century.

Students have access to all kinds of information instantaneously. Finding a solution to a problem can be as simple and quick as a click of a button. Creativity and creative thinking compel us to take time, think things through, wait until we have considered all the different options, stand back to see our ideas from a distance, and finally to ponder "what next." From the invention of the light bulb to space travel, creativity is what has enabled our society to advance and succeed. Demanding that our students master creative thinking will ensure our continued success.

1 "The Creativity Crisis" by Po Bronson and Ashley Merryman, *Newsweek*, July 10, 2010. Cited research by Dr. Kyung Hee Kim at the College of William and Mary.

What Is Creative Thinking?

Creativity is an essential ingredient that makes entrepreneurs, mathematicians, business leaders, artists, musicians, teachers, doctors, lawyers, and everyday people successful. Being able to think creatively is what distinguishes those who can do the job from those who can do the job better. But what exactly *is* creativity? We may "know it when we see it," but how do we help students master it if we can't specifically define it? This chapter provides some descriptions of creativity and strategies for how to engage students in being more creative and thinking more creatively.

Creative Thinking Is Making Something New or Improved

In general, creativity is the mental process used to imagine or invent through combining, changing, or reshaping existing ideas. In the simplest term: it is *the ability to make something new.* Creative individuals see multiple ways to solve problems. They are limber thinkers who are able to produce innovative products, ideas, and solutions. Creativity is also a process of refining and improving ideas and solutions. Creative ideas and products usually do not happen in a flash. The most creative innovations are the result of hard work, patience, persistence, and perseverance.

Creative Thinking Is the Opposite of Critical Thinking

Creative thinking can also be thought of as the flip side to critical reasoning. Whereas the main goal of critical reasoning is to come to one conclusion, the goal of creative thinking is to explore many ideas, generate several possibilities, and look for many "right" answers. Both types of thinking are vital to a successful life and required in solving problems. Providing students the opportunity to hone the skills of creative thinking will help them develop tools to deal with new problems and situations. These tools will allow them to find answers that are not in books or at websites, create ideas that have not been considered, and apply new information in constructive ways.

Creative Thinking Is Inclusive and Aware

The act of creative thinking requires us to look, ask, and seek new ideas and answers. It inspires us to open our eyes to the world around us and see it with wonder. Creative thinkers have an awareness of those things that others miss. Creativity also requires the use of all our senses to accept many kinds of stimuli. Most importantly, creativity does not happen in a vacuum; it requires the multiple voices and views of others. Sir Kenneth Robinson, a leading authority in creativity, states that most original thinking comes through collaboration and being stimulated by other people's ideas.[2] Collaboration, diversity, the exchange of ideas, and building on others' achievements is at the heart of the creative process.

> Creativity does not happen in a vacuum. It requires the multiple voices and views of others.

Creative Thinking Is Both Convergent and Divergent

In Chapter 7, two types of thinking were discussed: convergent thinking and divergent thinking. In summary, convergent thinking is the thinking that brings together information from various sources so that a solution can be found. Decisions are based on the facts coming toward an answer (see Figure 7.1). Whereas divergent thinking is intuitive, open-minded, and generative of many solutions (see Figure 7.2). Creativity is not always about coming up with the wackiest or most far-fetched ideas, nor is it aimless thinking. For an idea to work, it has to be doable, reasonable, and provide an outcome that is reliable. Therefore, to be an effective creative thinker, both convergent and divergent thinking are required. Divergent thinking opens up the possibilities and convergent thinking ensures the solution or idea is workable.

2 Azzam, Amy M. "Why Creativity Now? A Conversation with Sir Ken Robinson." *Teaching for the 21st Century.* September 2009, Volume 67, No. 1, pp. 22–26.

Characteristics of Creative Individuals

Dr. Robert Sternberg promotes the idea of making creativity a habit, something that all students should be expected to do. He states, "The main things that promote the habit are (a) opportunities to engage in it, (b) encouragement when people avail themselves of these opportunities, and (c) rewards when people respond to such encouragement and think and behave creatively."[3] Following are the general characteristics of creative individuals as well as ideas for developing these characteristics in your students.

Creative Individuals Are Motivated

Students who are internally motivated are driven to seek out problems and find interesting solutions to those problems. Creative thinkers are motivated to know how things work, why things don't work, and how to make things work better. Creativity takes that drive to solve problems in a new way. Chapter 4 explains motivation in more detail.

Creative Individuals Have a Solid Knowledge Base

To be effective at creativity, a student must have a solid understanding of the content area. One cannot solve problems or make things better without a wide range of knowledge, both within the content area as well as across other content areas. This interconnectivity of knowledge allows the individual to create variations or combinations of ideas. For instance, having a solid knowledge base is especially important for creativity in mathematics. Mathematicians think flexibly and are able to efficiently problem solve because of their insights into and understanding of the workings of mathematics, not just due to their computational skills.

Creative Individuals Enjoy Challenges

Being creative is not necessarily an easy act. Creativity usually requires a lot of trial and error. If students do not have the inclination toward challenge, or have not faced intellectual challenges throughout their learning, creativity may be difficult. This is why some gifted or advanced learners are unwilling to be creative. They lack the resourcefulness of being able to cope with challenge and not succeeding instantly. Creative individuals must be willing to take on the challenge of finding new solutions and question their own beliefs, ideas, and assumptions. They also must be aware that they may not reach a conclusion quickly, nor come up with the right solution initially.

Creative Individuals Show Patience, Persistence, and Perseverance (P^3)

Our world today is one of instant gratification. We don't have to wait long before we find an answer (Google.com, Ask.com), eat a meal (fast food, microwave dinners), hear from a friend (social media, text messages, cell phones), or watch our favorite show whenever we want (TiVo, Hulu). Today's students have generally become less patient and often lack persistence and the ability to persevere at a task that doesn't have a quick and easy solution.

Creativity is hard work and requires the P^3 behaviors of patience, persistence, and perseverance. (See page 76). While there are no quick and easy answers, being able to stimulate creative thinking quickly is necessary. However, as previously stated, creative thinking requires a solid knowledge base—this takes time and patience to build. Creative thinkers also must enjoy the challenge of creating—this takes determination. And they must not settle for the single "right" answer—this takes perseverance and stick-to-it-ness.

Creative Thinking Strategies

Building creativity in the classroom takes many forms. From brainstorming ideas for a writing assignment, to predicting an outcome of a science experiment, to an independent study, students are using creative thinking skills and talents every day in the classroom. In many cases students don't even know they are being creative. By raising the students' awareness of creativity, you can help them understand the power of creative thought. To raise your students' creative consciousness, you must infuse specific and directed creative thinking activities and exercises into your daily lessons. Introduce the activities as "creativity building" activities. Students need to be consciously aware of these activities and know there is an expectation of open-mindedness, novelty, and unconventional thought.

One approach to developing creative thinking is through the four best-known creative thinking strategies: *fluency, flexibility, originality,* and *elaboration* (or, *FFOE*). These strategies may be used individually or in combination. The following activities and ideas can be used as "sponge" activities (to be used when you have a few minutes left and you want students to soak up all

3 Sternberg, Robert. "Creativity Is a Habit." *Education Week*, February 22, 2006.

the learning they can), warmups to thinking, or as "brain breaks" (see Chapter 4, page 47). Engaging students in these strategies, both imbedded within the curriculum and as independent activities, can develop their habits of creative thinking and provide incentive for them to use creative thinking more often.

Encourage Fluency

Fluency is the action of coming up with as many ideas as possible. Encouraging fluency can help students overcome their anxiety of finding that "one right answer." Fluency activities can also be thought of as brainstorming. Brainstorming requires that in a group:

1. All members participate in some way, either in generating ideas or respectful listening.
2. All ideas are considered; there is no judgment (either positive or negative) and no put-downs.
3. All members work as quickly as possible; taking time to think through an idea may stifle creativity and encourage self-criticism.
4. All members listen to others' ideas and build on them.

Activities That Stimulate Fluency

- List as many [insert color] things as you can.
- List all the things you can think of that are [insert adjective].
- List all the things that come in pairs [or in threes, fours, etc].
- List as many compound words as you can.
- List as many three-syllable words as you can.
- List words that start with the letter [insert letter].
- List words that end with the letter [insert letter].
- List words with the [insert vowel or consonant] sound.
- List all the things that involve [insert concept; for example, truth, love, justice, independence].
- List things that are framed.
- List things that shine.
- List things that inspire.
- List things that open [or close].
- List activities for [insert season].
- List the possible uses for [insert object].
- List ways to represent [insert number or math concept].
- List the questions you would ask [insert person; for example, the President of the United States, Albert Einstein, Georgia O'Keefe].
- List all the things you might see at a [insert place].
- List things that can only be used once.
- List things that come in multiple colors.
- List items included on a road map.
- List things that are uneven.
- List ways our culture has been influenced by ideas or inventions of ancient civilizations.
- List items that use the metric system as a method of measurement.
- List ways to say hello in as many languages as you can.
- List all the ways to solve [insert problem].

Develop Flexibility

Flexibility is the ability to adapt to new situations and try various ways to approach and solve problems. It means not accepting the first and most obvious solution. It teaches students to look at problems and ideas from many different angles and perspectives. Questions that can stimulate flexibility are, "What other kinds of . . . ?" "What else does . . . ?" "What's another way to . . . ?

Activities and Questions That Stimulate Flexibility

- How many different ways can you categorize these items?
- Create a metaphor for . . .
- Use a metaphor/simile/analogy to describe . . .
- What items could be bought at a discount store that could be used to build a house?
- What items could be bought at a grocery store that could be used to stop a flood?
- What items could be bought at a hardware store that could be used to make a dress?
- What items might you find in a garage that could be used to tame a lion?
- How many different ways can you use a pencil?
- What's another way to solve this problem?
- What's another way to look at . . . ?
- What's another way to use . . . ?
- How else can you . . . ?
- Where else might you find . . . ?
- Show a different way to represent your answer.

Emphasize Originality

The concept of *lateral thinking*—the process of consciously changing your perspective in order to come up with an original idea—is another valuable strategy in creative thinking. Originality is the development of unique, unusual, and novel ideas. Novelty in thinking can be difficult for students because they may believe that "everything has already been thought of," or they may take the easy way out by using others' ideas. Being original or novel does not always mean coming up with something totally new. It can also mean taking an old idea or product and giving it a twist so that the outcome is distinctive.

Activities and Questions That Stimulate Originality

- From your list of items, which item did no one else think of?
- From your list of items, which item do you think is the most unique?
- Create a new use for a [insert object].
- Design a new use for [insert object].
- Share the most unusual occasion for writing a note or letter to someone.
- Create a new ending for [insert novel or film].
- Construct a workable plan for a new gardening tool.
- Design a device to clean a messy room.

Inspire Elaboration

Elaboration is the process of providing extensive and extended details. When students are pushed to "color in all the white spaces," they develop a more holistic sensibility for solution finding. Elaboration requires expanding, embellishing, extending, refining, and stretching ideas. Creativity demands this refinement and continual improvement. For any common product or utensil, manufacturers are constantly making improvements by building upon the collective creativity of the previous model. Take, for instance, a car—each year, the new model includes improvements over the previous year's model. Car companies make these improvements based on continual evaluation to make their cars faster, sleeker, more comfortable, more efficient, and more tuned to our needs. Creative thinkers never stop trying to make their ideas better.

Activities and Questions That Stimulate Elaboration

- Choose a word from your list and elaborate on it by creating a story, picture, poem, or song.
- How can you make a pencil more effective or interesting?
- Elaborate on this shape [show a circle, squiggle, line, square, or other shape].
- Write what happened before the story begins of the *Three Little Pigs*, *Romeo and Juliet*, or *Call of the Wild*.
- Elaborate on the sentence: "The dog barked in the night."
- How would you change the game of [insert game] so it could be played . . . ? (for example, How would you change the game of baseball so it could be played under water?)
- Write a technical manual to build the world's best peanut butter and jelly sandwich.
- Explain how you arrived at your answer to [insert problem].
- Using numbers only, give someone directions to a location.
- A thief has stolen the "Mona Lisa" painting from the Louvre Museum in Paris. She used three items to help her steal the painting [list three unrelated items such as an ice cube, piano, and crowbar]. How did she do it?
- Which month is the heaviest? Why?
- Which day is the sweetest/most sour? Why?
- What hour is the tallest/widest/narrowest? Why?

Creative Thinking Activities

In addition to the activities listed under each *FFOE* strategy (fluency, flexibility, originality, elaboration), the following activities also help develop creative thinking skills by stimulating multiple *FFOE* strategies at once.

Activity: SCAMPER with Sparking Words

▶ Stimulates: flexibility, originality

(*sparking words* = words to spark kids' thinking)

S = Substitute

What could you substitute on a . . . to make it better?
Instead of . . . I could use . . .
What if I change . . . ?

Sparking words: alternate, exchange, fill-in, rename, replace, reposition, change, stand in for, swap, switch, take the place of, proxy, use instead of

C = Combine

What would you combine with . . . to make it better?
If I put . . . with . . . it will create . . .

Sparking words: merge, blend, bring together, commingle, conjoin, unite, join, coalesce, mix, associate, package

A = Adapt

What could you adapt on a . . . to make it better?
How can you adapt the idea of . . . ?
If I change . . . it will . . .

Sparking words: Change, alter, adjust, vary, amend, bend, fit, adapt, conform, copy, emulate, incorporate, transform

M = Modify (maximize/minimize)

How can I modify . . . to make it better?
Where might I put greater emphasis to make . . . better?
If I make . . . larger/smaller it will . . .

Sparking words: adapt, adjust, alter, change, grow, amend, vary, transform, mutate, curb, control, temper, modulate, make the most of, exploit, capitalize on, get the most out of, take advantage of, enlarge, increase, expand, amplify, make bigger, raise, enlarge, lengthen, heighten, boost, augment, extend, reduce, diminish, lessen, curtail, decrease, play down, make light of, shorten, stretch out, overemphasize, overstress, underemphasize

P = Put to other use

How might I use . . . differently to make it better?
I can use . . . in this way:_____.
How might . . . use . . . ?

Sparking words: employ, utilize, exercise, apply, exploit, draw on, operate, work, handle, treat, manipulate, manage, spend, expend, exhaust, use up, consume, function, purpose

E = Eliminate

What can I eliminate from . . . to make it better?
What could I simplify to make . . . better/more efficient?
If I eliminate . . . it will . . .

Sparking words: get rid of, do away with, eradicate, abolish, remove, reduce, purge, exclude, excrete, expel, exterminate, jettison, kill, lessen, limit, liquidate, lower, moderate, minimize, modulate, pass over/on, remove, reject, reduce, restrict, throw out, waste, wipe out/away

R = Revise (rearrange/reorder/reverse)

What can I revise to make . . . better?
If I revise . . . it can . . .

Sparking words: overturn, turn around, undo, annul, invalidate, repeal, quash, swap, transpose, switch, invert, change, opposite, contrary, converse, inverse, antithesis, other side, alter, modify, adjust, amend, correct, improve, rework, reorganize, reschedule, delay, reshuffle, regroup, restructure, sort out, alter, mix up, move around, mess up, upset, change around, undo, withdraw, transpose, move backwards/forwards/around

Activity: Squiggle

▶ Stimulates: fluency, flexibility, originality, elaboration

(*Variation:* Dot—the same activity but using a single sticky dot.)

1. With a black felt pen or marker, draw a random "squiggle" on a piece of paper for each student. The squiggle can be identical for every student or completely different for each student.
2. Give the paper to the students and direct them to elaborate on their squiggle to create an original drawing.
3. Be sure to encourage your students to turn the paper around to get a different perspective of the squiggle until an idea is sparked in their head.
4. Direct students to fill in "all the white spaces" and be as elaborate as they can.

5. Students should spend at least five minutes elaborating on their drawing. For those students with the "I'm done" syndrome, say:
   - Where might you add more colors or lines?
   - What objects could you add that might be around your object?
   - What objects could you add that might *not* typically be around your object?
   - How could you use SCAMPER to make your drawing more elaborate?
6. Have students share their drawings.
7. To extend the learning, ask:
   - What was most difficult about this activity?
   - What would make this task easier?
   - Why did you do what you did?
   - How could you use this technique in other classes?

Activity: Think Fast!

▶ Stimulates: fluency, flexibility

1. Collect an assortment of odd objects (such as: empty tin can, one foot of plastic tubing, spoon, slinky, drumstick, hair brush, paper towel tube, tennis ball), and place them into a large bag.
2. Arrange students in small groups of no more than 10.
3. To warm up, give each group one of the objects.
4. Have them pass the object around the group once without saying anything. They are to appraise the object using all of their senses (for example, What does/might it smell/taste/sound/look/feel like?) and then come up with at least one idea of what the object *could* be (not what it really is). For instance, the group with the drumstick may think of ideas such as a microphone, baton, or stirring rod.
5. On the second pass around, the students share with each other their idea. No one can repeat what someone else has said. If their idea was used, they will need to come up with another idea.
6. After students are warmed up, change the objects in the group and begin again.
7. This time have the students pass the object around the group instantly sharing their idea of what the object could be.
8. Again, change the object in each group and this time students must pass the object around stating what it could be, but doing it as quickly as possible. I use: "Ready, set, think fast!" to begin this round of the game.
9. The group that passes the object around fastest and comes up with all different ideas is considered the "winner."

Variations on this activity

- Instead of only passing the object around once, have the students try to pass it around the circle as many times as they can without repeating an idea. (flexibility, elaboration)
- After each round have the students decide which of the ideas was the most original. (originality)
- Have one student suggest what the object could be, and then the others elaborate on their idea (for example, drumstick = a baton . . . used by a world famous conductor . . . who was captured by evil spies . . . and taken to an underground hideaway . . . where he was found and rescued because his baton had magic powers that could lull his captors to sleep . . . and so on. (elaboration)
- Each group member gets a different object and must create a new idea for his or her object. The students then collaborate with each other to use the objects in a play-acted scene. (fluency, flexibility, originality, elaboration)
- Each group member gets a different object and works together with the group to come up with one combined object or new idea. (fluency, flexibility, originality, elaboration)
- Each group member must pantomime (using no words or sounds) their idea for an object to get others to guess what the student has created. (fluency, flexibility, elaboration)

Activity: ROLE Cards

▶ **Encourages: fluency, flexibility, originality, elaboration**

1. Using four different color index cards, create four categories:

ROLE	OCCASION	LOCATION	EMOTION
Farmer	Birthday	At a lake	Happy
Banker	Wedding	In a castle	Sad
Server	Funeral	In a car	Tired
Dog catcher	Party	In a cave	Angry
Writer	Religious event	In a haunted house	Bored
Artist	Dinner	In a restaurant	Disgusted
Scientist	Breakfast	On a bus	Calm
Mathematician	Senate hearing	In the woods	Crabby
Inventor	Business meeting	In a grocery store	Smug
Juror	Trial	In school	Snide
Judge	Fundraiser	In a hospital	Excited
Historian	Prom	On a street	Frightened
Reporter	Halloween	In the zoo	Kind
Soldier	Kentucky derby	In a barn	Jealous
Therapist	Book signing	In an office	Worried
Journalist	Graduation	At the beach	Upset
Character from a novel	Event in a novel	Location in novel	Emotion in a novel

2. Divide the students into groups of four or small teams.
3. Have the groups pull one card randomly from each of the four ROLE categories.
4. Each group develops a scene based on the ROLE cards they have drawn.
5. Allow the groups 5 to 10 minutes to collaborate on their scene. Tell the groups they are *not* to use the words written on the ROLE cards.
6. Have students present their scene to the other groups.
7. The other groups try to guess what ROLE cards the group chose.

Variations on this activity

- Each student draws one card from each category and writes his or her own story using the ROLE cards as guides. (elaboration, originality)
- In teams, students create their own ROLE cards and swap with another team. (flexibility, originality, elaboration)
- Using a work of literature, students create ROLE cards to rewrite the ending (elaboration) or create the prequel (elaboration, originality).
- After all groups have performed, the class votes on which scene was the most original. (originality)
- The class receives the same randomly drawn ROLE cards and each student must create a story or scene based on the four cards. (elaboration, originality)
- Each student in a small group draws one ROLE card from each category and must create one scene using all the descriptors. (elaboration, originality)

Activity: What's the Question?

▶ Stimulates: fluency, flexibility, originality, elaboration

This game, like the game Jeopardy, begins with the answer and requires the students to provide the question. The intent of this game is to help students understand and appreciate that there may be more than one right answer to any question. Using the ROLE cards, give the "answer" to the students. Individually, in pairs, in small groups, or as a whole class, students come up with the most original, unique, or novel "question" to match the answer.

Example:

You: "Farmer."

Students: "Who is outstanding in their field?"

Variations on this activity

- Instead of using the ROLE cards, have students create their own "answers" using the most obscure information they can find. For example, Answer: "Westmoreland." Question: "Ralph deNeville was the First Earl of what?" (*Note:* This variation requires substantial research. Therefore, students will need ample time to find the questions—up to one week.)
- For younger students, use content information as a form of review. For example, Answer: "Winter." Question: "What season is the sun closest to the Earth?"
- For a math variation: use equations. For example, Answer: "9." Question: "What is (3 x 12) – (3 x 9)?"

Activity: Everyday Art View

▶ Stimulates: fluency, flexibility, originality, elaboration

1. Post a reprint of a famous work of art.
2. Next to the work of art, post a list of questions that are used as either "sponge" activities, writing prompts, or discussion builders/guides.

Sample fluency activities

- List all the things you identify in this painting.
- List all the feelings you have when you view this painting.
- List all the colors you see in this painting.
- List questions for the artist about this painting.
- List all the things you think about when you view this painting.

Sample flexibility activities and questions

- Put the items you have identified from this painting into categories.
- Create a metaphor, simile, or analogy to describe this painting.
- The artist titled this painting _____. What other title might you give the painting, and why?
- If we turn the painting on its side, what might you see?
- Besides a museum, where might you find a painting like this?

Sample originality questions

- What is the most unique component of this work of art?
- Where is the most unusual place you might find a work of art such as this?
- What would be the most original way to view this work of art?
- Why is this work of art original?
- How does this work of art stimulate your imagination?

Sample elaboration activities and questions

- Write a poem, story, song, or sentence about this painting.
- What happened right before/after the scene represented in this painting?
- On a blank piece of paper, use two of the colors from this painting to create an extension of the painting.
- Why do you think the artist used the colors or ideas he or she did?
- Design a frame that would highlight the most important aspects of this painting, and explain your design.

Activity: Name 5

▶ Stimulates: flexibility, fluency, elaboration

1. Have students sit in a circle, with one student sitting in the center.
2. Give a tennis ball or other small, soft object to a random student in the circle.
3. The student in center of the circle closes his or her eyes and says, "begin."
4. The object is quickly passed around the circle counter-clockwise, while everyone is perfectly silent.

5. At any point the student in the center says, "stop," and keeping his or her eyes closed, says to the person holding the object, "Name five _____."

   Sample Name 5 items:

   - Animals in the zoo
   - Facts that are devisable by 5
   - Terms from the unit of study
   - Compositions by Tchaikovsky
   - Students in the classroom (a great way to get students to know each other's names)
   - Important dates during the Civil War

6. The object is passed again while the person tries to complete the list of five before the object returns to him or her.

7. If the student is unable to complete the list of five before receiving the object again, he or she goes into the center of the circle.

Variations on this activity

Reverse the activity by having the student holding the object say "Name 5 . . . " to the student in the center of the circle.

Creative "Sponge" Activities

The following activities can be done when small bits of time remain, such as when students are waiting in the lunch line, waiting for the bell to ring, or waiting for you to collect lunch money or take attendance.

Activity: What If . . . ?

▶ Stimulates: fluency, flexibility, originality, elaboration

Use hypothetical thinking to warm up students' creativity. (See Chapter 9, page 139 for more on hypothetical thinking.)

- What if there was no rain this summer?
- What if there was no music?
- What if school lasted until 6 p.m. every day?
- What if we didn't use numbers?
- What if everyone spoke the same language?
- What if cars could fly?
- What if there was no gravity?
- What if houses were built entirely from inflexible materials?
- What if there was no Internet?
- What if time stood still?
- What if no one went to school?

Activity: Then What Happened?

▶ Stimulates: elaboration, originality

1. Write a beginning sentence on the board, such as: *We all boarded the bus for the field trip.*
2. Ask students, "Then what happened?"
3. Students take turns calling out the next sentence. To each one you respond, "Then what happened?"
4. This continues until all students have made a sentence contribution.

Variation on this activity:

Students can either write their next sentence on the board, in their journal, or on a sheet of paper that is passed around the room.

Additional Creative Activity Ideas

Activity: Living Timeline

▶ Stimulates: elaboration

Students choose a point along a timeline and then act out or narrate it.

Activity: Role Play, Skits, or Plays

▶ Stimulates: fluency, flexibility, elaboration

To highlight their understanding of a character in a novel or in history, students take on the character's role and create a two- to five-minute presentation of a moment in the character's life.

Activity: Readers Theater

▶ Stimulates: elaboration

Students read from a script to dramatize a piece of literature. No memorization, costumes, sets, or acting skills are required. Students use their voice to elaborate on the words.

Activity: Research on a Creative Individual

▶ Stimulates: elaboration

Researching a creative individual in history or the present day can help students understand the complex nature of creativity and the successes and struggles creative people face.

In the differentiated classroom, creativity is an integrated tool necessary for success in the twenty-first century. When you enrich the learning environment with varied creative activities, students grow "smarter" because they naturally become more engaged in the learning process. Creativity requires the use of both content knowledge (facts and skills) and conceptual connections (linking ideas across the disciplines). Nurturing your students' creative potential does not stand in opposition to teaching in support of standards and assessments. It can be a complementary tool that highlights effective thinking and encourages achievement.

Building a Creative Classroom

Every classroom should be a creative classroom. Students learn best by playing with ideas. To engage students in a creative classroom, we need to actively encourage students to question, make connections, and visualize what might be. We must value, promote, and reward imagination and originality. This engagement comes through authentic experiences with problems that have multiple ambiguous solutions. Ambiguity is a fact of life and students must develop cognitive tools for dealing with it rather than avoiding it. Students can become accustomed to and work through ambiguity by being immersed in authentic activities—real-world examples and experiences. A creative classroom also encourages a willingness to be in the moment. So when real-world experiences happen, they are transformed into "teachable moments."

A classroom that nurtures creativity is one where there is never only one right answer. There is openness to finding new problems; new solutions and varied perspectives are expected. Students find it fun and adventurous to explore ideas and get involved in discussing problems. They are encouraged to share ideas with others and to talk about their progress. They learn to appreciate the different qualities in others' work and to value ways of working that are different from their own.

Students feel relaxed, supported, and "at home" in a creative classroom. Their thinking is valued and honored. They take intellectual risks and respond creatively to new situations. Teachers also know when to stand back and let students take the lead. However, the teacher is always there to make sure students are prompted and supported when needed. Students are guided through the process with the assistance of formative feedback provided by the teacher and other students.

Phrases That Encourage Creativity

Interesting.

I'm enjoying all your answers.

Keep going.

Keep thinking.

Dig deeper.

Tell me more.

Hmmmmmmm.

Carry on.

Exciting!

Fascinating!

Noted.

Elaborate on that idea.

Rich!

Expand on that.

Go on.

Continue.

Teachers in a creative classroom must model creative thinking, behaviors, and attitudes. Show students that you are a learner as well. Don't fear being creative with and for your students. This will create an open, constructive learning environment. On page 161 is a list of norms to strive for in a creative classroom. You might find a place to display this list in your classroom.

Norms of the Creative Classroom

1. Curiosity and questions are encouraged.

2. Problems can be solved in many ways.

3. Necessity is the mother of invention.

4. Judgment and criticism are suspended.

5. Patience, perseverance, and persistence are mandatory.

From *Advancing Differentiation: Thinking and Learning for the 21st Century* by Richard M. Cash, Ed.D., copyright © 2011. Free Spirit Publishing Inc., Minneapolis, MN; 800-735-7323; www.freespirit.com. This page may be reproduced for use within an individual school or district. For all other uses, contact www.freespirit.com/company/permissions.cfm.

Chapter 11

Problem Finding, Problem Solving, and Decision Making

> Education is the most powerful weapon that you can use to change the world.
>
> —*Nelson Mandela, civil rights leader*

Effective thinking and learning skills ultimately lead to making sound decisions. Good decisions are necessary for a productive and successful life. Making decisions often involves rooting out problems and devising solutions. People who have the ability to identify potential problems before they arise are better equipped to proactively approach a solution. Unfortunately, many people do not foresee problems, and when problems arise, they approach them in a reactionary, stressful way, relying on past practice and automatic "knee-jerk" responses to deal with them. Effective problem finders, problem solvers, and decision makers anticipate problems, strategize their decisions, and take action toward the best solution.

Simply teaching students how to find answers to problems is no longer enough in today's complex world. Only teaching problem solving suggests to our students that "if it isn't broken, don't fix it." This line of thinking is analogous to putting out fires rather than preventing them. Whereas problem finding helps students better define problems, think more proactively, and achieve higher quality solutions. Once a problem has been found, the act of decision making begins. Decision making should not be thought of as a linear process. When identifying and choosing alternatives, we all base our decisions on the values and preferences that fit best with our desires, goals, needs, or wants. Decision making can be defined as *the act of reducing uncertainty or doubt to produce the most reasonable choice.*[1]

This chapter provides you with a list of characteristics of effective problem finders, problem solvers, and decision makers; offers various steps to achieving quality outcomes; and includes graphic organizers that can assist students in the process. At the end is a list of barriers students face in making good decisions, and strategies to help them overcome these barriers.

Characteristics of Effective Problem Finders, Problem Solvers, and Decision Makers

Successful problem finders, problem solvers, and decision makers view problems through many lenses. They look at issues from multiple perspectives, seek out information from various sources, and foresee roadblocks that may arise. Their traits include the following:

1 Robert Harris, www.virtualsalt.com.

They Are Curious

Curiosity, rather than kill the cat, can often save it. Curious people are open to all evidence and activity surrounding them; they do not quickly ignore or discount new information.

They Are Flexible

They take "old" problems and look at them with "new" eyes. This outside-the-box thinking can create outside-the-box solutions that are more effective and efficient.

They Listen to What's *Not* Being Said and See What's *Not* Being Shown

A common error people make in solving problems is they do not pay attention to the unspoken, or negative space. Anticipating problems before they arise, discovering unique possibilities, and identifying what has been previously overlooked can lead to better solutions.

They Are Persistent and Patient

As is often repeated, there are no easy answers. The most difficult problems are also often the most challenging to find and solve. Therefore, students must put forth effort, persist, and be patient until a good solution can be found.

They Defer Judgment

It may take students a long time to think through ideas, issues, or information. Successfully solving problems and coming to good decisions often requires us to "sleep on it." Our brains need time to process, consider possible outcomes, and choose alternatives. Reaching a sound decision might mean delaying closure and taking the time to fully think things through.

They Are Reflective

Once a conclusion has been reached, good problem solvers review what they did, how they did it, and in what ways the outcome could have been different.

Finding Problems

The first step to arriving at good solutions and decisions is finding potential problems. Finding problems should not be seen as looking for trouble, but instead looking for ways to improve a situation, anticipate potential failures, or intercept an issue before it becomes negative. Following are examples of questions and activities that help build students' skills in problem finding.

- Come up with a list of improvements for how this classroom and school operates.
- What are some issues we can address in our classroom now in order to prevent them from becoming bigger problems in the future?
- Seek out potential problems the characters may face in this story.
- If we implement an all-electronic financial system in our government, what problems might we anticipate?
- Suppose we limit each person on Earth to one gallon of water per day. What problems can we expect?
- What problems could occur if school were held four days a week rather than five?
- What issues could arise if we were required to post all public signs in two languages?
- Scientists are considering creating a pill that can increase intelligence. What issues might we anticipate?

Activity suggestion: Take a current issue in your school or community, and frame the issue in a similar manner to these questions and activities.

Solving Problems

A common problem-solving process, known as the "I-FORD," guides students through five steps to identify a problem, gather facts, list and rank options, and make a decision.

Steps to Problem Solving: I-FORD

Identify: Define or shape the problem. What is the goal you want to achieve?

Facts: Gather the facts and data you need to make the best decision.

Options: List possible solutions or strategies to solve the problem.

Rank your options: Rate, rank, and test your options and strategies.

Decide: Make your decision, and implement and evaluate your solution.

The most effective problem solvers often follow these steps in both a linear and cyclical process (see **Figure 11.1**). In this process, the solver can always back up to the previous step and should continually evaluate each step along the way to see if he or she is coming close to a solution.

Within each of the five I-FORD steps, detailed in the next section, the dozen specific problem-solving strategies listed to the right are embedded and described, along with several graphic organizers.

STRATEGIES FOR PROBLEM SOLVING

1. **Frame** the problem to its core in simple, descriptive language.
2. **Use graphics** (pictures, tables, diagrams) to dig deeper into the issues.
3. **Work backwards** from possible outcomes.
4. **Use a different symbol system** to represent the problem in a new way.
5. **Share** your defined/refined problem with another person.
6. **Gather data** that may be helpful in solving the problem.
7. **Rephrase and confirm** the problem.
8. **Brainstorm** possible solutions or strategies.
9. **Test** possible solutions.
10. **Select** the best course of action.
11. **Implement** the action.
12. **Evaluate** your success.

The I-FORD Process Described

Step 1: Identify the Problem

Along with problem finding comes the art of shaping or defining the problem so that a quality solution can be found. In the problem-defining stage, students apply the strategy of *framing the problem to its core*. A technique to get to the core of a problem is the 5 Whys to Therefore chart on page 165. See **Figure 11.2** for an example. After completing the example chart, I realized that my original problem, "I want a new car," had another problem embedded within it: "I need a new job." Simply stating that I needed a new car did not get to the real core of my problem. Once students reach their core problem, make sure they state it in simple descriptive language. Using overly elaborate or sophisticated language can muddy what needs to be accomplished and potentially aim the solution at the wrong issue.

Figure 11.1 A Linear-Cyclical Problem-Solving Process

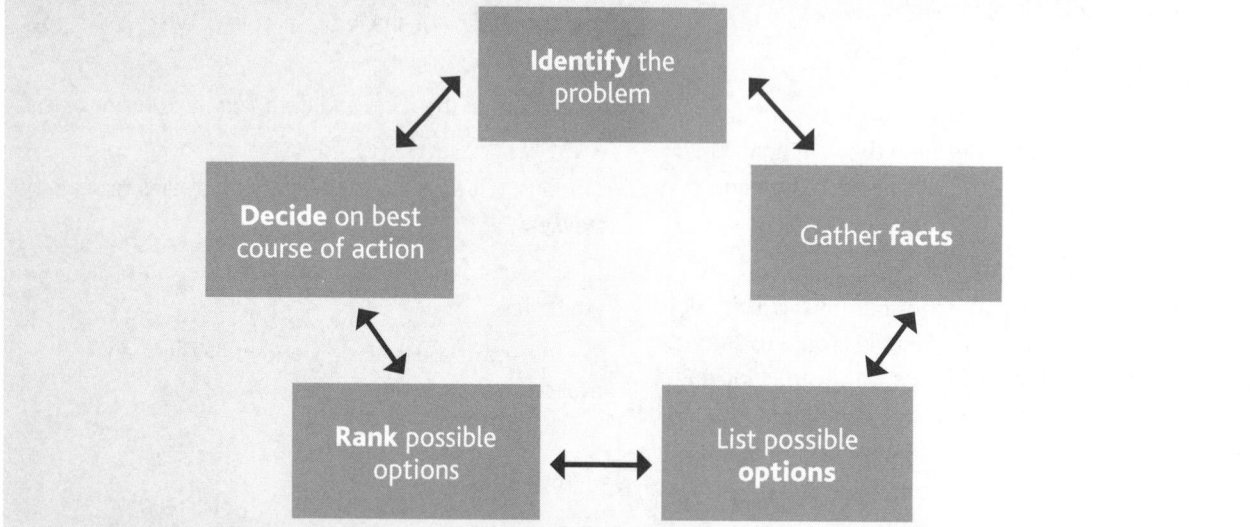

5 WHYS TO THEREFORE

Statement:

Why:

Why:

Why:

Why:

Why:

Therefore:

From *Advancing Differentiation: Thinking and Learning for the 21st Century* by Richard M. Cash, Ed.D., copyright © 2011. Free Spirit Publishing Inc., Minneapolis, MN; 800-735-7323; www.freespirit.com. This page may be reproduced for use within an individual school or district. For all other uses, contact www.freespirit.com/company/permissions.cfm.

Figure 11.2 **5 Whys to Therefore: Example**

Statement:
I want a new car.

Why:
Because I don't like paying for repairs.

Why:
Because it is costing me too much.

Why:
Because I don't have the extra cash.

Why:
Because I am not making enough money.

Why:
Because my current position doesn't pay what it should.

Therefore:
I need to find a job that pays better.

Another strategy for shaping or defining the problem is to *use graphics,* such as pictures, diagrams, or tables. Examples include the If-Then Mind Map for Decision Making (see **Figure 11.3** on page 171), the What Would Happen If . . . ? diagram (see **Figure 11.4** on pages 173–174), and the What? So What? Now What? chart (see **Figure 11.5** on page 176). All of these graphic organizers help the learner dig deeper into the issues, predict possible outcomes, or define possible obstacles. These graphics can also help identify potential causes for the problem.

Figure 11.3 can be used when there are multiple situations or issues that could arise or that need to be resolved. Remember, when having students do any sort of mind mapping, instruct them to keep their notations simple, clear, and concise. Mind maps are note-taking devices that provide an overview of a situation, offer keywords in solution finding, and help keep ideas organized. See a blank template on page 172.

Figure 11.4 is useful in hypothetical thinking situations or in predicting outcomes from actions. It offers the thinker a way to see how one situation can have an effect on or cause other interrelated situations or issues. From the example, you will see how one event leads to multiple secondary issues or situations. Have students select one of the secondary issues and do an additional mind map to find tertiary issues of situations that can or may arise.

A blank template is provided on page 175.

The graphic organizer in Figure 11.5 was discussed previously in Chapter 8 as depicting the three stages of the Understand level of Bloom's Revised Taxonomy (see Figure 8.6 on page 119). A What? So What? Now What? chart helps students frame an issue, define ways the issue is important, and then describe actions that should be taken to solve or mitigate the situation. This model is an excellent tool to use for thinking through current events or coming up with local issues students could act upon. The model gives students a format for creating doable solutions.

A blank template is provided on page 177.

Students can also use the previous graphics in the strategy of *working backwards*. With this strategy, they would identify possible solutions or outcomes to a problem and, using the graphic organizers, cite possible domino, or ripple, effects of implementing each alternate solution.

In some problem situations, a stumbling block may lie in the way we are looking at the particular information or data. In this case, students can employ the strategy of *using a different symbol system* to clarify the issue. Sometimes the way the problem is represented (verbally, for instance) can distract or confuse its solver. When problems are framed in only one system or code (such as words), this can limit the ability to think creatively or broadly. Words convey many meanings and can confuse their receiver. For instance, take this problem:

Mary is six times the age of Sam. Sam is three times the age of Tina. Tina just celebrated her fourth birthday. How old are Mary and Sam?

Using a different symbol system (numbers versus words) can make the solution appear much simpler:

Tina (T) = 4

Sam (S) = 3T = 3 x 4 = 12

Mary (M) = 6S = 6 x 12 = 72

The following questions can be used to define a problem:

Questions Students Ask

- What is the problem?
- How can I describe it in my own words?
- What specific elements are involved?
- What am I being asked to do?
- What am I asked to show?
- Can I draw a picture or make a table, graph, or chart to better understand the problem?

- Can I show the problem using another symbol system (such as numbers versus words)?

Questions Teachers Ask

- Can you tell me, in your own words, what the problem is?
- What are your missing pieces of information?
- What information can you safely ignore?
- What assumptions are you making about this problem?
- What are you not defining about the problem that you should be?

Finally, another great idea for defining the problem is to *share the defined problem with another person*. Students must ensure they've captured the true essence of the issue. Enlisting another set of eyes or ears is very helpful in the problem-defining process.

Step 2: Find the Facts

Once the problem has been defined, students begin to *gather data* that may be helpful in the process of solving the problem. This may be as simple as listing information or creating graphic representations of what is known and unknown. In the Mary-Sam-Tina problem just described, we simply list each of the individual's ages as stated in the problem. Here, students should also check to see if they have enough information to solve the problem. The solver must analyze the problem to check for information that is not stated or that may be taken for granted, and also check that all information is in the same form or unit type. At this point, it is a good idea for solvers to step back from the problem and rephrase it to confirm what actually needs to be changed or corrected. (Use the 5 Whys to Therefore chart on page 165.)The following questions can be used to find the facts of a problem:

Questions Students Ask

- What can be causing the problem?
- Where is it happening?
- When is it happening?
- How is it happening?
- With whom is it happening?
- Why is it happening?
- What are the (smaller) parts of this problem?
- What are the unknowns?
- What information can I gather from the problem?
- What information is missing or unnecessary?
- Is there a pattern in the information?
- Are there other problems like this that I can use as a model?
- Can I make a graph, chart, table, diagram, or equation with the information I have?

Questions Teachers Ask

- Define the possible causes of this problem.
- What are the smaller problems embedded within this problem?
- Define patterns that you see in this problem.
- Show me a graph, chart, table, diagram, or equation that you have created to help you define the problem.

Step 3: List Your Options

Next comes the strategy of *listing possible solutions or strategies to solve the problem*. Here is where students' brainstorming skills come in handy. Brainstorming involves the following process:

1. Generate as many ideas a possible.
2. Eliminate evaluation of ideas until all ideas have been shared.
3. Work quickly so as not to allow time for judgment.
4. Piggyback on others' ideas.

It is also helpful at this point for students to involve others in listing possible solutions. Other people may see the problem from a different point of view and may have a solution not already considered.

Step 4: Rank Your Options

After several ideas have been generated, students begin to analyze or *test possible solutions*. A list of the pros, cons, and additional questions that arise from each possible solution is created. A helpful tool at this point is to use either the PNI or CAI (see pages 142 and 144). Students should be careful not to evaluate any of the solutions at this point so they can keep an open mind about solutions that may have been previously unconsidered. After reviewing the various solutions, students are ready to *select the best course of action or strategy to solve the problem*. Here is a list of possible problem-solving strategy options students might test and rank:

- Guess and check
- Make a list
- Draw a picture, diagram, table, or chart
- Look for patterns
- Solve a similar/simpler problem
- Use a different symbol system

- Act out the problem
- Create a simulation
- Work backwards
- Look at the problem from a different perspective

The following questions can be used to rank strategy options:

Questions Students Ask

- What should happen first, second, third, fourth, and so on, in this process?
- What resources will I need?
- How much time will the action take?
- Who is responsible for which steps?
- Which approaches are timely, appropriate, reasonable, realistic, cost-effective, efficient, and doable?
- What will the situation look like when the problem has been solved?
- How will I know when I've reached a solution?
- How do I check to see that each step has been followed?
- What might happen if I implement this solution? (Use the If-Then Mind Map for Decision Making or the What Would Happen If . . . ? templates on pages 172 and 173–174.)

Questions Teachers Ask

- Can you explain your plan to me?
- What have you tried so far?
- In what ways did you organize your information?
- What problems have you encountered before that resemble this problem?
- Why do you think your plan will work?
- How have you made sure that you have all the information you need?
- How will you know that you have reached a solution?
- In what ways have you checked your progress each step along the way?

Step 5: Decide on a Solution

Once the best course of action has been selected, problem solvers are now ready to *implement the action*. As they are implementing the action, have students check each step for accuracy along the way. After the action has been implemented, students must *evaluate* what changed, how it changed, and to what degree they will need to make adjustments to their actions. Also, they must determine if the solution makes sense in relation to the original problem. Critical at this stage are the P^3 behaviors: persistence, patience, and perseverance (see page 76).

The following questions can be used when deciding on a solution:

Questions Students Ask

- Did I solve the problem? If not, what do I need to do differently?
- Was the action I took effective and efficient?
- What did I learn from this problem-solving activity?
- Does my answer make sense?
- Could I have solved this problem another way?

Questions Teachers Ask

- How have you solved the problem?
- If you haven't solved the problem, what new direction will you take?
- How effective and efficient was your plan and solution?
- What have you learned from this experience?
- In what ways does your answer make sense?
- Could you have solved the problem in a different way?

If the problem has not been solved satisfactorily, students must begin the process again, making sure they have defined the problem well, gathered the appropriate data, listed all possible solutions, selected and implemented the right plan of action, and evaluated their success. Encourage students to look forward to a new decision, not to look back in regret. Remind them: If at first you don't succeed, try, try again!

Decision Making

Skills in decision making are required throughout the problem finding and solving process. Every step along the way requires students to produce reasonable choices based on the information available. However, making decisions is a complex process and is often one in which students have difficulty. They may be apprehensive about being creative or decisive because of stumbling blocks that get in the way of their thinking. In some cases this is because students haven't been taught strategies to overcome these difficulties, or they have not met prior challenges that required them to work hard at solving a problem. Many very bright students struggle with decision making because of the lack of rigor or challenge in their early years of schooling.

Decision-making stumbling blocks include the following: (*Note:* You'll notice this list is similar to the list of reasons students underachieve on pages 36–37, because in many cases underachieving students have limited practice in the art of thinking.)

- Fear of failure ("If I fail people will know I'm not that smart.")
- Fear of success ("If I succeed people will expect me to succeed all the time.")
- Lack of problem-solving skills
- Lack of understanding the problem
- Lack of challenge
- Lack of interest
- Lack of motivation
- Lack of self-efficacy
- Lack of perseverance
- Too much or too little self-confidence
- Spreading oneself too thin (taking on too many things)
- Using the wrong abilities
- Inability to translate thought into action
- Lack of follow-through for getting the job done
- Inability to complete tasks
- Failure to initiate
- Procrastination
- Blaming others
- Excessive self-pity
- Excessive dependency
- Focusing on personal difficulties
- Being highly distractible or lacking in concentration

Overcoming Barriers to Decision Making

One major reason why students are reluctant to make decisions and risk failure is due to what cognitive psychologist Dr. Carol Dweck calls the *fixed mindset* (discussed previously in Chapter 5 on page 73). Students with a fixed mindset believe their intelligence and abilities are fixed traits they are born with and cannot develop further. These students believe all the tests and documentations (grades, trophies, and certificates) are what define their success. Dweck states, "When people believe in fixed traits, they are always in danger of being measured by a failure."[2] Conversely, students with a *growth mindset* believe that all skills and abilities can be developed through dedication and hard work. A person with a growth mindset knows that what they are born with can be cultivated and built upon. "When people believe their basic qualities can be developed, failures may still hurt, but failures don't define them," writes Dweck.[3] When we teach students that they can improve their performance through a growth mindset, they are better able to overcome negative labels, bullying, difficult situations, stereotyping, and other perceived or real barriers. This may be especially valuable for students from culturally, linguistically, socially, or economically diverse backgrounds.

Develop Growth Mindset Conventions

A strategy to help students overcome difficult decision-making situations is to develop classroom conventions that address a growth mindset. Classroom conventions are different from rules; conventions are a way of doing business or acting within a given setting. Classroom conventions to encourage a growth mindset include the following:

Growth Mindset Conventions for the Teacher

As the teacher, I will . . .

- Present all skills and processes as learnable
- Model patience, persistence, and perseverance (P^3)
- Present all feedback as constructive toward future success

Growth Mindset Conventions for the Student

As the student, I will . . .

- Tackle all skills and processes as learnable
- Employ patience, persistence, and perseverance (P^3)
- Welcome all feedback as constructive toward my future success

Display these conventions in your classroom and have students (and yourself) recite them daily.

Support Students' Self-Confidence

Building students' confidence in themselves as learners and thinkers is another crucial strategy in helping them make sound decisions. As a teacher you can help build their confidence in the classroom, and you can also encourage parents to participate in confidence building.

2 Dweck, Carol S. *Mindset: The New Psychology of Success*. New York: Ballantine Books, 2006, p. 29.

3 Ibid, p. 39.

Suggestions for parents to build their child's confidence:

- Show your child that you love challenges.
- Use your own mistakes as a learning tool.
- Discuss the effort you put forth each day.
- Display your continued learning.
- Provide constructive criticism to your child.
- When your child comes home from school, ask questions like:
  - What is one specific thing that you learned today?
  - What mistake did you make today that taught you something about yourself?
  - What did you try hard at today?
  - What is one thing that you were proud of in your learning today?
  - What is one thing that you would change about your learning today?
  - What specific goal will you set for yourself tomorrow?
- Give your child compliments that can build confidence, such as:
  - I'm proud of how much effort you put forth to achieve what you did.
  - Wow, you worked hard and that hard work paid off!
  - Your perseverance shows in your work.
  - I'm impressed at how patient you are when you face a challenge.
  - Even though you may not have achieved your goal, I can tell you tried your hardest.

Notice that all of the above statements focus *not* on ability but on *hard work* and *effort*.

Teach Students to Mobilize Their Resources

Another idea for helping students overcome decision-making barriers is to teach them how to mobilize their resources. When students know what they have and/or where to find what they need, they are better able to be creative and solve problems.

Steps to Mobilize Your Resources

1. Believe in yourself as the most valuable resource.
2. Utilize those around you (teachers, classmates, parents, or other adults).
3. Utilize the materials available.
4. Ask questions or ask for help.
5. Request, require, and/or advocate for more support, information, or resources.

Encourage Students to Take Risks

Finally, students need to know that making good decisions involves risk taking. Taking risks and making mistakes are actually valuable skills to be learned. Without risk and failure there is no growth; any success without risk or failure is pure luck. In fact, everything in life requires some level of risk and there will be some chances for failure. For example: Because I fear flying, I will decide to drive to my vacation destination. By avoiding my fear of flying, I've now increased my risk of being involved in a car crash. In another case, to avoid all risk, I will sit on the couch and watch TV. This choice will increase my risk for obesity, heart attack, or even an airplane crashing though my roof onto my sofa. Risk is a natural part of life and involves some levels of fear. This is a good thing, because it shows that we are human.

Practice decision making as a class by using the 12 Steps to Group Decision Making (see page 178).

A quality curriculum encourages students to develop and use problem finding and solving and stimulates good decision making. Effective instruction models and promotes successful problem finding and solving and supports students in making sound decisions. As stated at the beginning of Chapter 3, only quality curriculum and effective instructional practices can be differentiated. All students can problem find and solve; the distinction in a differentiated classroom is that varying levels of curricular activities are used to scaffold students so they are confident problem finders and to provide support structures for all students so they are willing to take risks to solve complex problems. Using the strategies and ideas listed in this chapter will help you find those "just right" activities to build students' abilities to problem find and solve so they are better equipped to make good decisions.

Figure 11.3 **If-Then Mind Map for Decision Making: Example**[4]

Based on *Charlotte's Web* by E.B. White

IF Wilbur hadn't been the runt of the litter . . .

THEN Fern wouldn't have been able to keep him as a pet . . .

THEN he would have been raised for slaughter.

THEN he would never have become friends with Charlotte.

THEN he would not have made so many friends in the barnyard.

THEN Wilbur might not have met Charlotte . . .

THEN he wouldn't have gone to the State Fair.

THEN Wilbur would not have found a great friend.

THEN she wouldn't have worked so hard to write her words.

Going further:
IF Charlotte hadn't worked so hard to write her words . . .

THEN she might not have died so soon.

THEN Wilbur might not have learned how to be such a good friend.

THEN Wilbur might not have realized how much she loved him.

4 Courtesy of Barbara Dullaghan, Bloomington Public Schools, Bloomington, MN

If-Then Mind Map for Decision Making

Topic:

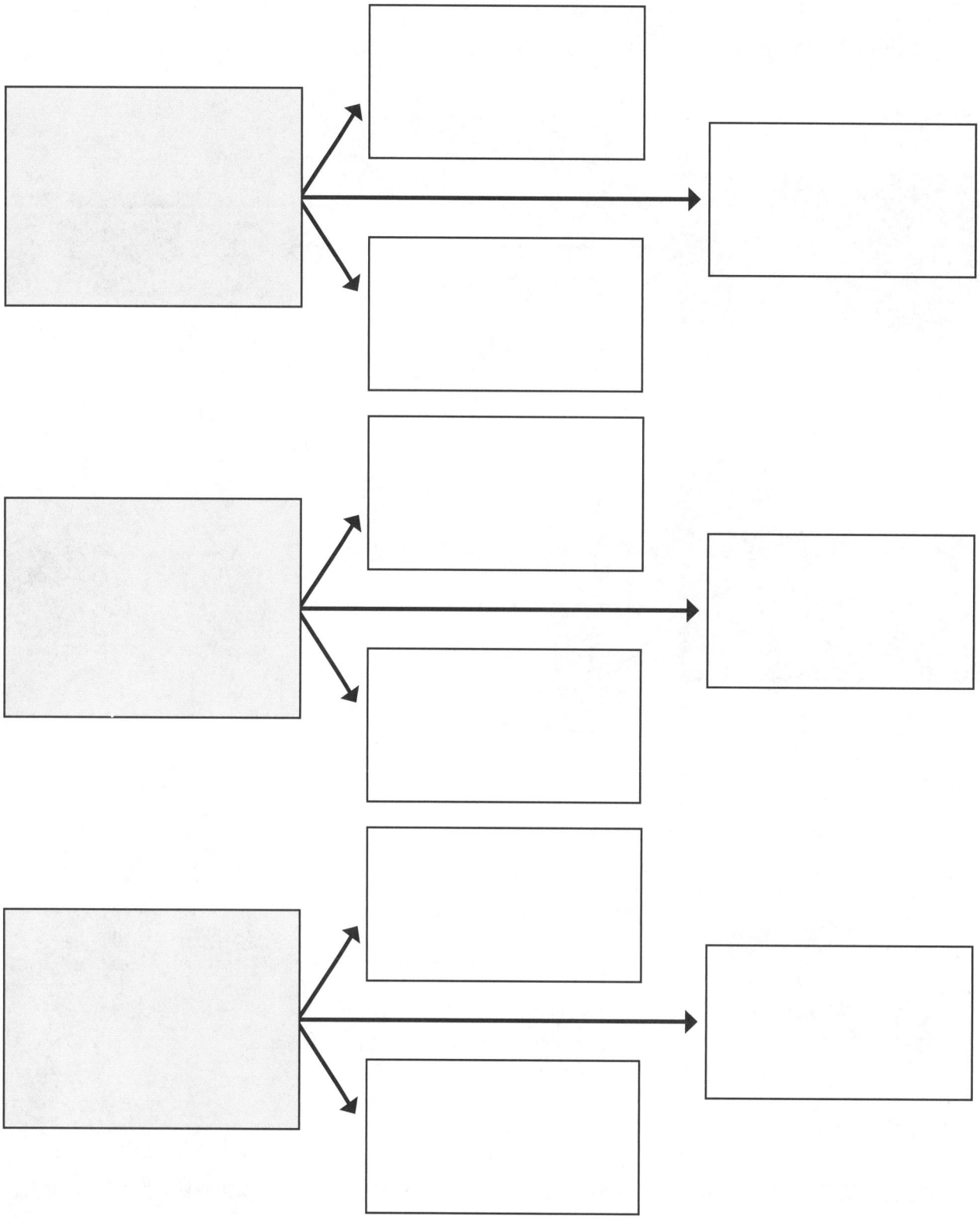

From *Advancing Differentiation: Thinking and Learning for the 21st Century* by Richard M. Cash, Ed.D., copyright © 2011. Free Spirit Publishing Inc., Minneapolis, MN; 800-735-7323; www.freespirit.com. This page may be reproduced for use within an individual school or district. For all other uses, contact www.freespirit.com/company/permissions.cfm.

Figure 11.4 What Would Happen If . . . ? Example

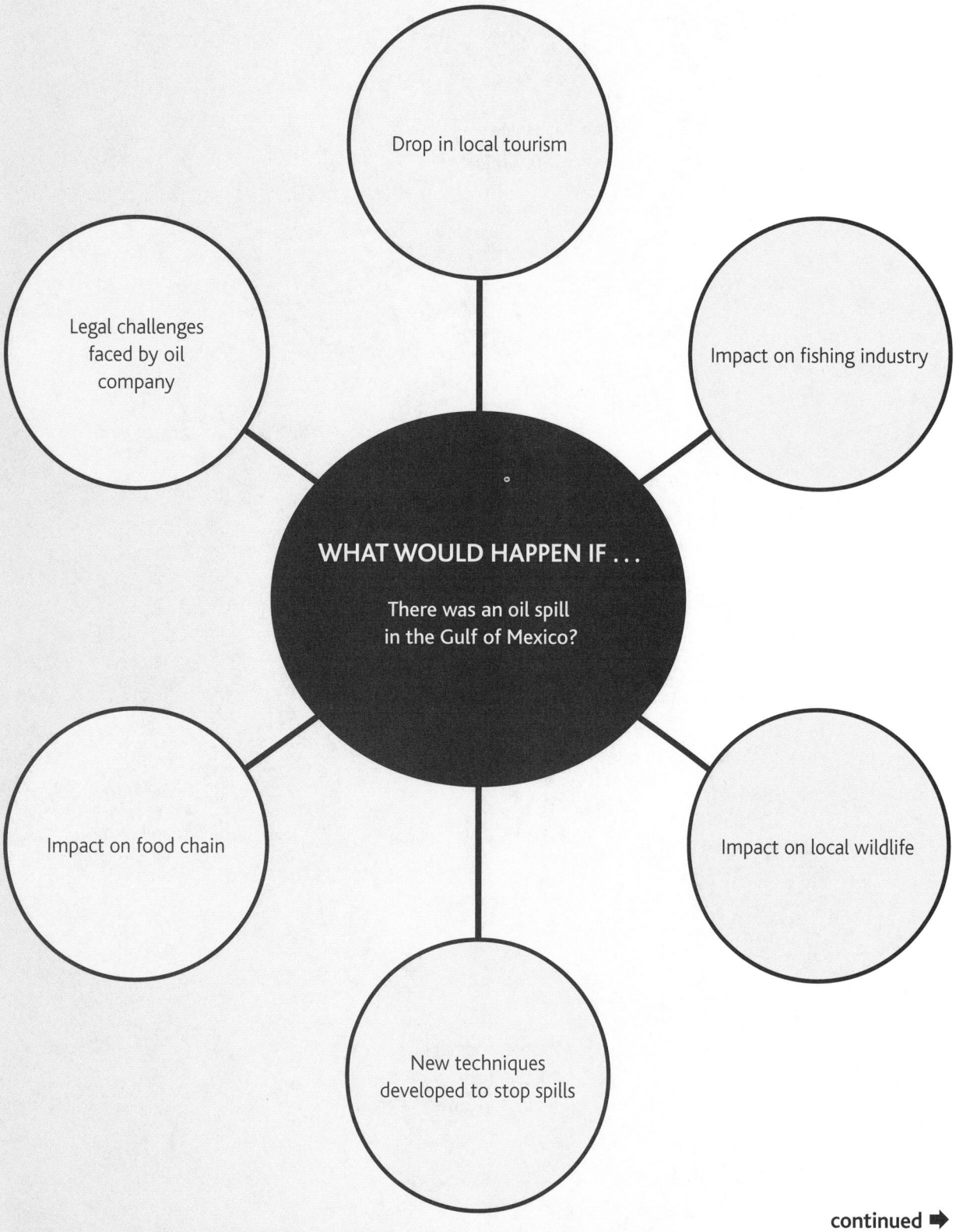

continued ➡

Figure 11.4 What Would Happen If . . . ? Example (continued)

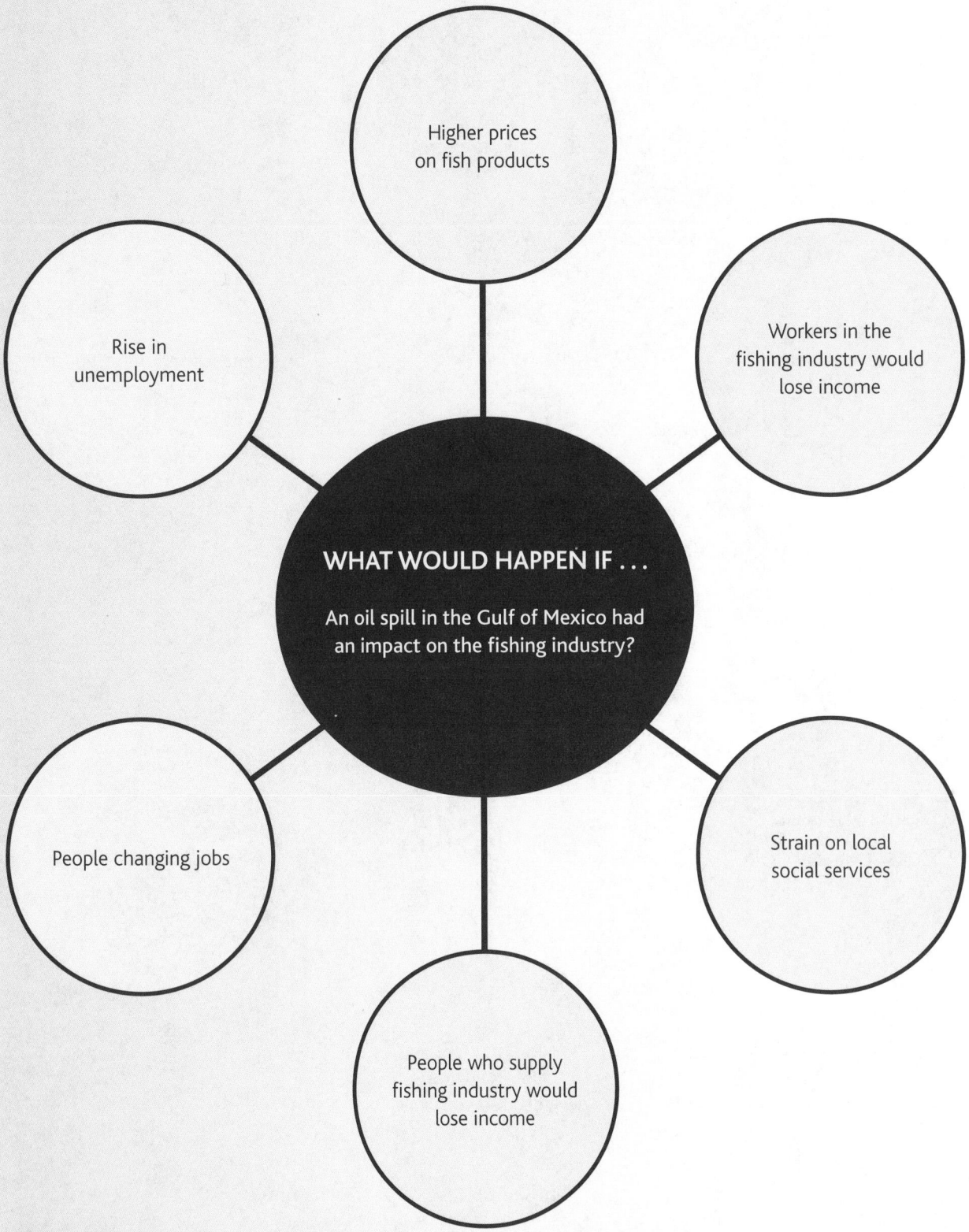

What Would Happen If . . . ?

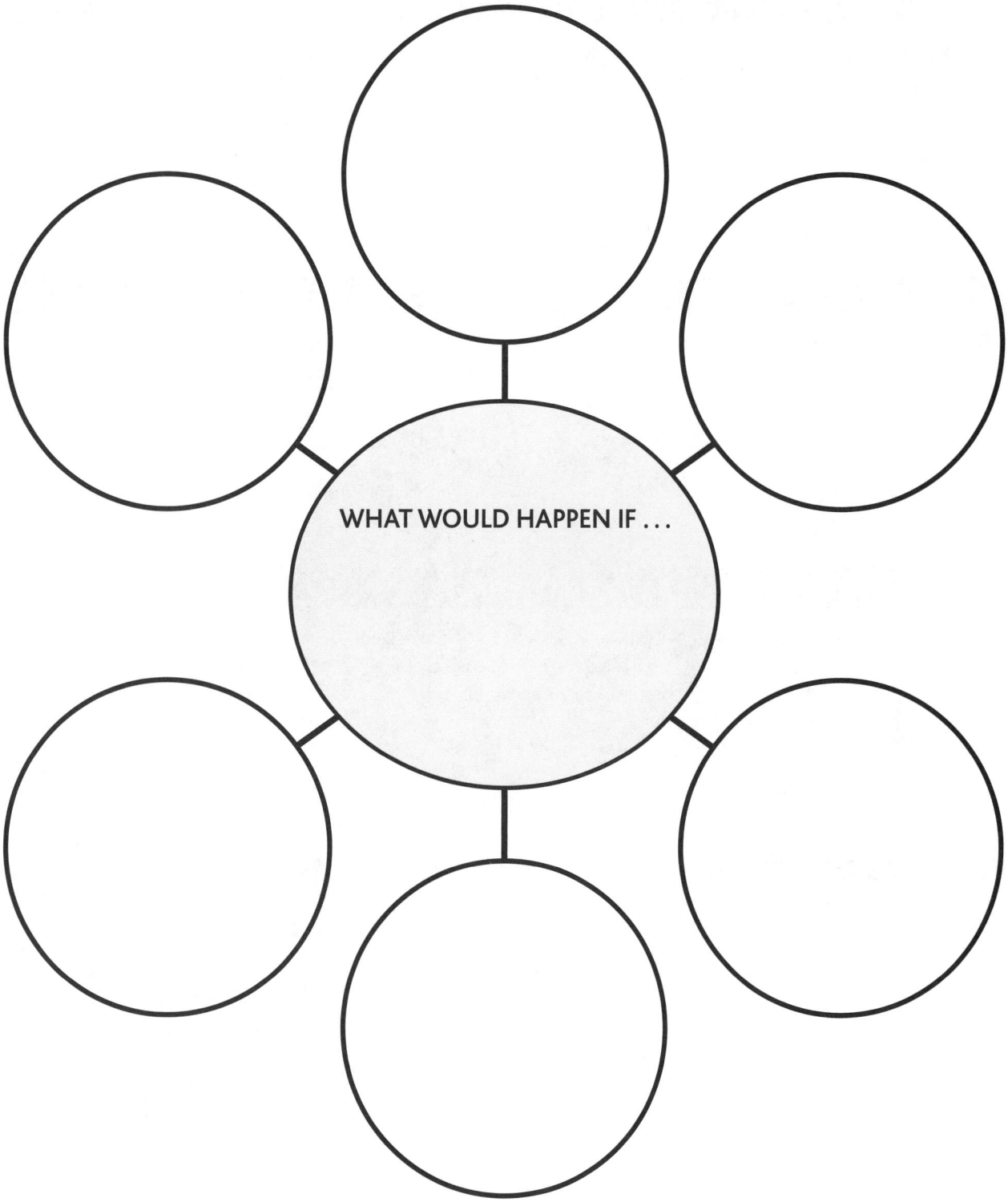

From *Advancing Differentiation: Thinking and Learning for the 21st Century* by Richard M. Cash, Ed.D., copyright © 2011. Free Spirit Publishing Inc., Minneapolis, MN; 800-735-7323; www.freespirit.com. This page may be reproduced for use within an individual school or district. For all other uses, contact www.freespirit.com/company/permissions.cfm.

Figure 11.5 What? So What? Now What? Example

WHAT?	SO WHAT?	NOW WHAT?
Flash floods destroy camping ground and kill 13 people.	Lives were lost due to the recreational use of local watersheds.	Early warning systems should be put into place to save people's lives. Limitations should be placed on recreational use of watershed areas.
WHAT?	**SO WHAT?**	**NOW WHAT?**
Heart disease is the number one killer of women in the United States.	Heart disease in women may increase without more prevention and research.	More preventative information should be given to women.
WHAT?	**SO WHAT?**	**NOW WHAT?**
Ethnic clashes in eastern Europe result in civil war.	Civil war in eastern Europe may lead to a major economic crisis that could impact the entire world.	The United Nations should form a negotiating team to help resolve the conflict as well as send in peace-keeping troops to support the local government.

What? So What? Now What?

WHAT?	SO WHAT?	NOW WHAT?
WHAT?	**SO WHAT?**	**NOW WHAT?**
WHAT?	**SO WHAT?**	**NOW WHAT?**

From *Advancing Differentiation: Thinking and Learning for the 21st Century* by Richard M. Cash, Ed.D., copyright © 2011. Free Spirit Publishing Inc., Minneapolis, MN; 800-735-7323; www.freespirit.com. This page may be reproduced for use within an individual school or district. For all other uses, contact www.freespirit.com/company/permissions.cfm.

12 Steps to Group Decision Making

Materials

Large chart paper

Colored adhesive dots (red, yellow, green)

Roles

Leader (keeps group on task)

Recorder (writes and records)

Timer (manages the time for each step)

1. Divide class into small groups of 5–8 students and designate 1 leader, 1 recorder, and 1 timer in each group.
2. Group leader defines the problem. *(1 minute)*
3. Each group member silently generates solutions. *(2 minutes)*
4. Using a round-robin format, group members share one idea. Recorder writes on a large sheet of paper exactly what was shared. Do not restate the individual's idea. No discussion other than clarifying questions is permitted at this point. The round-robin continues until all ideas have been shared. *(Maximum 10 minutes)*
5. Discussion and clarification. At this point individuals may ask clarification questions, discuss the particular implications of each idea, defend their ideas, compare ideas, or persuade others to favor their idea. *(5 minutes)*
6. Group members then rank the various ideas by assigning each idea one of the colored dots. *(1 minute)*

   Red: Most likely will NOT work

   Yellow: May be a possible solution

   Green: Most likely WILL work
7. Group leader then selects the ideas that generated the most green dots, or the ideas that generated the greatest likelihood of success.
8. Small groups come together and each group leader reports on the group's green dot decisions to the class. *(Maximum 5 minutes)*
9. The class votes on the various small group decisions, ranking them the same way as in Step 6. *(1 minute)*
10. In case of a tie, groups may encourage others to vote for their solutions in a debate-style round-robin. *(1 minute)*
11. Repeat the class vote, this time using one red and one green dot. *(1 minute)*
12. Report the final decision to the class.

From *Advancing Differentiation: Thinking and Learning for the 21st Century* by Richard M. Cash, Ed.D., copyright © 2011. Free Spirit Publishing Inc., Minneapolis, MN; 800-735-7323; www.freespirit.com. This page may be reproduced for use within an individual school or district. For all other uses, contact www.freespirit.com/company/permissions.cfm.

A Final Note

Pulling It All Together

Differentiation involves providing students with a variety of avenues through the content, enabling them to make sense and take ownership of the information through the process, guiding them to create products that represent their knowledge, and offering a nurturing environment that builds learner autonomy. **Figure 12.1** on page 180 connects these four aspects of differentiation with the essential twenty-first century thinking and learning tools presented in this book.

A quality curriculum is defined by content that clearly identifies major concepts that connect within and across disciplines, so students are better able to grasp conceptual meanings and form deep understandings. Additionally, as a teacher you must be fully aware of the factual and procedural foundations embedded within the discipline and units of study. With this knowledge, you can effectively assess your students' knowledge base in facts, procedures, and concepts, and deliver content that encourages greater levels of problem finding and solving.

The processes of effective instruction are designed to build on students' prior knowledge and innate creativity to stimulate skill development for application within the discipline and in complex ways. Teachers know where students are in their ability to use critical, creative, and higher level thinking tools. If students need more scaffolding or more complexity when using these tools, teachers have multiple resources and strategies to support these needs. Students are then encouraged to develop products that represent their learning through unique and original performances. These performances can look very different from student to student, depending on his or her learning style or necessity of expression.

The hallmark of success in the twenty-first century is the ability to generate unique and original ideas or products and be able to put them to use in practical ways.

The hallmark of success in the twenty-first century is the ability to generate unique and original ideas or products and be able to put them to use in practical ways. We must develop these abilities in our students by promoting various ways for students to express their thinking and learning. In the classrooms of the future, learning will take place in many different types of settings and venues. Students will be learning beyond the classroom walls. They will be communicating and collaborating with others around the world with the click of a button. Educators must be able to differentiate the learning environment so it is structured in ways that respect the learners' differing brain requirements, and it nurtures and supports the natural curiosity and creativity of our students.

Figure 12.1 Connecting Differentiation and 21st Century Thinking and Learning

Content

The curriculum is rich in deep concepts and ideas that encourage students to investigate beyond the facts. Some students expand on fundamental ideas, while others develop new ideas in the discipline. Students are encouraged to solve real-world problems using learned knowledge.

Process

Engaging instructional practices teach students the essential skills of the twenty-first century, such as critical and creative thinking. Some students require more direct instruction on these skills, while others develop risk-taking skills to expand on the usage of these tools.

DIFFERENTIATION

Product

Students construct meaningful products that represent their learning of new ideas, skills, and processes. Outcomes are designed to encourage students to problem solve through critical thinking and also to construct useful products. Some students are able to represent their ideas through music, drama, prose, or graphic representation, while others choose to represent their learning through speech, artistic design, multi-media, or other avenues.

Environment

The learning setting is designed to acknowledge brain compatibility and the need for enrichment and stimulation. Learning happens for some students inside of the classroom, while for others it may happen via the Internet or in authentic nonclassroom locations. In the twenty-first century, learning is increasingly occurring beyond the classroom walls.

Conclusion

My parents went to school in the late 1930s and early 1940s. My mother graduated from high school with only the prospects of going to college to become a teacher or nurse. My mother's strength was in math, so she was encouraged to proceed to clerical school to become a secretary, which she did. My father left school after completing eighth grade, because school held very little interest to him. In my father's day, a high school degree was not a necessity to getting a job. His only real prospect was to enter the military where he could earn his GED. My parents successfully raised five children without either of them attending a post-secondary institution.

My siblings and I graduated from high school in the mid-1970s. We all went on to college with career prospects far different than those afforded our parents. Avenues were opening up in the computer sciences—the first computer I saw took up an entire classroom and required its own air conditioner—and healthcare. In addition, the options we had available to us post-college were greater and far more diverse than those available to our parents 30 years earlier. All of us ended up in the field of education, which is surprising given the fact neither of our parents attended college, and one did not even complete high school.

Students who will be graduating from high school in the coming decades of the twenty-first century will have many more options available to them than existed 30 years ago for my siblings and me, and exponentially more options than my parents had in the mid-twentieth century. The level of workforce needs has changed—and will continue to change—from skill application to knowledge development. Knowledge workers of the twenty-first century will be required to be FIT: **F**lexible, **I**nnovative thinkers, and they will also be expected to be **T**ech-savvy to increasingly greater degrees.

As discussed in Chapter 1, the use and application of technology in the classroom is essential for our students to be prepared for their future. Our role with students is to guide them in employing technology in a thoughtful manner to enhance and enrich all of our lives. If used in this way, computers, PDAs, video games, software programs, interactive white boards, projectors, clickers, graphic tablets, and other devices provide unparalleled learning tools that increase students' resourcefulness, productivity, and creativity. They also appeal to the visual, interactive learning preferences of many of today's students. However, while technology can benefit, improve, and enhance our lives and the lives of our students, it cannot do our thinking for us.

All students can learn and think at advanced levels, and they will need practice and coaching to get there. To assist them in our full capacity as teachers, we must remember these key points:

- We must model our own thinking and learning processes for our students.
- We must infuse thinking and learning processes into the classroom and curriculum on a daily basis.
- We must expect students to use and discuss their thinking.
- We must honor, value, and celebrate all kinds of student thinking, even if we don't agree with it.
- We must support students in their ability to connect what is learned in the classroom to what goes on outside the classroom walls.

All students can learn and think at advanced levels, and they will need practice and guidance to get there.

By embracing this book's ideas for infusing effective twenty-first century thinking and learning skills into your classroom and curriculum, and implementing its strategies, templates, and models, you can be assured that your students will be more actively engaged in learning and will advance their thinking processes to increase their chances of success in this rapidly advancing society.

References and Resources

Anderson, Lorin W. and David R. Krathwohl, eds. *A Taxonomy for Learning, Teaching, and Assessing: A Revision of Bloom's Taxonomy of Educational Objectives*. New York: Addison Wesley Longman, 2001.

Beecher, M. *Developing the Gifts and Talents of All Students in the Regular Classroom*. Mansfield Center, CT: Creative Learning Press, 1995.

Bellanca, J. and R. Fogarty. *Catch Them Thinking*. Kankakee, IL: Imperial International Learning Corporation, 1986.

Ben-Hur, M. *Concept-Rich Math Instruction: Building a Strong Foundation for Reasoning and Problem-Solving*. Alexandria, VA: ASCD, 2006.

Cole, R. W., ed. *Educating Everybody's Children: Diverse Teaching Strategies for Diverse Learners*. Alexandria, VA: ASCD, 1995.

———. *More Strategies for Educating Everybody's Children*. Alexandria, VA: ASCD, 2001.

Colvin, G. *Talent Is Overrated: What Really Separates World-Class Performers from Everybody Else*. New York: Portfolio Publishing, 2008.

Cox, A. J. *No Mind Left Behind: Understanding and Fostering Executive Control—The Eight Essential Brain Skills Every Child Needs to Thrive*. New York: Perigee Books, 2007.

Csikszentmihalyi, M. *Finding Flow: The Psychology of Engagement with Everyday Life*. New York: Basic Books, 1997.

Dweck, Carol S. *Mindset: The New Psychology of Success*. New York: Ballantine Books, 2006.

Elder, L. and R. Paul. *Guide to Critical Thinking*. Dillon Beach, CA: Foundation for Critical Thinking, 2009.

Elliot, Andrew J. and Carol S. Dweck, eds. *Handbook of Competence and Motivation*. New York: The Guilford Press, 2005.

Erickson, H. Lynn. *Concept-Based Curriculum and Instruction: Teaching Beyond the Facts*. Thousand Oaks, CA: Corwin Press, 2002.

———. *Concept-Based Curriculum and Instruction for the Thinking Classroom*. Thousand Oaks, CA: Corwin Press, 2007.

Erlauer, L. *The Brain-Compatible Classroom: Using What We Know About Learning to Improve Teaching*. Alexandria, VA: ASCD, 2003.

Erwin, J. C. *The Classroom of Choice: Giving Students What They Need and Getting What You Want*. Alexandria, VA: ASCD, 2004.

Fisher, D. and N. Frey. *Checking for Understanding: Formative Assessment Techniques for Your Classroom*. Alexandria, VA: ASCD, 2007.

Gentry, M. and R. K. Gable. *My Class Activities: A Survey Instrument to Assess Students' Perceptions of Interest, Challenge, Choice and Enjoyment in Their Classroom*. Mansfield Center, CT: Creative Learning Press, 2001.

Girsch, M. and C. Girsch. *Fanning the Creative Spirit: Two Toy Inventors Simplify Creativity*. St. Paul, MN: Creativity Central, 2005.

Given, B. K. *Teaching to the Brain's Natural Learning Systems*. Alexandria, VA: ASCD, 2002.

Gurian, M. and K. Stevens. *The Minds of Boys: Saving Our Sons from Falling Behind in School and Life.* San Francisco, CA: Jossey-Bass, 2005.

Guskey, T. R., ed. *The Teacher as Assessment Leader.* Bloomington, IN: Solution Tree Press, 2009.

Heacox, Diane. *Differentiating Instruction in the Regular Classroom: How to Reach and Teach All Learners.* Minneapolis: Free Spirit Publishing, 2012.

———. *Making Differentiation a Habit: How to Ensure Success in Academically Diverse Classrooms.* Minneapolis: Free Spirit Publishing, 2009.

Jensen, E. *Brain-Based Learning.* San Diego, CA: The Brain Store, 2000.

———. *The Arts with the Brain in Mind.* Alexandria, VA: ASCD, 2001.

Johnson, E. B. *Contextual Teaching and Learning: What It Is and Why It's Here to Stay.* Thousand Oaks, CA: Corwin Press, 2002.

Jukes, Ian, Ted McCain, and Lee Crockett. *Understanding Digital Kids.* Thousand Oaks, CA: Corwin Press, 2010.

Marzano, R. J. *Transforming Classroom Grading.* Alexandria, VA: ASCD, 2000.

———. *Designing a New Taxonomy of Educational Objectives.* Thousand Oaks, CA: Corwin Press, 2001.

Marzano, R. J., D. J. Pickering, and J. E. Pollock. *Classroom Instruction that Works: Research-Based Strategies for Increasing Student Achievement.* Alexandria, VA: ASCD, 2001.

McTighe, J. and G. Wiggins. *Understanding by Design.* Alexandria, VA: ASCD, 2004.

Murphy, P. K. and P. A. Alexander. *Understanding How Students Learn: A Guide for Instructional Leaders.* Thousand Oaks, CA: Corwin Press, 2006.

Newmann, F. M., W. G. Secada, and G. C. Wehlage. *A Guide to Authentic Instruction and Assessment: Vision, Standards and Scoring.* Madison, WI: Wisconsin Center for Educational Research, 1995.

O'Connor, K. *How to Grade for Learning: Linking Grades to Standards.* Thousand Oaks, CA: Corwin Press, 2002.

Piirto, J. *Understanding Those Who Create.* Scottsdale, AZ: Great Potential Press, 1998.

———. *Understanding Creativity.* Scottsdale, AZ: Great Potential Press, 2004.

Reeves, D. B. *Making Standards Work: How to Implement Standards-Based Assessment in the Classroom, School, and District.* Englewood, CO: Advanced Learning Press, 2004.

Renzulli, Joseph, Marcia Gentry, and Sally Reis. *Enrichment Clusters: A Practical Plan for Real-World, Student-Driven Learning.* Mansfield Center, CT: Creative Learning Press, 2003.

Robinson, K. *Out of Our Minds: Learning to Be Creative.* Oxford, United Kingdom: Capstone Publishing Limited, 2001.

———. *The Element: How Finding Your Passion Changes Everything.* New York: Penguin Group, 2009.

Ryan, R. M. and E. L. Deci. "Self-Determination Theory and the Facilitation of Intrinsic Motivation, Social Development, and Well-Being." *American Psychologist* (January 2000): 68–78.

Savery, J. R. and T. M. Duffy. "Problem-Based Learning: An Instructional Model and Its Constructivist Framework." In *Constructivist Learning Environments: Case Studies in Instructional Design,* edited by B. G. Wilson. Englewood Cliffs, NJ: Educational Technology Publications, 1998: 135–148.

Sheffield, L. J. *Extending the Challenge in Mathematics: Developing Mathematical Promise in K–8 Students.* Thousand Oaks, CA: Corwin Press, 2003.

Smilkstein, R. *We're Born to Learn: Using the Brain's Natural Learning Process to Create Today's Curriculum.* Thousand Oaks, CA: Corwin Press, 2003.

Sousa, D. A. *How the Brain Learns.* Thousand Oaks, CA: Corwin Press, 2001.

Sternberg, R. J. *Successful Intelligence: How Practical and Creative Intelligence Determine Success in Life*. New York: Plume Books, 1997.

———. "Schools Should Nurture Wisdom." In *Teaching for Intelligence*, edited by B. Z. Presseisen. Arlington Heights, IL: Skylight Training and Publishing, 1999: 55–82.

———. *Wisdom, Intelligence and Creativity Synthesized*. New York: Cambridge University Press, 2003.

———. "Creativity Is a Habit." *Education Week* (February 22, 2006): 47–64.

Sternberg, R. and R. Subotnik, eds. *Optimizing Student Success with the Other Three Rs: Reasoning, Resilience, and Responsibility*. Greenwich, CT: Information Age Publishing, 2006.

Sternberg, Robert J. and Elena L. Grigorenko. *Teaching for Successful Intelligence: To Increase Student Learning and Achievement*. Thousand Oaks, CA: Corwin Press, 2007.

Strong, Richard W., Harvey F. Silver, and Matthew J. Perini. *Teaching What Matters Most: Standards and Strategies for Raising Student Achievement*. Alexandria, VA: ASCD, 2001.

Sylwester, R. *How to Explain a Brain: An Educator's Handbook of Brain Terms and Cognitive Processes*. Thousand Oaks, CA: Corwin Press, 2005.

Taba, Hilda. *Curriculum Development: Theory and Practice*. New York: Harcourt Brace and World, 1962.

Tomlinson, Carol Ann. *The Differentiated Classroom: Responding to the Needs of All Learners*. Alexandria, VA: ASCD, 1999.

———. *How to Differentiate Instruction in Mixed Ability Classrooms*. Alexandria, VA: ASCD, 2001.

———. *Fulfilling the Promise of the Differentiated Classroom: Strategies and Tools for Responsive Teaching*. Alexandria, VA: ASCD, 2003.

Tomlinson, Carol Ann and Jay McTighe. *Integrating Differentiated Instruction & Understanding by Design: Connecting Content and Kids*. Alexandria, VA: ASCD, 2006.

Treffinger, D. J., ed. *Creativity and Giftedness*. Thousand Oaks, CA: Corwin Press, 2004.

VanTassel-Baska, J. and C. A. Little. *Content-Based Curriculum for High-Ability Learners*. Waco, TX: Prufrock Press, 2003.

Vygotsky, L. S. *Mind in Society: The Development of Higher Psychological Processes*. Cambridge, MA: Harvard University Press, 1978.

Walters, K. S., ed. *Re-Thinking Reason: New Perspectives on Critical Thinking*. Albany, NY: State University of New York Press, 1994.

Wolfe, P. *Brain Matters: Translating Research Into Classroom Practice*. Alexandria, VA: ASCD, 2001.

Wormeli, Rick. *Fair Isn't Always Equal: Assessing and Grading in the Differentiated Classroom*. Portland, ME: Stenhouse Publishers, 2006.

Zimmerman, B. J. "Becoming a Self-Regulated Learner: An Overview." *Theory Into Practice, 41, No. 2* (Spring 2002): 64–70.

———. "Investigating Self-Regulation and Motivation: Historical Background, Methodological Developments, and Future Prospects." *American Educational Research Journal, 45* (2000): 166–183.

Zimmerman, B. J., S. Bonner, and R. Kovach. *Developing Self-Regulated Learners: Beyond Achievement to Self-Efficacy*. Washington DC: American Psychological Association, 1996.

Zimmerman, B. J. and A. Kitsantas. "Developmental Phases in Self-Regulation: Shifting from Process to Outcome Goals." *Journal of Educational Psychology, 89* (1997): 29–36.

Index

A

Abstract conceptual knowledge, 15, 16
Achievement
  cycle of progression, 72
  intrinsic motivation, 37, 84
  reasons for underachievement, 36–37
Advanced thinking levels, *See* Thinking
Ambiguous topics, 30
Amygdala, 39
Analogous thinking, developing, 137–138
Analytical learning dimension, 57
Analyze level, Bloom's revised taxonomy, 114–118, 120–121
Anderson, Lorin, 112
Annotating, as reading strategy, 136
Apply level, Bloom's revised taxonomy, 114–118, 120
Assessments
  autonomy, building, 88–89
  in Bloom's revised taxonomy, 112–113, 114–118, 122
  of factual knowledge, 15
  grading, 10, 64, 65
  types of, 10, 62, 64–65
Authentic audiences, presentations to, 81
Authentic tasks, creating, 30–31
Automatic performance, 39, 112
Autonomy
  assessment and, 88–89
  in goal setting, 73
  importance of, 80–81, 84
  See also Teaching and Learning Continuum (TLC)

B

Bill of rights, classroom, 74
Bloom, Benjamin, 15, 111
Bloom's taxonomy
  overview, 111–112
  revision, 112–122
Boy-friendly classrooms, 44–45
Brain breaks, 47
Brain-compatible learning environments
  characteristics of, 36
  community of scholars as, 74
  strategies for creating, 46
Brain domains, 38–41
Brain stem, 38
Brainstorming, 167
Buddy systems, 75

C

CAI, *See* Consider All the Issues (CAI) tool
Cerebellum, 38–39
Cerebral cortex, 40–41
Check-ins, 98
CIM, *See* Cross-Impact Matrixes (CIMs)
Classroom practices
  for advancing learning, 34
  bill of rights, 74
  boy-friendly classrooms, 44–45
  community of scholars, developing, 74
  conventions, developing, 74, 169
  creativity, building, 160, 161
  motivating classroom, pathway to building, 42–43
  "No Easy Answers" bulletin board, 141
  oversight councils, 74
  restorative justice, 74
  student-centered classrooms, 73–77
  supportive environments, 75
  thinking skills, promoting, 94, 101
  See also Brain-compatible learning environments
Coached instruction, 66, 81, 82, 86–87
Collaboration of students
  authentic tasks, 31
  creativity and, 151
  promoting, 56
  See also Grouping practices
Communities of scholars, establishing, 74
Comparing and contrasting in critical thinking, 127, 130, 131
Competence/competencies
  autonomy and, 80
  motivation and, 37, 42
  self-regulation and, 84
  types of for twenty-first century, 2, 14
Concept development
  effective curricula and, 29
  lesson sample, 18–19
  relationships-rigor-relevance model, 17
  worksheet, 20, 21
Conceptual knowledge
  abstract concepts, 16
  in Bloom's revised taxonomy, 113, 114–115
  defined, 14, 15
Concrete knowledge, 15
Confidence, *See* Self-confidence
Connectedness, 42
Conscious performance, 112
Conscious thinking, *See* Critical thinking
Consider All the Issues (CAI) tool, 140, 145
Consultative instruction, 81, 82, 87, 88

Content standards
history example, 118
math example, 26
science examples, 24, 25, 117
Contextualizing, as reading strategy, 136
Conventions
classroom, 74
mindset, 169
Convergent thinking, 93, 151
Conversations, substantive, 31–32
Create level, Bloom's revised taxonomy, 114–118, 121–122
Creativity/creative thinking
activities, 155–160
in Bloom's revised taxonomy, 112
characteristics of creative individuals, 152
compared to critical thinking, 125, 151
creative classroom, building, 160, 161
decline in, 150
defined, 151
importance of, 150
learning preferences and, 57
strategies, 152–154
Critical thinking
compared to creative thinking, 125, 151
defined, 125–127
in mathematics, 137
Positive, Negative, Interesting (PNI) tool, 140, 142, 143, 144
questioning strategies, 137–139
reading strategies, 136
in science, 137
writing strategies, 136–137
Cross-Impact Matrixes (CIMs), 127, 132, 133
Cross-lateral brain activities, 47
Culturally diverse students, 42
Curricula
adapting and enhancing, importance of, 1–2
goals, 14
hierarchy of knowledge, 14, 15
key components, defining, 15, 17
objectives, 22
principles for advancing learning, 33
quality, defining, 179
rigor, infusing, 28–32, 122–123, 124
thinking skills, promoting, 94–95, 102
twenty-first century model, 15

D

DDM, *See* Digging Deeper Matrix (DDM)
Dean, Ben, 75
Deci, Edward, 81
Decision making
characteristics of effective decision makers, 162–163
critical thinking and, 126
group decision-making steps, 178
overcoming barriers to, 169–170
stumbling blocks, 168–169
Deductive reasoning, 126
Didactic instruction, 81, 83, 85–86
Differentiated instruction
connecting to twenty-first century thinking and learning, 1–2, 179, 180
elements of a differentiated classroom, 11
myths and characteristics of, 8–10
technology use, impact of, 12, 181
Digging Deeper Matrix (DDM), 122–123, 124
Direct instruction, *See* Didactic instruction
Discovery-based lessons and content, 70
Discrimination, 42
Discussions
group discussion, 136
substantive conversations, 31–32
Divergent thinking, 93, 151
Dweck, Carol, 37, 73, 85, 169

E

E^4 curricula, 29–31, 32
Editing, as writing strategy, 136
Elaborate rehearsal (ER), 61
Elaboration, inspiring, 154
Elliott, Andrew, 37
Empathy, building, 75
Engagement of students, 29–30, 42
See also Motivation
ER, *See* Elaborate rehearsal (ER)
Essential questions, 17, 23–24
Ethnicity/race diversity, 42
Evaluate level, Bloom's revised taxonomy, 114–118, 121
Evaluating arguments, as reading strategy, 136
Everyday Art View activity, 158
Expert sources, consulting, 31
Extrinsic motivation, 37

F

Facilitated instruction, 81, 83, 86, 87
Factual knowledge
in Bloom's revised taxonomy, 113, 114–115
defined, 14, 15
Feldhusen, John, 8
Fixed mindsets, 73, 169
Flexibility, creativity and, 152
Flexible grouping practices, *See* Grouping practices
Fluency, creativity and, 152
Formative assessments, 10, 64
Four square concept maps, 62, 63, 64
Framework for 21st Century Learning, x
Free writing, 136
Frontal lobe, 40

G

Gender differences, 41
Generalizations, 17, 18–19
Gifted and talented students
creativity, 152
fixed mindsets, 73
strategies for, 8, 9–10, 53
Goals
building self-regulation, 72–73
curricular, 14
SMART goals, 97–98

Grading
in differentiated classrooms, 10
as extrinsic motivation, 37
formative assessments, 64
summative assessments, 65
See also Assessments
Gradual Release of Responsibility Model, 84
Graphic organizers
critical thinking and, 127, 130–133
for problem solving, 166, 172–177
Group activities
concept development, 18–19
decision-making steps, 178
group discussion, 136
special interest groups (SIGs), 56
See also specific activities
Grouping practices
flexible grouping, 10
motivation and, 49, 56, 61, 70
Growth mindsets, 73, 85, 169
Guided thinking, 97, 105, 106–107

H

Heacox, Diane, 80
Higher order thinking skills, 8, 31, 99
Highlighting, as reading strategy, 136
High-stakes testing, *See* Standardized tests
Hindbrain, 38–39
Hippocampus, 39
History instruction, *See* Social Studies instruction
Hollingworth, Leta, 8
Hypothetical thinking, 139, 166

I

I Chart, 48
I-FORD problem-solving process, 163–168
If-Then Mind Map for Decision Making, 166, 171, 172
Incompletions, as questioning strategy, 138
Independence, *See* Autonomy
Inductive reasoning, 126
Interdisciplinary themes, 2
Interests of students, using, 49–56
Intrinsic achievement motivation, 37, 84
Inventories and surveys, 49

J

Journaling
as motivation strategy, 61
thinking journals, 76

K

KIQ charts, 49, 51, 75
Kitsantas, Anastasia, 71
Knowledge
in Bloom's revised taxonomy, 112, 114–115
conceptual, 14, 15, 16, 113, 114–115
creativity and, 152
factual, 14, 15, 113, 114–115
procedural, 14, 15, 113, 114–115
pyramid of, 22
Krathwohl, David, 112

L

Lateral thinking, 154
Learning
ability dimensions, 57–58
brain domains, 38–41
differences, types of, 1
gender differences, 41
learning preferences, 57–61
learning styles activity, 59–61
motivation and, 57–61
self-regulation and, 71–72
types of, 14
Learning environments, *See* Brain-compatible learning environments
Learning materials, 70
Learning styles instruments, 61
Linguistically diverse students, 42
Living Timeline activity, 159

M

Mathematics instruction
creativity and, 152
critical thinking strategies, 137
guided thinking example, 106
math standards example, 26
Metacognitive skills, 75–76, 97
Midbrain, 39–40
Mindsets, 73, 85, 169
Motivation
assessment and, 62–70
creativity and, 152
defined, 37
intrinsic achievement motivation, 37, 84
learning preferences and, 57–61
pathway to building a motivating classroom, 42–43
strategies, 49, 56
student interests and, 49–56
types of, 37

N

Name 5 activity, 158–159
"No Easy Answers" bulletin board, 141
Note taking, as reading strategy, 136

O

Objectives, curricular, 22
See also Goals
Occipital lobe, 41
Open-ended questions, 23
Originality, creativity and, 154
Oversight councils, classroom, 74

P

P^3 (persistence, patience, and perseverance), 76–77
creativity and, 152
Parents
as homework coaches, 45
suggestions for supporting self-confidence, 169–170
Parietal lobe, 40
Partnership for 21st Century Skills, 2, 14

Passion projects, 53, 54–55
Peer review, as writing strategy, 136
PL, *See* Priority Ladder (PL) tool
PNI, *See* Positive, Negative, Interesting (PNI) tool
Point of view, analyzing, 138
Positive, Negative, Interesting (PNI) tool, 140, 142, 143, 144
Practical learning dimension, 58
Preassessments, 10, 62
Prefrontal cortex, 39, 40
Previewing, as reading strategy, 136
Principles, in concept development, 21
Priority Ladder (PL) tool, 140–141, 146, 147
Problem finding
  characteristics of effective problem finders, 162–163
  example activities, 163
Problem solving
  characteristics of effective problem solvers, 162–163
  graphic organizers, 166, 172–177
  I-FORD process, 163–168
  strategies, 164
  student/teacher questions, 166–167, 168
Procedural knowledge
  in Bloom's revised taxonomy, 113, 114–115
    defined, 14, 15
Provocative topics, 30
Publication, as writing strategy, 137

Q

Questions
  adjusting questioning practices, 70
  critical thinking questions, 137–139
  essential questions, 17, 23–24
  ill-formed vs. well-formed, 23
  for problem solving, 166–167, 168
  sequential questioning, 74
  for students before turning in work, 77
  unit questions, 24

R

Race, *See* Ethnicity/race diversity
Rank Your Interests forms, 49, 52, 53
Readers Theater activity, 159
Reading instruction
  CIM example, 133
  critical thinking strategies, 136
  If-Then Mind Map for Decision Making example, 171
  PNI example, 143
Read-write-pair-share activity, 65
Recall level, Bloom's revised taxonomy, 113–118
Reciprocal teaching, 70
Reflection
  as achievement phase, 72
  encouraging, 76
  as reading strategy, 136
Reflection logs, 98, 110
Renzulli, Joe, 8
Reptilian brain, 39–40
Research on a Creative Individual activity, 159–160
Research strategies, student, 31
Resources, mobilizing, 170
Response to Intervention (RTI) model, 84
Responsibility for learning, 42
Restorative justice, 74
Reversal of thinking, 139
Rigorous curriculum
  defined, 28
  Digging Deeper Matrix, using, 122–123, 124
  E^4 curricula, 29–31
Risk taking, encouraging, 170
Robinson, Kenneth, 151
ROLE Cards activity, 157
Role play activity, 159
Roundtable review, 68–69
Ryan, Richard, 81

S

SCAMPER activity, 96, 155
Scanning, as reading strategy, 136
Science instruction
  critical thinking strategies, 137
  Digging Deeper into Bloom's example unit, 117
  Rank Your Interests example, 53
  Spider Diagram example, 128
  standards examples, 24, 25
Self-confidence, 81, 169–170
Self-determination theory, 84–85
Self-efficacy, 72
Self-esteem, 97
Self-evaluation, 76
Self-reflection, *See* Reflection
Self-regulation
  achievement motivation and, 84–85
  phases of, 71
  strategies, 72–73
  theoretical background, 71–72
  Sequence Chain, 135
Sequencing and prioritizing in critical thinking, 127, 134–135
Sequential questioning, 74
Series of Events tool, 135
Skimming, as reading strategy, 136
SMART goals, 97–98
Social Studies instruction
  Advanced Compare and Contrast Graphic Organizer examples, 131
  CIM example. 133
  Digging Deeper into Bloom's example unit, 113, 118
  guided thinking example, 107
  PNI example, 144
  Priority Ladder example, 146
  What? So what? Now what? example, 119, 176
  What Would Happen If . . . ? example, 173, 174
Special interest groups (SIGs), 56
Spider diagrams, 128, 129
"Sponge" activities
  creative thinking, 152–154, 159
  critical thinking, 137, 140
Squiggle activity, 155–156
Standardized tests, 9, 65

Stereotyping, 42
Sternberg, Robert, 57, 75, 80
Structured Thinking Organizer (STO) tool, 141, 149
Student-centered classrooms, 73–77
Student Perception Questionnaire, 97, 108
Student Reflection Log, 98, 110
Students
  characteristics of thinking students, 94, 100
  critical elements for student-centered classrooms, 74, 78
  culturally diverse students, 42
  gender differences, 41
  growth mindset conventions, 169
  interests of, using, 49–56
  learning preferences, 57–61
  problem-solving questions for, 166–167, 168
  reasons for underachievement, 36–37
  See also Gifted and talented students; Motivation
Substantive conversations, 31–32
Successful intelligence, 57
Summative assessments, 10, 64–65
Support of students, need for, 42
Surveys and inventories, 49
Symbol systems, 139, 166
Synthesis 3 +1 tool, 141, 148

T

Taxonomy of Educational Objectives, The Classification of Educational Goals, Handbook I: Cognitive Domain (Bloom), 111
T-Charts, 127, 131
Teachers
  autonomy development and, 81, 84
  growth mindset conventions, 169
  key points for, 181
  nurturing creativity, 160, 161
  problem solving questions for, 166–167, 168
  responsibilities in student-centered classrooms, 74, 79
Teaching and Learning Continuum (TLC)
  levels of, 82–83, 85–88
  overview, 81
  theoretical framework, 84–85
Technology use, impact of, 12, 181
Temporal lobe, 41
10:2/20:2 Rule, 76
Terman, Lewis, 8
Textbooks, 32
Then What Happened? activity, 159
Theories, in concept development, 21
Think Fast! activity, 156
Thinking
  classroom characteristics, 94, 101
  curriculum characteristics, 94–95, 102
  defined, 92
  divergent vs. convergent, 93
  guided thinking, 97, 105, 106–107
  higher order thinking skills, 8, 31, 99
  lateral thinking, 154
  lesson formats, 96, 103–104
  student characteristics, 94, 100
  teaching methods and strategies, 95–99
  types of thinkers, 92–93
Thinking journals, 76
Think-pair-share activity, 65
3-2-1 Exit Slip/Entrance Ticket, 67
Tiered review/practice, 66
TLC, *See* Teaching and Learning Continuum (TLC)
Tomlinson, Carol Ann, 28
Topic previews, 49, 50
Torrence, Paul, 8
Tracking, 10

U

Unconscious thinking, 125
Understand level, Bloom's revised taxonomy, 114–120
Unit questions, 24

V

Validating information for critical thinking, 127, 128, 129
Venn diagrams, 127, 131
Verbal repetition, 76
Vygotsky, Lev, 29

W

Wait-time, 61
Walkthroughs, 32, 35
Webbing, as questioning strategy, 139
What If . . . ? activity, 159
What? So What? Now What? chart, 166, 176, 177
What's the Question? activity, 158
What Would Happen If . . ? diagram, 166, 173–174, 175
Wisdom, building, 75
Workforce skills, 13, 181
Working backwards, for problem solving, 166
Work plans, creating, 97, 109
Writing
  critical thinking strategies, 136–137
  See also Journaling

Z

Zimmerman, Berry, 71
Zone of proximal development theory, 29